DOMESTIC VIOLENCE AND PARENTAL CHILD ABDUCTION

THIS BOOK HAS BEEN PREPARED UNDER THE AUSPICES
OF THE POAM PROJECT

UNIVERSITY OF ABERDEEN   PRAVOS   Pravni fakultet Osijek
Sveučilište J. J. Strossmayera u Osijeku   LMU   BICOCCA

This project has received funding from the European Union's Rights, Equality and Citizenship Programme 2014–2020 under grant agreement No. 810373.

An open access online version of this book is also available.
Visit www.intersentiaonline.com for more information.

INTERSENTIA | ONLINE

DOMESTIC VIOLENCE AND PARENTAL CHILD ABDUCTION

The Protection of Abducting Mothers in Return Proceedings

Edited by

Katarina TRIMMINGS
Anatol DUTTA
Costanza HONORATI
Mirela ŽUPAN

INTERSENTIA

Cambridge – Antwerp – Chicago

Intersentia Ltd
8 Wellington Mews
Wellington Street | Cambridge
CB1 1HW | United Kingdom
Tel: +44 1223 736 170
Email: mail@intersentia.co.uk
www.intersentia.com | www.intersentia.co.uk

Distribution for the UK and
Rest of the World (incl. Eastern Europe)
NBN International
1 Deltic Avenue, Rooksley
Milton Keynes MK13 8LD
United Kingdom
Tel: +44 1752 202 301 | Fax: +44 1752 202 331
Email: orders@nbninternational.com

Distribution for Europe
Lefebvre Sarrut Belgium NV
Hoogstraat 139/6
1000 Brussels
Belgium
Tel: +32 (0)800 39 067
Email: mail@intersentia.be

Distribution for the USA and Canada
Independent Publishers Group
Order Department
814 North Franklin Street
Chicago, IL 60610
USA
Tel: +1 800 888 4741 (toll free) | Fax: +1 312 337 5985
Email: orders@ipgbook.com

Domestic Violence and Parental Child Abduction. The Protection of Abducting Mothers in Return Proceedings

Artwork on cover: Danny Juchtmans

ISBN 978-1-83970-245-7
D/2022/7849/46
NUR 828

British Library Cataloguing in Publication Data. A catalogue record for this book is available from the British Library.

FOREWORD

The changing context that the Hague Child Abduction Convention has had to operate in has been well-documented. It has emerged that the type of abduction that is most prevalent is not the type that was in the minds of the drafters. Thanks to statistics collected by the central authorities of State Parties and their regular analyses by Professor Nigel Lowe and his colleagues, we now know that mothers are the abducting parents in around 70% of cases. From other research, we also know that the reasons underlying these abductions are diverse.

Today, between the fortieth birthday of the Hague Child Abduction Convention's creation and the fortieth birthday of its entry into force, the Convention has over 100 State Parties. It has solicited a wealth of literature and case law on all possible levels. The European Court of Human Rights has issued no less than 78 judgments on the Child Abduction Convention and its application in light of the European Convention on Human Rights. The Court of Justice of the EU, through its interpretation of the Brussels IIa Regulation (2201/2003), has ruled on matters of child abduction in 17 cases. Add to this the numerous policy meetings, briefings and documents, and practice guides, at international, European Union and national levels, as well as EU-funded and postgraduate research; one would think that everything has been said.

Yet, sticky issues remain. The one addressed by this book is one that is pervasive and difficult to tackle. When mothers take their children and go to another country to get away from domestic violence, how can the law protect the children against the negative effects of abduction and, at the same time, protect the mothers from the violence they set out to guard themselves and their children against? Can the law provide an adequate response? Can the Hague Child Abduction Convention operate in such situations at all? Some courts have devised legal mechanisms such as undertakings or mirror orders to accompany return orders. These are meant to protect the returning parent, most frequently the mother. They are, however, not always easy to implement in the country to which the child (and parent) return(s).

The European Union legislator has, over the past twenty years, been thoroughly committed to cooperation in the fields of civil and criminal law. Many regulations and directives have resulted. Some of these might be underused. The editors of this book, and the researchers involved in the POAM project that led to it, identified two underused instruments in EU law that might help to solve the problem of abducting mothers fleeing from domestic violence. Their approach was to look not only at what the current law does, but also at its potential. Their research confirmed the perceived underuse of the Regulation for the Recognition of Protection Orders in Civil Law and the Directive on the European Protection Order in child abduction cases, but they went further. They investigated the ways in which protection orders could, and perhaps should, be used to provide protection to abducting mothers. If the legal instruments can be used in this manner, the Hague Child Abduction Convention can continue to operate, but with the aid of newer instruments that are adapted to the newer reality of child abduction cases. Getting more than a hundred States to agree to an amendment or an addition to an international convention is nearly impossible, and perhaps not desirable. Using guides and soft law to convince State Parties to operate in a particular way is feasible but strenuous and time-consuming. So why not use what we have in terms of other legislation, at least at the level of the European Union? That is what this book is seeking to do.

In what has become a good tradition for EU-funded research projects, outputs provide knowledge in an accessible way to practitioners of various domains and, in addition, advance the state of legal knowledge for academia. The contributions published in this book are only a part of the outcome of the project: the partners have also published national reports about the current state of affairs. They have made available the POAM Best Practice Guide, which will assist with improving the situation of mothers abducting, or considering abducting, their children due to violence that they face at home.

Thalia Kruger
Professor of Private International Law, University of Antwerp
Honorary Research Associate, University of Cape Town

PREFACE

This book marks the conclusion of the POAM (Protection of Abducting Mothers in Return Proceedings) project, a collaborative research project conducted between 2019 and 2021, which explored the intersection between domestic violence and international parental child abduction within the European Union. The project, which was funded by the European Union's Rights, Equality and Citizenship Programme (2014–2020), was concerned with the protection of abducting mothers who had been involved in return proceedings under the 1980 Hague Abduction Convention and the Brussels IIa Regulation, in circumstances where the child abduction had been motivated by acts of domestic violence from the left-behind father. In the project, we examined the usefulness of Regulation 606/2013 on Mutual Recognition of Protection Measures in Civil Matters and Directive 2011/99/EU on the European Protection Order – which both allow cross-border circulation of protection measures and, so far, have not attracted much attention in practice – in the context of such return proceedings.

The volume mainly collects the ideas given at our final conference, where the POAM research team presented the results of the project: the event was held online due to the pandemic, and not, as initially planned, in Munich. During this conference, each project partner presented a part of the project, and distinguished external speakers commented on each part presented. Based on these presentations and comments, the contributions of this book, highlighting some of the topics of our project, were drafted. Furthermore, the Best Practice Guide developed during the project for the application of Regulation 606/2013 and Directive 2011/99/EU in child abduction cases committed against the background of domestic violence will be documented as an annex.

We have to thank many individuals and institutions for their invaluable help during the project: the European Union for the generous funding (and our EU project officer for flexibility in adapting our project to the needs of the pandemic), our four universities (the University of Aberdeen, the Ludwig Maximilian University of Munich, the University of Milano-Bicocca and the Josip Juraj Strossmayer University of Osijek) for the constant support, the POAM research team for their excellent work, and many colleagues from academia and practice for their valuable participation during the many workshops and training sessions held. Finally, we are deeply indebted to the authors for their manuscripts, Onyója Momoh and Tatjana Tertsch for their editorial work, and Intersentia for publishing this book.

Aberdeen, Munich, Milan and Osijek, December 2021
Katarina Trimmings, Anatol Dutta, Costanza Honorati
and Mirela Župan

CONTENTS

PART II. PROTECTIVE MEASURES IN THE CONTEXT OF INTERNATIONAL PARENTAL CHILD ABDUCTION

LIST OF CASES

COURT OF JUSTICE OF THE EUROPEAN UNION

EUROPEAN COURT OF HUMAN RIGHTS

AUSTRALIA

CANADA

GERMANY

NEW ZEALAND

UNITED KINGDOM

UNITED STATES OF AMERICA

LIST OF CONTRIBUTORS

Anatol Dutta
Prof. Dr., M. Jur. (Oxford), Ludwig Maximilian University of Munich, Germany

Marilyn Freeman
Prof. Dr., University of Westminster, United Kingdom

Jan von Hein
Prof. Dr., University of Freiburg, Germany

Costanza Honorati
Prof. Dr., University of Milano-Bicocca, Italy

Onyója Momoh
Dr., Barrister (England and Wales), University of Aberdeen, United Kingdom

Marin Mrčela
Judge at the Supreme Court of the Republic of Croatia and Prof. Dr., Josip Juraj Strossmayer University of Osijek, Croatia

Johanna Niemi
Prof. Dr., Dean, Faculty of Law, University of Helsinki, Finland

Laura-Maria Poikela
Legal Counsel, Doctoral Student, University of Turku, Finland

Nicola Taylor
Prof. Dr., University of Otago, New Zealand

Tatjana Tertsch
Ludwig Maximilian University of Munich, Germany

Katarina Trimmings
Dr., University of Aberdeen, United Kingdom

Michael Wilderspin
Former Legal Adviser to the European Commission

Mirela Župan
Prof. Dr., Josip Juraj Strossmayer University of Osijek, Croatia

PART I

CROSS-BORDER PROTECTIVE MEASURES IN THE EU

Weaknesses of the Current Regime

THE CROSS-BORDER CIRCULATION OF PROTECTION MEASURES UNDER REGULATION 606/2013

Anatol DUTTA*

1. INTRODUCTION

Since 2015, two EU instruments have tried to improve the cross-border effects of protection measures within the Union. The Regulation 606/2013,[1] which provides for a cross-border recognition and enforcement of protection measures in civil matters, has applied since then, and the deadline for the implementation of the Directive 2011/99/EU[2] has passed. This Directive, which will be analysed in the next contribution,[3] introduces

* This contribution is based on earlier papers published in German ('Grenzüberschreitender Gewaltschutz in der Europäischen Union' (2015) *Zeitschrift für das gesamte Familienrecht* 85) and English ('Cross-border protection measures in the European Union' (2016) 12 *Journal of Private International Law* 169).

1 Regulation (EU) 606/2013 of the European Parliament and of the Council of 12 June 2013 on mutual recognition of protection measures in civil matters [2013] OJ L181/4.

2 Directive 2011/99/EU of the European Parliament and of the Council of 13 December 2011 on the European protection order [2011] OJ L338/2.

3 See the contribution by T. TERTSCH in this volume.

a European protection order, which the authorities of one Member State can issue in criminal matters, and which the other Member States are bound to recognise, and to transform into a protection measure under their own national law.

By introducing the Regulation and Directive, the EU legislator's aim was to strengthen the area of freedom, security and justice. The main purpose of these instruments was to safeguard the freedom of movement of persons within the Union, as guaranteed by Article 21(1) of the Treaty on the Functioning of the EU and Article 3(2) of the EU Treaty. Persons benefiting from protection measures shall not be prevented from moving and residing freely within the European Union because they fear that, by exercising their freedom of movement, they will be losing the protection against the person causing the risk or danger, due to a lack of any cross-border recognition and enforcement of those measures.[4] These rules are intended to improve the cross-border effects of protection measures throughout the European Union.

As protection measures may be issued, in the Member States, in either civil or criminal proceedings, the EU legislator did not want to interfere with the national provisions on protection measures,[5] and therefore felt compelled to divide the cross-border enforcement of protection measures between two instruments. Protection measures in civil matters are subject to Regulation 606/2013, and protection measures in criminal matters lie within the scope of Directive 2011/99/EU or the implementing provisions of the Member States, respectively.

2. ISSUES COVERED BY THE INSTRUMENTS

Both instruments deal with the cross-border effects of protection measures, rather than covering all aspects of private international law. Both instruments do not deal with the jurisdiction for, and the law applicable to, protection measures, by contrast to an earlier Commission proposal for Regulation 606/2013, which at least contained a provision on the courts competent for protection measures in civil matters.[6]

---

4 See Recital 6 of Dir. 2011/99/EU, and Recital 3 of Reg. 606/2013.

5 Recital 10, sentence 4, of Dir. 2011/99/EU, and Recital 12 of Reg. 606/2013.

6 See Art. 3 of the Proposal of the Commission for a Regulation of the European Parliament and of the Council on mutual recognition of protection measures in civil matters COM(2011) 276 final, which stated: 'The authorities of the Member State where the person's physical and/or psychological integrity or liberty is at risk shall have jurisdiction.'

This silence of the EU legislator is surprising for two reasons. On the one hand, the private international law dimensions of protection measures remain in the dark, especially on the level of EU private international law.[7] It would have been advisable for the EU legislator to create legal certainty in this area by adopting common provisions; furthermore, protection measures in cases with international links are not far-fetched.[8] On the other hand, by virtue of Regulation 606/2013 and Directive 2011/99/EU, the EU legislator has introduced a duty to enforce foreign protection measures, even without an exequatur requirement in some cases. So far, there has been consensus at the EU level that the pertinent jurisdictional rules (and quite possibly even the conflict rules) have to be harmonised if decisions in a certain area of law are to circulate freely within the EU. This applies even more so if there is no review, or only a limited review, in the Member State of enforcement. Furthermore, protection measures not only limit the freedom of the person causing the risk or danger considerably, but are also – as the EU legislator has observed, at least if one can trust Recitals 12, 13 and 15 of Regulation 606/2013 – characterised by a great variety of solutions in the different Member States' systems.

3. SCOPE OF THE REGULATION

Article 1 of Regulation 606/2013 states that the Regulation creates 'rules for a simple and rapid mechanism for the recognition of protection measures' ordered in a Member State of origin in another Member State, the so-called 'Member State addressed': cf. also Recital 4. The term 'recognition' is, of course, not to be understood technically. The Regulation focuses mainly on the cross-border enforcement of protection measures: see also Article 4(1) of Regulation 606/2013.

---

7 See the contributions by J. von Hein and C. Honorati in this volume.

8 See, however, for a different view, E. de Götzen, 'Protection Orders Across Europe: First Remarks on Regulation No. 606/2013' in K. Boele-Woelki, N. Dethloff and W. Gephart (eds), *Family Law and Culture in Europe*, Intersentia, Cambridge 2014, pp. 277, 283. Cf. also M. Wilderspin, 'Règlement (UE) n° 606/2013 relatif à la reconnaissance mutuelle des mesures de protection en matière civile' (2014) *Annuaire de droit de l'Union européenne* 520, 523, who supposes that '*en pratique une mesure de protection n'est prise que s'il y a un lien de proximité entre la juridiction ordonnant la décision et la personne protégée (résidence habituelle ou présence sur le territoire national)*', and that harmonised rules would be '*superflue*'.

3.1. THE AUTONOMOUS CONCEPT OF PROTECTION MEASURES

The duty to enforce relates only to protection measures that fall within the scope of the Regulation. The Regulation, according to its Articles 1 and 2(1), covers only protection measures in 'civil matters': an open concept which, as Recital 10 of the Regulation clarifies, has to be interpreted autonomously, and, hence, without reverting to national law. The rich case law of the Court of Justice of the European Union (CJEU) interpreting the term 'civil and commercial matters' within the Brussels I regime[9] can probably only be used to a limited extent here. For example, in terms of the Brussels IIa Regulation, the CJEU has already pointed out that the delineation of civil and non-civil matters in family law – where public law and private law often intertwine – can be different from such delineation in other areas of law. According to the Court, measures by the State protecting children can also be regarded as civil matters, although under the Brussels I criteria they would clearly be characterised as non-civil matters, as far as the State exercises public authority.[10] The same will also apply once the Brussels IIb Regulation is applicable.

In interpreting the term 'civil matters' within Regulation 606/2013, one also has to consider Directive 2011/99/EU. Both instruments are expected to supplement each other, and to safeguard a cross-border enforcement of protection measures without any gaps: cf. Recital 9 of the Regulation. Hence, one probably has to characterise all protection measures that are not issued in criminal proceedings and, thus, are not subject to the Directive, as civil matters: a dichotomy which is also indicated in Recital 9 of the Regulation. The EU legislator did, however, mitigate the characterisation issue. Member States have to identify, and communicate to the Commission, the authorities competent to issue protection measures, in the sense meant by the Regulation, the so-called issuing authorities (see Articles 3(4) and 18(1)(a)(i) of Regulation 606/2013), and the Commission has to publish this information (see Article 18(2) of the Regulation).[11] Protection measures (the exact meaning of this term will be addressed shortly) issued by the issuing authorities designated by the Member States should be regarded as civil matters without further inquiry; a similarly pragmatic approach was also employed by the CJEU with reference to the Brussels IIa Regulation,

---

9 See, e.g. Case C-49/12, *Sunico*, EU:C:2013:545, para 33 et seq.

10 Case C-435/06, C, EU:C:2007:714, [2007] ECR I-10141.

11 These authorities need not necessarily be courts; other authorities – with the exception of police authorities – can also be nominated by the Member States, cf. also Recital 13.

where the Court of Justice, in effect, characterised all child protection measures as civil matters, for purposes of Brussels IIa.[12]

However, not every measure of an issuing authority that has been designated by a Member State can be enforced throughout the European Union. The measure to be enforced must qualify as a 'protection measure', as defined in Article 3(1) of Regulation 606/2013. According to that statutory definition, a protection measure imposes on the person causing the risk an obligation 'with a view to protecting another person, when the latter person's physical or psychological integrity may be at risk'; not surprisingly, according to Articles 3(2) and 3(3), the protected person and the person causing the risk both have to be natural persons. The statutory definition does not explicitly refer to personal freedom as a potential object to be protected by the protection measure, unlike some Member States' laws.[13] However, an interference with personal freedom will often also entail a risk to the person's psychological integrity, protected under Article 3(1). In addition, the recitals of the Regulation appear to assume that a risk to personal freedom can be the object of a protection measure in the sense of Regulation 606/2013; actually, the wording of the recitals and the provisions of the Regulation – which, furthermore, deviate from Directive 2011/99/EU in this respect[14] – do not concur here.[15] Yet, not every obligation imposed on the person causing the risk suffices. Rather, the Regulation contains a list of possible prohibitions (or, in more moderate terms, possible regulations) that can be imposed by a protection measure. Measures covered include prohibitions on entering certain places (Article 3(1)(a)), and prohibitions on contacting (Article 3(1)(b)) and approaching (Article 3(1)(c)) the protected person. The fact that the Regulation only applies to prohibitions and regulations 'ordered by the issuing authority' excludes, of course, cross-border enforcement of private undertakings given by the person causing the risk.

---

12 Case C-435/06, *C*, EU:C:2007:714, [2007] ECR I-10141, para. 48 et seq.

13 See, e.g. § 1 of the German Gesetz zum zivilrechtlichen Schutz vor Gewalttaten und Nachstellungen.

14 Cf. Art. 2(2) and Art. 5 of the Directive.

15 See Recital 6 of Reg. 606/2013: 'This Regulation should apply to protection measures ordered with a view to protecting a person where there exist serious grounds for considering that that person's life, physical or psychological integrity, personal liberty, security or sexual integrity is at risk, for example so as to prevent any form of gender-based violence or violence in close relationships such as physical violence, harassment, sexual aggression, stalking, intimidation or other forms of indirect coercion. It is important to underline that this Regulation applies to all victims, regardless of whether they are victims of gender-based violence.'

It is rather surprising that the Regulation does not include a provision in respect of the family home, for example in cases of domestic violence, which is regarded in some Member States as a protection measure.[16] Such measures do not fall within the statutory definition in Article 3(1) of the Regulation. Notably, prohibitions on entering certain places, according to Article 3(1)(a) of the Regulation, do not cover such a provision comprehensively; they can only safeguard the absence of the person causing the risk, but do not allow the protected person to stay in the family home. It is regrettable that the European legislator did not address this point.

Finally, it is noticeable that the protection measure, according to the definition in Article 3(1) of Regulation 606/2013, has to be issued by the competent authority 'in accordance with its national law'. Does this qualification exclude measures that have been taken by the issuing authority based on foreign law (because, according to its private international law, foreign law applies)? There is no legitimate reason for such a limitation. Rather, this element of the statutory definition should be understood in the sense that the measure is based on the national procedural law and private international law, which have – as has already been seen – not been harmonised by Regulation 606/2013.

3.2. IS A CROSS-BORDER ELEMENT NECESSARY?

Regulation 606/2013 only applies to protection measures from other 'Member States'. Recitals 40 and 41 of the Regulation stress that Ireland and the United Kingdom are bound by the Regulation, but not Denmark.[17] Although the wording of the Regulation, unlike some other EU instruments (see, for example, Article 2(3) of the Brussels IIa Regulation), does not define the term 'Member State', it can be assumed that a duty to 'recognise' exists only between participating Member States and, hence, not regarding protection measures taken by authorities in Denmark.[18] Rather strange is

---

16 See, e.g., for Germany, § 2 of the Gesetz zum zivilrechtlichen Schutz vor Gewalttaten und Nachstellungen; see also § 1361b of the Bürgerliche Gesetzbuch.

17 Despite Brexit, the Regulation still applies in the United Kingdom, according to s. 3(1) of the European Union (Withdrawal) Act 2018 (c. 16) and s. 5 of The Mutual Recognition of Protection Measures in Civil Matters (Amendment) (EU Exit) Regulations 2019, SI 2019/493. Cf. C. v. Bary, 'Internationales Familienverfahrensrecht im Vereinigten Königreich nach dem Ende des Brexit-Übergangszeitraums' (2021) *Zeitschrift für das gesamte Familienrecht* 342, 345 and T. Tertsch in this volume.

18 See, for Germany, § 13 No. 1 of the Gesetz zum Europäischen Gewaltschutzverfahren, which clarifies that Denmark is not to be regarded as a Member State for the purposes of the Regulation.

the alleged limitation of the Regulation's scope to 'cross-border cases', in Article 2(2)(1) of the Regulation. According to the second sentence of that provision, it is sufficient to constitute a cross-border case if an application for recognition has been made in another Member State, without, of course, requiring the case to have any connection to that Member State. Obviously, by this 'non-requirement', the EU legislator wanted to reflect the competence basis for Regulation 606/2013 in Article 81 of the Treaty on the Functioning of the EU (cf. Recital 2 of the Regulation), which only allows legislative measures, in the field of judicial cooperation, in civil matters 'having cross-border implications'.

4. PRECONDITIONS FOR A CROSS-BORDER RECOGNITION AND ENFORCEMENT

Measures falling within the scope of Regulation 606/2013 have to be recognised and enforced pursuant to Article 4(1) of the Regulation, without any special procedure requiring a review as to the substance of the measure. Article 13 provides that recognition and enforcement can only be refused based on certain statutory grounds (see *infra* section 6).

The only precondition for cross-border enforcement of a protection measure is that certain formalities, defined in Article 4(2)–(4) of the Regulation, have been met. Apart from an 'application' and an 'authentic copy of the measure', the protected person must provide, according to Article 4(2)(b) of the Regulation, a 'certificate' that has been issued in the Member State of origin, under Article 5 of Regulation 606/2013. The certificate summarises the protection measure in a multilingual standard form. As required in Articles 5(3) and 19 of the Regulation, the European Commission has drafted a specimen for this form in an Implementing Regulation.[19] If necessary, the certificate (for the issuing of the certificate, see *infra* section 5) has, according to Articles 4(2)(c) and 16(1) of the Regulation, to be transliterated and/or translated in an official language (and, presumably, script) of the Member State addressed, unless that Member State has indicated that it will also accept certificates in other official languages of the EU. Transliterations and translations of certificates have to comply with the requirements for official translations in the Member State addressed, under Article 16(2) of the Regulation.

---

19 Annex I of the Commission Implementing Regulation (EU) 939/2014 of 2 September 2014 establishing the certificates referred to in Articles 5 and 14 of Regulation (EU) No 606/2013 of the European Parliament and of the Council on mutual recognition of protection measures in civil matters [2014] OJ L263/10.

The Article 5 certificate is, however, not independent of the certified protection measure. Under Article 4(3) of the Regulation, the certificate 'shall take effect only within the limits of the enforceability of the protection measure'. The legislator, apparently, tries to clarify that the certificate does not attribute the protection measure with having wider effects than the protection measure already has within the Member State of origin. This is a matter of course because Regulation 606/2013 only extends the effects awarded by the protection measure in the Member State of origin to the Member State addressed.[20] Nevertheless, unfortunately, the wording of Article 4(3) of the Regulation cannot be fully trusted. If there is a later decision in the Member State of origin which suspends, withdraws or limits the enforceability of the measure, Article 14(1) of the Regulation requires a new certificate on the suspension, withdrawal or limitation, and the authorities in the Member State addressed have, according to Article 14(2) of the Regulation, to suspend or withdraw the effects of the recognition or enforcement only after this new certificate has been submitted. The Commission has also drafted a multilingual form for this Article 14 certificate.[21] Hence, the Article 5 certificate has effects exceeding the certified protection measure.

It should be stressed that the Article 5 certificate has an expiry date. Irrespective of a potential time limitation of the measure to be enforced, the 'effects of recognition' (which surely include the enforceability) are limited to one year after the issuing of the certificate, under Article 4(4) of the Regulation. The relevant expiry date has to be specified in the certificate, under Article 7(h) of the Regulation. If the cross-border enforcement of the measure is extended beyond this expiry date, the protected person either has to apply for a new certificate in the Member State of origin, or rely on other EU instruments, or – more obviously, because it is probably less complicated – the protected person has to apply for a new protection measure in the Member State addressed: cf. also Recital 16 of the Regulation. The cross-border effects of protection measures under the Regulation secure only a transitional period.

5. THE ISSUING OF THE ARTICLE 5 CERTIFICATE

How does the protected person obtain the certificate in the Member State of origin, which is, as seen above, crucial for the cross-border enforcement of

---

20 Cf. also Recital 4, sentence 2, of the Regulation.

21 Annex II of the Commission Implementing Regulation 939/2014.

the protection measure? The certificate is displayed by the issuing authority 'upon request' of the protected person, based – as already mentioned – on the multilingual standard form drafted by the Commission. The issuing authority shall only issue an Article 5 certificate if the protection measure falls within the scope of the Regulation and is enforceable. Furthermore, the issuing of the certificate requires a minimum level of participation of the person that caused the risk in the proceedings giving rise to the protection measure. The certificate shall only be issued if the protection measure 'has been brought to the notice' of the person causing the risk, in accordance with the law of the Member State of origin, as per Article 6(1). Hence, the requirements for 'bringing to the notice' are not to be established by an autonomous interpretation of Article 6(1) but are instead, based on the clear wording of the Regulation, subject to the law of the Member State of origin. In so far as enforcement of the protection measure is admissible in the Member State of origin before a 'bringing to the notice' of the person causing the risk (as is the case in some Member States), the effects of the measure are restricted to that Member State only, as an Article 5 certificate cannot be obtained. This is not unproblematic,[22] as in proceedings giving rise to protection measures, the address of the person causing the risk might not be known and, thus, problems of formally serving the measure might arise. Regulation 606/2013 also contains special rules to safeguard a minimum level of participation of the person causing the risk, if that person did not enter an appearance, or was deliberately excluded from the proceedings (for example, in the case of *ex parte* proceedings). In such situations, it has to be ensured that the person causing the risk has been duly informed about the introduction of the proceedings (Article 6(2) of the Regulation), or has been able to challenge the measure in the Member State of origin (Article 6(3) of the Regulation). Article 8 of Regulation 606/2013 requires the certificate to be brought to the notice of the person causing the risk, while safeguarding the security of the protected person (cf. Article 8(3)).

It is noteworthy that the issuing authority, according to Article 5(3) of Regulation 606/2013, also has to provide a 'transliteration or translation' of the certificate. This duty relates only to a transliteration or translation into one of the official languages of the EU; here, also, the provision refers to the multilingual standard form in the Commission

22 M. Wilderspin, 'Règlement (UE) n° 606/2013 relatif à la reconnaissance mutuelle des mesures de protection en matière civile' (2014) *Annuaire de droit de l'Union européenne* 520, 525.

Implementing Regulation. This duty is, according to Article 16(1), restricted to languages that are accepted in the Member State addressed; a general duty to preventively transliterate or translate the certificate into all official languages of the EU (for example, because the protected person does not yet know whether, and where, the measure will have to be enforced) would surely go too far, even if the duty to bear the translation costs is a question of the law of the Member State of origin, as Recital 23 of Regulation 606/2013 indicates.

Article 5(2) of Regulation 606/2013 provides that an 'appeal' – for example, by the person causing the risk – 'against the issuing of the certificate' is not admissible. This is rather misleading, because the person causing the risk can challenge the protection measure itself in accordance with the law of the Member State of origin and, hence, refute the cross-border enforcement of the measure. Also, Article 9(1) of the Regulation allows, upon request of the protected person or the person causing the risk, or *ex officio*, not only a rectification of the certificate (Article 9(1)(a)), but also a withdrawal of the certificate by the issuing authority, if the certificate 'was clearly wrongly granted' (Article 9(1)(b)), even if it is rather unclear what this – at least on first sight – qualified degree of wrongfulness requires in detail.[23] Also, the decision on a rectification or withdrawal can be challenged by an appeal on the basis of the law of the Member State of origin, under Article 9(2) of Regulation 606/2013. Reading Article 5(2) of the Regulation *e contrario*, one can assume that Regulation 606/2013, in itself, does not exclude an appeal of the protected person against refusal of the certificate but, rather, following the principle in Article 9(2), refers that question to the procedural law of the Member State of origin.

A certificate has to be issued not only as to the protection measure itself, but also, as already mentioned, as to measures of the issuing authorities which 'suspend, withdraw or limit the enforceability of the protection measure' in the Member State of origin, or 'withdraw the certificate', as per Article 14(1) of the Regulation. Regulation 606/2013 is silent on the question of whether an appeal is admissible against those certificates; this question probably has to be answered by the law of the Member State of origin.

---

23 See also Recital 29 of the Regulation, which says that the certificate has to be withdrawn, 'if it was clearly wrongly granted, for example where it was used for a measure that falls outside the scope of this Regulation or where it was issued in breach of the requirements for its issuing', which seems to involve a full review of the issuing of the certificate.

6. ENFORCEMENT IN THE MEMBER STATE ADDRESSED

The enforcement of the protection measure is governed, according to Article 4(5) of the Regulation, by the law of the Member State addressed. If the circumstances change, for example because the protected person relocates his or her domicile or place of work, due to his or her moving to the Member State addressed, the protection measure might not cover the new situation and, thus, might become meaningless. Against this background, Article 11 of the Regulation allows an 'adjustment' of the foreign protection measure by the authorities of the Member State addressed: see also Recitals 19–21 of the Regulation. The adjustment procedure is governed by the law of the Member State addressed, under Article 11(2) of the Regulation. Article 11(3) and (4) of the Regulation, however, provide that the adjustment has to be brought to the notice of the person causing the risk. Again, according to Article 11(5), either the protected person or the person causing the risk can appeal against the adjustment, on the basis of the law of the Member State addressed, without the appeal having suspensive effects.

As already mentioned, no exequatur is necessary in the Member State addressed, but merely a check of the formalities. However, the Member State addressed might refuse recognition and enforcement of the protection measure, but, according to Article 13(1) of the Regulation, only upon request of the person causing the risk, and only as far as there is a statutory ground for refusal. Recognition and enforcement might be refused if the protection measure violates public policy (Article 13(1)(a), see also Article 13(3)) or is irreconcilable with a judgment having effects in the Member State addressed (Article 13(1)(b)).

7. CONCLUSION

Even those people most enthusiastic about the Europeanisation of private international law will have to concede that, in relation to the rules on the cross-border enforcement of protection measures, the results hardly justify the effort. Furthermore, as shown, the rules are not very convincing as to their substance.[24] Against this background, one is tempted to advise

24 See also the conclusion of M. Wilderspin, 'Règlement (UE) n° 606/2013 relatif à la reconnaissance mutuelle des mesures de protection en matière civile' (2014)

protected persons to apply directly, if necessary, in the other Member State for parallel protection measures, instead of using the rather complicated cross-border enforcement procedures. However, the rules could prove valuable in the context of child abduction proceedings.[25]

Annuaire de droit de l'Union européenne 520, 525: *'On a sans doute rarement vu un instrument "communautaire" aussi bâclé'*. For a more positive evaluation, however, see E. de Götzen, 'Protection Orders Across Europe: First Remarks on Regulation No. 606/2013' in K. Boele-Woelki, N. Dethloff and W. Gephart (eds), *Family Law and Culture in Europe*, Intersentia, Cambridge 2014, p. 288. See also the results of S. van der Aa, J. Niemi, L. Sosa and A. Ferreira, *Mapping the legislation and assessing the impact of Protection Orders in the European Member States*, Wolf Legal Publishers, Oisterwijk 2015, p. 218 et seq.

25 See the contributions by O. Momoh, M. Župan and M. Mrčela, K. Trimmings and M. Wilderspin in this volume.

CROSS-BORDER RECOGNITION UNDER DIRECTIVE 2011/99/EU

Tatjana Tertsch

1. INTRODUCTION

The European Protection Order Directive[1] introduces a mechanism for mutual recognition of protection measures issued in the context of criminal matters. In this respect, it complements Regulation 606/2013, which applies only to protection measures issued in civil matters. The goal of the Directive is 'to ensure that the protection provided to a natural person in one Member State is maintained and continued in any other Member State to which the person moves'.[2] If victims fear that they will lose their protection if they move from one Member State to another, they might refrain from exercising their right to move and reside freely within the territory of the Member States.[3] Therefore, the Directive, like the Regulation,[4] aims to ensure that moving within the EU does not have a negative effect on the protection of the victim. A victim should not have to go through the whole process of having to produce evidence again, as if the decision in the other Member State did not exist.[5] To achieve this aim, the Directive introduced a European protection order (EPO) that can be issued by a Member State that has ordered a criminal protection measure before, and which has to be converted into a national protection measure by another Member State where the victim seeks the continuation of its protection.

However, the practical relevance of the instrument is, so far, very limited: according to a report of the Commission, presented on 11 May 2020,[6] only 37 EPOs had been issued, and only 15 had been executed.

1 Directive 2011/99/EU of the European Parliament and of the Council of 13 December 2011 on the European protection order [2011] OJ L338/2.

2 Dir. 2011/99/EU, Recital 6.

3 Dir. 2011/99/EU, Recital 6. A similar provision is in Regulation 606/2013, Recital 3. Also compare A. Dutta, 'Cross-border protection measures in the European Union' (2016) 12 *Journal of Private International Law* 169, 171.

4 Regulation (EU) No 606/2013 of the European Parliament and of the Council of 12 June 2013 on mutual recognition of protection measures in civil matters [2013] OJ L181/4.

5 Compare Recital 7 of the Initiative of the Kingdom of Belgium, the Republic of Bulgaria, the Republic of Estonia, the Kingdom of Spain, the French Republic, the Italian Republic, the Republic of Hungary, the Republic of Poland, the Portuguese Republic, Romania, the Republic of Finland and the Kingdom of Sweden with a view to the adoption of a Directive of the European Parliament and of the Council on the European Protection Order (2010/C 69/02) OJ C69/5 ('avoiding the need for the victim to start new proceedings or to produce the evidence in the executing State again as if the issuing State had not adopted the decision').

6 Report from the Commission to the European Parliament and the Council on the implementation of Directive 2011/99/EU of the European Parliament and of the Council of 13 December 2011 on the European protection order, COM(2020) 187 final.

There is no indication that the practical significance has changed since then. The report assumes that the reason for the low number of applications is that the competent authorities, and the persons in need of protection, are not fully aware of the possibility of requesting an EPO. One of the aims of this contribution is to examine the usefulness of the Directive, as the limited practical significance could also be due to the fact that the instrument has too many deficiencies.

Directives, unlike regulations, are not directly applicable but, rather, oblige the Member States to transpose the provisions into their national law. The deadline for the transposition of the European Protection Order Directive expired on 11 January 2015, the same date that the Regulation came into force. All participating Member States have fulfilled their obligations, and have implemented the rules in their national laws.[7] The participating Member States include all Member States except for Ireland and Denmark. Thus, the international scope of the Directive is not identical to that of the Regulation:[8] while Denmark participates in neither the Directive nor the Regulation,[9] Ireland opted out of the Directive, but participates in the Regulation.[10] Originally, i.e. before Brexit, the UK declared that it wished to take part in the application of the Directive[11] and, thus, England and Wales,[12] Northern Ireland[13] and Scotland[14] have each enacted rules to implement the Directive. However, after the UK left the EU, the implementing rules of England, Wales and Northern Ireland were revoked.[15] This is rather surprising, given the fact that the

7 A list of all national transpositions can be found here: <https://eur-lex.europa.eu/legal-content/EN/NIM/?uri=CELEX:32011L0099> accessed 19.08.2021. For details regarding the transposition, see also the Report from the Commission to the European Parliament and the Council on the implementation of Directive 2011/99/EU of the European Parliament and of the Council of 13 December 2011 on the European protection order, COM(2020) 187 final.

8 A. Dutta, 'Cross-border protection measures in the European Union' (2016) 12 *Journal of Private International Law* 169, 183.

9 Dir. 2011/99/EU, Recital 42 and Regulation 606/2013, Recital 41.

10 Dir. 2011/99/EU, Recital 41 and Regulation 606/2013, Recital 40.

11 Dir. 2011/99/EU, Recital 40.

12 The Criminal Justice (European Protection Order) (England and Wales) Regulations 2014, SI 2014/3300.

13 The Criminal Justice (European Protection Order) (Northern Ireland) Regulations 2014, SI 2014/320.

14 The European Protection Order (Scotland) Regulations 2015, SI 2015/107, and the Act of Adjournal (Criminal Procedure Rules Amendment No. 2) (European Protection Orders) 2015, SI 2015/121.

15 Ss. 4 and 10 of The Criminal Justice (Amendment etc.) (EU Exit) Regulations 2019, SI 2019/780. See also C. v. Bary, 'Internationales Familienverfahrensrecht im Vereinigten

Regulation continues to apply.[16] Apparently, the English legislator believed the Regulation to be more useful than the Directive. However, Scottish implementing laws have not yet been revoked and, thus, are still in force.[17]

2. THE ACTUAL NEED FOR TWO INSTRUMENTS

The reason for adopting two instruments with the same goal – the recognition of protection measures across the Union – can be better understood by taking a glance at the legislative procedure.[18] The original initiative envisaged only one instrument: the Directive on the protection order.[19] The Directive was intended to cover both criminal and civil protection measures. Even the initiators were aware of the different legal systems providing for criminal, civil or mixed measures, 'it was decided to base the Directive on criminal cooperation [i.e. Article 82 Treaty on the Functioning of the European Union (TFEU)] because the legal interests to be protected, such as life, physical or mental integrity, or sexual freedom, have traditionally been safeguarded under criminal law'.[20] Some countries, and the Commission, however, questioned whether this legal basis would be sufficient to cover civil protection measures as well. Thus, the scope of the Directive was limited to criminal matters, and a second instrument, the Regulation, was introduced to ensure the recognition

---

Königreich nach dem Ende des Brexit-Übergangszeitraums' (2021) *Zeitschrift für das gesamte Familienrecht* 342, 345.

16 S. 3(1) of the European Union (Withdrawal) Act 2018 (c. 16) and s. 5 of The Mutual Recognition of Protection Measures in Civil Matters (Amendment) (EU Exit) Regulations 2019, SI 2019/493.

17 The Criminal Justice (EU Exit) (Scotland) (Amendment etc.) Regulations 2020, SI 2020/339 is, unlike its equivalent for England, Wales and Northern Ireland, silent on the revocation.

18 See, for more details, S. van der Aa and J. Ouwerkerk, 'The European Protection Order: No time to waste or a waste of time?' (2011) 19 *European Journal of Crime, Criminal Law and Criminal Justice* 267, s. 7 <https://pure.uvt.nl/ws/portalfiles/portal/1370573/Aa_The_European_Protection_Order_final_111202_postprint_embargo_1_y.pdf> accessed 19.08.2021; N. Oliveras, 'Directive 2011/99/EU on the European Protection Order' in T. Freixes and L. Roman (eds), *The European Protection Order: Its Application to the Victims of Gender Violence*, Editorial Tecnos, Madrid 2015, pp. 34, 35 et seq.

19 Initiative with a view to the adoption of a Directive of the European Parliament and of the Council on the European Protection Order (2010/C 69/02) OJ C69/5.

20 N. Oliveras, 'Directive 2011/99/EU on the European Protection Order' in T. Freixes and L. Roman (eds), *The European Protection Order: Its Application to the Victims of Gender Violence*, Editorial Tecnos, Madrid 2015, p. 36.

of civil protection measures. The result was the co-existence of two instruments with the same goal, i.e. the continuation of the protection of the victim across the European Union. However, this co-existence is rather confusing,[21] and not fully convincing, especially with regard to the fact that both instruments introduce different recognition mechanisms: while the Regulation provides an automatic recognition for civil protection measures,[22] the Directive, in contrast, introduces a unique procedure that requires the executing Member State to transpose the original protection measure into a national protection measure (see *infra* section 4).

This raises the question of whether two instruments were necessary, or if it would have been possible to adopt one instrument for all protection orders. The original initiative argued that all protection measures fall under the legal basis for criminal matters, 'provided that the infringement of such obligations or prohibitions constitutes a criminal offence'.[23] The ensuing European Parliament legislative resolution went even further: it argued that all protection measures which had been imposed to protect a person against a criminal act fall under the legal basis of Article 82 TFEU.[24] However, this interpretation is very questionable. Just because a protection measure is imposed to protect a person against a criminal act, or because the infringement of such an obligation constitutes a criminal offence, is probably not enough to constitute a 'decision in criminal matters', as required by Article 82(1)(a) TFEU. If a protection measure is issued within a civil court – even where the protection order aims to protect the victim against behaviour that is criminalised, or the infringement of such obligation is criminalised – it is not convincing to argue that such a civil decision falls within the scope of Article 82(1)(a) TFEU, especially with regard to the existence of Article 81 TFEU. Thus, the adoption of one instrument for all kinds of protection measures solely on the legal basis of Article 81 TFEU was, indeed, impossible. On the other hand, some scholars argue that it would have been possible to identify protection measures issued in criminal matters within the judicial cooperation in

21 Same assessment by N. Oliveras, in ibid., p. 37.

22 See the contribution by A. Dutta in this volume.

23 Art. 1(2) of the Initiative with a view to the adoption of a Directive of the European Parliament and of the Council on the European Protection Order (2010/C 69/02) OJ C69/5.

24 Art. 2(2) of the European Parliament legislative resolution of 14 December 2010 on the draft directive of the European Parliament and of the Council on the European Protection Order (2012/C 169 E/35) OJ E/175; see also S. van der Aa and J. Ouwerkerk, 'The European Protection Order: No time to waste or a waste of time?' (2011) 19 *European Journal of Crime, Criminal Law and Criminal Justice* 267, s. 7.

civil matters.[25] The representatives of this approach also argue that criminal protection measures are 'structurally aimed to protect private interests and not the public interest of the State to punish wrongs'.[26] Further, they refer to the Brussels Ia Regulation,[27] in particular to its Article 7(3), which also encompasses private law 'islands' in criminal proceedings.[28] However, this approach is not fully persuasive, as most criminal protection measures were developed as alternatives to detention or prison[29] and, hence, interpreting criminal protection measures as decisions in civil matters cannot be recommended either.

To sum up, because of the different national approaches to protection measures, neither Article 81 TFEU nor Article 82 TFEU is sufficient as the sole legal basis for all protection measures. However, this does not mean that the EU was, therefore, obliged to introduce two instruments; rather, it could have been adopted one instrument on the legal basis of Articles 81 and 82 TFEU.[30] As will be shown later in this contribution (*see infra* section 5), the Regulation outperforms the Directive, and thus it would have been preferable to base the Regulation on Articles 81 and 82 TFEU, extending its scope to all protection measures. From a legal perspective, this would have been possible, as Article 82 TFEU does not oblige the EU to use a Directive rather than a Regulation.[31]

---

25 A. Dutta, 'Cross-border protection measures in the European Union' (2016) 12 *Journal of Private International Law* 169, 184.

26 A. Dutta, 'Cross-border protection measures in the European Union' (2016) 12 *Journal of Private International Law* 169, 184.

27 Regulation (EU) No 1215/2012 of the European Parliament and of the Council of 12 December 2012 on jurisdiction and the recognition and enforcement of judgments in civil and commercial matters [2012] OJ L351/1.

28 A. Dutta, 'Cross-border protection measures in the European Union' (2016) 12 *Journal of Private International Law* 169, 184.

29 S. Van der Aa, et al., *Mapping the Legislation and Assessing the Impact of Protection Orders in the European Member States*, Wolf Legal Publishers, AH Oisterwijk 2015, p. 242.

30 Compare S. van der Aa and J. Ouwerkerk, 'The European Protection Order: No time to waste or a waste of time?' (2011) 19 *European Journal of Crime, Criminal Law and Criminal Justice* 267, s. 7 ('For this reason, it would be more accurate if the EPO would not only refer to Art. 82(1)(a) and (d) TFEU as the legal basis for mutual recognition of protection measures, but also to Art. 81 TFEU.').

31 Only for the establishing of minimum rules according to Art. 82(2), the Treaty dictates the adoption of directives: G. Hochmayr, 'Art. 82 AEUV' in M. Pechstein, C. Nowak and U. Häde (eds), *Frankfurter Kommentar zu EUV, GRC and AEUV*, vol. 2, Mohr Siebeck, Tübingen 2017, paras. 23, 35. Differently, see N. Oliveras, 'Directive 2011/99/EU on the European Protection Order' in T. Freixes and L. Roman (eds), *The European Protection Order: Its Application to the Victims of Gender Violence*, Editorial Tecnos, Madrid 2015, 36, fn. 32.

3. SCOPE OF THE DIRECTIVE

As mentioned above, the Directive only applies to protection measures adopted in criminal matters, and does not cover civil protection measures, as these are already covered by the Regulation. However, the Directive – like the Regulation – does not define what constitutes a criminal protection measure in comparison to a civil protection measure. In any event, the nature of the authority issuing the protection measure is not determinative for the classification of the protection measure. The Directive explicitly states that the nature of the authority is not relevant and, thus, it does not necessarily have to belong to the criminal justice system, but can instead be an administrative or civil authority.[32] In some States like Denmark and Sweden, the distinction can be difficult, as these countries adopt 'quasi-criminal measures'.[33] On the one hand, the protection orders are imposed by the Chief of the Police (Denmark), or by the public prosecutor (Sweden), but, on the other hand, they are not necessarily linked to criminal proceedings.[34] At present, there is no case law of the CJEU on how to qualify a protection measure as a civil or criminal measure, thus it is suggested here that if a Member State issues an EPO in accordance with the Directive, the other Member State is bound by that decision, and should, therefore, apply the recognition procedure under the Directive.[35]

To fall under the scope of the Directive, the protection measure must be adopted to protect a person against a criminal act.[36] This means that the underlying conduct must be criminalised in the State that issued the protection measure, and that it is not sufficient that violations of the protection order are subject to criminal sanctions. The criminal acts include all crimes that endanger the life, physical or psychological integrity, dignity, personal liberty or sexual integrity of the victim.[37] It is, however, not necessary for the protection measure to have been adopted as part of a final decision in criminal proceedings; rather, a protection measure can also be adopted in the investigation or pre-trial stage, as a precautionary

32 Dir. 2011/99/EU, Recital 10 and Regulation 606/2013, Recital 10.

33 S. Van der Aa, et al., *Mapping the Legislation and Assessing the Impact of Protection Orders in the European Member States*, Wolf Legal Publishers, AH Oisterwijk 2015, pp. 7, 46 et seq. (Denmark), 56 et seq. (Sweden), 59, 222 ('the "quasi-criminal" protection orders in Sweden, Denmark, and Finland could be problematic since the trajectories in these countries have both civil and public features').

34 Ibid.

35 See also *Best Practice Guide – Protection of Abducting Mothers in Return Proceedings* (hereafter 'POAM Best Practice Guide'), reprinted in this volume, at s. 4.3.3.e.

36 Dir. 2011/99/EU, Recital 9.

37 Ibid., Recital 9, Arts. 1 and 2(2).

measure.[38] Further, the protection measure must be adopted specifically with the aims of protecting a person against a criminal act, and preventing new criminal acts or reducing the consequences of previous acts.[39] It should be noted that the scope of the Directive is not limited to the protection of victims of gender violence, but extends to all victims of the above mentioned criminal acts.[40] This is persuasive as the national laws for protection measures, also, are not necessarily restricted to gender-based violence.[41] If, on the other hand, the protection measure primarily serves aims other than the protection of the victim, the Member States are not obliged to issue a European protection order.[42] Since, in some Member States, criminal protection measures are imposed with different motives in mind, such as witness protection[43] or the social rehabilitation of the offender,[44] these measures will not be recognised under the Directive. This narrows the scope of the Directive, and can also easily be used as an excuse not to transpose the Directive into national law, while it will be difficult for the European Commission, as the guardian of the Treaties, to prove the opposite. A good example is Germany, where the first part of the Directive dealing with the issuing of an EPO has not been transposed into national law, with the explanation that criminal protection orders, under the national law, primarily serve the rehabilitation of the offender.[45] This is very interesting, as the German provisions on criminal protection orders are very similar to the equivalent Austrian provisions,[46] but the Austrian legislator was of the opinion that its criminal protection measures fell under the scope of the Directive, and has, therefore, introduced provisions regarding the ordering of an EPO.[47] As the wording of the German national

---

38 Ibid., Recital 10.

39 Ibid., Recital 9.

40 Ibid., Recital 10.

41 See the overview at S. Van der Aa, et al., *Mapping the Legislation and Assessing the Impact of Protection Orders in the European Member States*, Wolf Legal Publishers, AH Oisterwijk 2015, p. 65.

42 Dir. 2011/99/EU, Recital 9.

43 Ibid., Recital 11.

44 Ibid., Recital 9.

45 Entwurf eines Gesetzes zur Umsetzung der Richtlinie 2011/99/EU über die Europäische Schutzanordnung, zur Durchführung der Verordnung (EU) Nr. 606/2013 über die gegenseitige Anerkennung von Schutzmaßnahmen in Zivilsachen und zur Änderung des Gesetzes über das Verfahren in Familiensachen und in den Angelegenheiten der freiwilligen Gerichtsbarkeit, BT-Drs. 18/2955, p. 23.

46 Compare § 51 of the Austrian Criminal Code (Strafgesetzbuch) and § 56c and 68b of the German Criminal Code (Strafgesetzbuch).

47 § 134 et seq. Bundesgesetz über die justizielle Zusammenarbeit in Strafsachen mit den Mitgliedstaaten der Europäischen Union.

law is silent on the motives of a criminal protection measure, it is very difficult to say whether the Directive applies or not.[48]

Lastly, similarly to the Regulation, not every prohibition or restriction imposed on the person causing the risk qualifies for recognition under the Directive. Rather, only the prohibitions set out in Article 5 are covered. These are:

a. the prohibition from entering certain localities, places or defined areas where the protected person resides or visits;
b. the prohibition or regulation of contact, in any form, with the protected person, including by phone, electronic or ordinary mail, fax or any other means; or
c. the prohibition or regulation on approaching the protected person closer than a prescribed distance.

Regarding the prohibition from entering certain places, the wording of the Directive differs slightly from that of the Regulation:[49] while the Regulation covers prohibitions from entering certain places where the person 'resides, works, or regularly visits or stays',[50] the Directive refers only to places 'where the protected person resides or visits'. The different wording raises the question whether the place of work is included in the Directive, as only the Regulation explicitly refers to it. As the place of work is also a place that the person visits, it is assumed, here, that the Directive covers this as well. Thus, the restrictions are the same as under the Regulation, even though the wording is slightly different.

4. RECOGNITION PROCEDURE UNDER THE DIRECTIVE

4.1. OVERVIEW OF THE RECOGNITION MECHANISM

The Directive creates a special mechanism for the recognition of criminal protection orders. Criminal protection measures are not recognised

---

48 The German Criminal Code states only that the protection measures are issued to prevent the offender from committing new criminal acts: § 56c of the German Criminal Code. However, it is not clear from the wording whether it serves the protection of the victim or the rehabilitation of the offender.

49 S. Van der Aa, et al., *Mapping the Legislation and Assessing the Impact of Protection Orders in the European Member States*, Wolf Legal Publishers, AH Oisterwijk 2015, pp. 215 et seq.

50 Reg. 606/2013, Art. 3(1)(a).

automatically but, rather, require a decision of the executing State, converting the original protection measure into a similar protection measure available under its national law.

After a criminal protection measure is issued by a Member State, this State has to inform the person about the possibility of requesting a European protection order.[51] If the person applies for it, the State will verify whether the requirements are met, and if so, will issue the EPO and transmit it to the competent authority of the executing State. The competent authority of the executing State will then recognise that order, as long as no grounds for non-recognition apply, and will adopt a protection measure that is available under its national law in a similar case. This does not have to be a criminal measure, as not all Member States have criminal protection measures, but can also be an administrative or civil measure.

4.2. REQUIREMENTS FOR ISSUING A EUROPEAN PROTECTION ORDER

The European protection order is a standard form, set out in Annex I to the Directive, that contains, inter alia, the following information:[52] a summary of the facts and circumstances that have led to the adoption of the original protection measure, the prohibitions or restrictions that have been imposed, the duration of the protection measure, and an indication of the penalty in the event of the breach of the prohibitions or restrictions. The EPO has to be translated by the issuing State into the official language of the executing State.[53] The requirements for issuing the EPO are set out in Article 6.

4.2.1. Existence of a Protection Measure within the Meaning of Article 5

Firstly, an EPO can only be issued when a national protection measure exists that meets the requirements set out in Article 5. Therefore, the protection measure must contain at least one of the following prohibitions: the prohibition from visiting certain places, the prohibition of contact, or the prohibition on approaching the protected person (see *supra* section 3).

51 Dir. 2011/99/EU, Art. 6(5).
52 Ibid., Art. 7.
53 Ibid., Art. 17.

4.2.2. *(Intended) Stay in the Executing State*

A further requirement for issuing an EPO is that the protected person plans to reside or stay in the executing State, or already resides or stays there. As the Directive explicitly states that a stay in the other Member State is enough, this may seem only a minor burden. The Directive, however, allows the issuing State to take into account the length of the period or periods for which the protected person intends to stay in the executing State, when deciding whether to issue an EPO.[54] This indicates that the issuing State can refuse to issue an EPO if the intended stay is not long enough. Thus, a short visit might not be sufficient for an EPO.[55] The question is how long a victim has to stay in another Member State in order to be entitled to apply for an EPO. The Directive does not specify the minimum length of the victim's stay and, thus, leaves room for interpretation, which might lead to different results depending on the Member State deciding upon the EPO. The Member States can even introduce a fixed minimum term, in their national laws, as a condition for decreeing an EPO.[56] In regard to the safety of the protected person and the effectiveness of the Directive, the threshold for this condition should, however, not be too high.

4.2.3. *Request of the Protected Person*

Moreover, a Member State can only take action at the request of the protected person. This means that an EPO cannot be issued *ex officio*. If the protected person has a guardian or representative, he or she can introduce the request on behalf of the protected person.[57] The request can

---

54 Ibid., Art. 6(1).

55 N. Oliveras, 'Directive 2011/99/EU on the European Protection Order' in T. Freixes and L. Roman (eds), *The European Protection Order: Its Application to the Victims of Gender Violence*, Editorial Tecnos, Madrid 2015, p. 41 ('[A] short stay during a weekend in another EU Member State may bring the competent authority of the issuing State to consider that the adoption of a protection order is disproportionate in relation to all the required procedural steps, even though the Directive does not establish a minimum period.').

56 See the Report from the Commission to the European Parliament and the Council on the implementation of Directive 2011/99/EU of the European Parliament and of the Council of 13 December 2011 on the European protection order, COM(2020) 187 final, p. 7 ('[A] few Member States have introduced specific deadlines for executing a EPO, obliging their competent authorities to recognise a EPO or take another decision on the measure. Depending on the Member State, the deadline is 2 days, 3 days, 10 days, 15 days, 7 + 10 days, or 28 days.').

57 Dir. 2011/99/EU, Art. 6(6).

be submitted either to the competent authority of the issuing State, or to the competent authority of the executing State.[58] If the request is submitted to the latter, it will forward the request as soon as possible to the issuing State. The competent authority of each State is defined by its national law.

4.2.4. *Right of the Person Causing Danger to be Heard*

A further condition of an EPO is that the person causing danger must have the chance to be heard, and to challenge the original protection measure. With this provision, the Directive intends to meet the standards set out in the European Convention for the Protection of Human Rights and Fundamental Freedoms, and in the Charter of Fundamental Rights of the European Union.[59] It is sufficient for these rights to have been granted in the process regarding the original protection measure. Only if the person causing the danger has not been heard, or has not had the chance to challenge the original decision, must this be done before issuing the EPO.

4.2.5. *Discretion of the Member State to Issue an EPO*

Even if the requirements mentioned above are fulfilled, Article 6(1) indicates that the issuing Member State has a discretion when deciding whether to issue an EPO. Article 6(1), sentence 2, states that '[w]hen deciding upon the issuing of a European protection order, the competent authority in the issuing State shall take into account, *inter alia*, the length of the period or periods that the protected person intends to stay in the executing State and *the seriousness of the need for protection*' (emphasis added). Given that the Member State is expected to consider the seriousness of the need for protection, the issuing of the EPO is unpredictable: the EPO can be refused simply because the Member State assumes that the danger will be eliminated when the victim moves to another State.[60] Accordingly, in the end, the victim will also have to prove their need for cross-border protection, and the assessment of this condition is left to the discretion of the issuing State.[61]

---

58 Dir. 2011/99/EU, Art. 6(3).

59 Dir. 2011/99/EU, Recital 17.

60 S. Van der Aa, et al., *Mapping the Legislation and Assessing the Impact of Protection Orders in the European Member States*, Wolf Legal Publishers, AH Oisterwijk 2015, p. 214.

61 S. Van der Aa, et al., *Mapping the Legislation and Assessing the Impact of Protection Orders in the European Member States*, Wolf Legal Publishers, AH Oisterwijk 2015, p. 214 ('This requirement … brings with it a "double" risk assessment for the victim who already had the seriousness of the need for protection recognized in the issuing state.').

4.3. RECOGNITION AND EXECUTION OF THE EPO

After the EPO has been transmitted to the executing State, the Member State has to recognise the order 'without undue delay', and replace the original protection measure with an equivalent measure available under its national law (Article 9(1)).

4.3.1. Grounds for Non-Recognition

The executing State can refuse recognition only on one of the grounds set out in Article 10. The grounds for non-recognition can be separated into those related to formal reasons, for example that the EPO has not been completed, and those related to the fact that the original protection measure has been ordered in criminal matters. The latter category includes grounds for non-recognition because:

- the underlying conduct does not constitute a criminal offence under the law of the executing State;
- the penalty or measure is covered by an amnesty, according to the law of the executing State;
- the person has immunity under the law of the executing State;
- the criminal prosecution is statute-barred under the law of the executing State;
- the recognition of the EPO would contravene the *ne bis in idem* principle;
- the person causing danger cannot be held criminally responsible under the law of the executing State because of his or her age; or
- the criminal offence is regarded as having been committed, wholly or for a major or essential part, within its territory.

The many possibilities for refusing the recognition can limit the effectiveness of the Directive. It is of particular significance that the recognition only ensues if the executing State criminalises the underlying behaviour as well. While this ground of refusal is of no relevance if the protection measure was imposed, on the person causing danger, in order to protect a victim of physical violence, as this behaviour is regarded as a crime in all Member States, other behaviour, such as stalking, may not be recognised as a crime in all Member States.[62] Although most Member States have criminalised

62 S. Van der Aa and J. Ouwerkerk, 'The European Protection Order: No time to waste or a waste of time?' (2011) 19 *European Journal of Crime, Criminal Law and Criminal Justice* 267, s. 6.

stalking,[63] the definition of the behaviour can vary across the Member States, as stalking is difficult to define, and thus, persons protected against stalking may experience difficulties in having their protection orders recognised.[64] Another example is the criminal offence of domestic abuse, as created in Scotland by the Domestic Abuse (Scotland) Act 2018. Under the Act, various types of behaviour can constitute domestic abuse, including those that have the purpose of making the victim dependent on the offender, isolating the victim from friends and relatives, or controlling the victim's day-to-day activities.[65] The scope of the Act is very wide, and not yet common among the Member States.[66] Consequently, it is likely that behaviour which is criminalised in Scotland as domestic abuse is not criminalised in a Member State and, thus, the recognition of an EPO ordered on the basis of such conduct might be refused.

The ground for refusal because the criminal offence is regarded as having been committed wholly, or for a major or essential part, within the territory of the executing State is of relevance in cases of extraterritorial jurisdiction. Again, the Scottish law is a good example:[67] the Scottish Domestic Abuse Act 2018 allows the prosecution of the offence of domestic abuse, even if the relevant behaviour has occurred in a State other than the UK. The only requirement is that the offender is a UK national, or is habitually resident in Scotland. Thus, if the Scottish courts adopt a protection measure, even though the underlying conduct has happened in the executing State, the latter can refuse the recognition.

However, the grounds for non-recognition only apply if the Member States have implemented them in their national laws. The wording, 'can refuse the recognition', included in the Directive, indicates that the Member States are not obliged to implement all reasons, but, rather, have discretion in this regard. For example, Germany has made use of this discretion, and has implemented only three reasons:[68] in particular, it has not

---

63 S. Van der Aa, et al., *Mapping the Legislation and Assessing the Impact of Protection Orders in the European Member States*, Wolf Legal Publishers, AH Oisterwijk 2015, pp. 212 et seq.

64 For example, Germany revised the requirements for stalking in 2017, and the German legislator is currently planning a new amendment of the provision: see <https://www.bmjv.de/SharedDocs/Gesetzgebungsverfahren/Dokumente/RegE_Cyberstalking.pdf?__blob=publicationFile&v=3> accessed 19.08.2021.

65 Domestic Abuse (Scotland) Act 2018, ss. 2(2)(b)(i), (3)(a)(b)(c).

66 See the POAM Best Practice Guide, s. 4.3.2.c.

67 Domestic Abuse (Scotland) Act 2018, s. 3. See also the POAM Best Practice Guide, ss. 4.3.1.a and 4.3.2.c.

68 § 6, Gesetz zur Umsetzung der Richtlinie 2011/99/EU über die Europäische Schutzanordnung und zur Durchführung der Verordnung (EU) Nr. 606/2013 über die gegenseitige Anerkennung von Schutzmaßnahmen in Zivilsachen.

implemented the reasons relating to the fact that the protection measure was adopted in a criminal matter. As an explanation, the German legislator pointed out that, in Germany, protection measures are not adopted in criminal measures and, therefore, these grounds for refusal would be of no relevance for Germany.[69] Most States, however, have implemented all grounds for non-recognition.[70]

If Member States adopt other grounds for refusal in their implementation laws, this would be a violation of EU law. An example from Germany is that, under the German implementing law, the competent authority can refuse the recognition if the person causing the danger has not been heard in either the proceeding leading to the original protection measure, or in the proceeding leading to the EPO.[71] Even if this is a requirement for issuing the EPO, it is not a ground on which the executing State can refuse the recognition. This means that compliance with this requirement is the sole responsibility of the issuing State, and it is not for the executing State to supervise this; rather, the executing State has to trust the issuing State in this regard. Mutual trust is important for the ability to guarantee a fast proceeding, which is essential for the safety of the victim.

4.3.2. *Execution of the EPO*

If the executing State has recognised the EPO, it then adopts a measure that is available under its national law in a similar case, and which corresponds, to the highest degree possible, to the protection measures of the issuing State.[72] Because of the national differences regarding protection measures, the executing State is not required to take the same protection measure as the issuing State but, rather, has discretion to adopt any measure under its national law that it considers to be adequate and appropriate, in a

69 Entwurf eines Gesetzes zur Umsetzung der Richtlinie 2011/99/EU über die Europäische Schutzanordnung, zur Durchführung der Verordnung (EU) Nr. 606/2013 über die gegenseitige Anerkennung von Schutzmaßnahmen in Zivilsachen und zur Änderung des Gesetzes über das Verfahren in Familiensachen und in den Angelegenheiten der freiwilligen Gerichtsbarkeit, BT-Drs. 18/2955, p. 29.

70 Report from the Commission to the European Parliament and the Council on the implementation of Directive 2011/99/EU of the European Parliament and of the Council of 13 December 2011 on the European protection order, COM(2020) 187 final, p. 8 ('Several Member States have transposed the grounds as optional and one has introduced them as mandatory.').

71 § 6(4), Gesetz zur Umsetzung der Richtlinie 2011/99/EU über die Europäische Schutzanordnung und zur Durchführung der Verordnung (EU) Nr. 606/2013 über die gegenseitige Anerkennung von Schutzmaßnahmen in Zivilsachen.

72 Dir. 2011/99/EU, Arts. 9(1) and 9(2).

similar case, in order to continue the protection of the victim.[73] Thus, the executing State can choose whether to apply criminal, administrative or civil measures, depending on its national legislation. In this regard, the Directive provides a high degree of flexibility.[74] As a result, the protected person will not necessarily be provided with the exact same protection as in the issuing State, but will have the same protection as if he or she had applied for a protection measure directly in the executing State.[75] The executing State informs all parties involved, i.e. the person causing danger, the issuing State and the protected person, of all the measures it has adopted on the basis of the EPO.[76]

If there is no protection measure available under the national law of the executing State in a similar case, the Directive does not oblige the Member States to adapt any measure. Instead, the executing State merely has to report any breach of the original protection measure to the issuing State.[77] The background to this rule is that the Directive was not intended to intervene with the national laws: in particular, it was not intended to oblige the Member States to implement new protection measures.[78]

4.4. LEGAL REMEDIES

The Directive does not contain any provisions regarding the question of whether the decision to issue an EPO, or the decision to reject the request to issue an EPO, can be challenged by the protected person or the person causing danger. The Directive only states, in Article 6(7), that if the issuing State has refused to order an EPO, it shall inform the protected person of any applicable legal remedies that exist under its national law. The wording of the provision indicates that Member States are not obliged to provide for legal remedies, but the provision makes it clear that the Member States are free to provide for legal remedies for the victim. Still, there is no indication as to whether the person causing the danger can also challenge the issuing of an EPO; the Directive only dictates that the person causing the danger

73 Ibid., Recital 20.
74 Ibid.
75 Council of the EU, Initiative for a Directive of the European Parliament and of the Council on the European Protection Order – Explanatory Memorandum, Brussels, 6 January 2010, p. 17. Thus, the person receives the same protection that the State provides for its own nationals in a purely national case.
76 Dir. 2011/99/EU, Art. 9(3), Recital 22.
77 Ibid., Art. 11(3), Recital 27.
78 Ibid., Recital 10.

must be granted the right to challenge the original protection measure.[79] As the Directive is not clear on this point, it is suggested that it is left to the Member States to regulate this in their national laws.[80] To ensure a fast procedure, and against the background that the person causing the danger had the chance to challenge the original protection measure, it would have been more convincing if the person causing the danger could not contest the decision. In Austria, for example, the protected person and the public prosecutor have the right to challenge any decision of the issuing State, while the person causing the danger may only challenge the decision if he or she was not heard before the protection measure was adopted.[81]

In relation to the decision taken by the executing state, the Directive explicitly states that the national law of that state applies to the rules on legal remedies.[82] This means that each Member State decides whether the decision to recognise the EPO, or to refuse the recognition, can be challenged. While, for example, in Austria[83] the public prosecutor, the protected person and the person causing danger can each challenge the decisions of the executing state, in Germany[84] only the protected person can contest the decision. The German law explicitly states that the decision to recognise the EPO cannot be contested.

As both decisions – that regarding the issuing of the EPO, and that regarding the recognition of the EPO – can be challenged, depending on

---

79 Ibid., Art. 6(4).

80 For a different opinion, see E. Cerrato, 'The Procedure for the Adoption of the Protection Measures' in T. Freixes and L. Roman (eds), *The European Protection Order: Its Application to the Victims of Gender Violence*, Editorial Tecnos, Madrid 2015, pp. 95, 121 ('Judging by the provisions of article 6(7) of the Directive, legal remedies are only available against a decision to reject the request for a European protection order to be issued, but not against a decision to grant such as request.').

81 § 134(5) des Bundesgesetzes über die justizielle Zusammenarbeit in Strafsachen mit den Mitgliedstaaten der Europäischen Union. In the event that the perpetrator was not given the right to be heard, either in the procedure leading to the adoption of the original protection measure or in the following procedure leading to the EPO, the issuing State is not allowed to issue the EPO. Thus, it makes sense that, in this case, the person can challenge the EPO.

82 Dir. 2011/99/EU, Art. 9(1). If the recognition of the EPO has been refused, the executing State has to inform the protected person of any applicable legal remedies that are available under its national law (Art. 10(2)). Again, this provision cannot be interpreted as an obligation to provide for legal remedies, but only obliges the Member States to inform the protected person whether any such legal remedies exist under its national law.

83 § 127(3) des Bundesgesetzes über die justizielle Zusammenarbeit in Strafsachen mit den Mitgliedstaaten der Europäischen Union.

84 § 8 Gesetz zur Umsetzung der Richtlinie 2011/99/EU über die Europäische Schutzanordnung und zur Durchführung der Verordnung (EU) Nr. 606/2013 über die gegenseitige Anerkennung von Schutzmaßnahmen in Zivilsachen.

the implementing laws of the Member States, this might retard the whole process and, thus, limit the effectiveness of the Directive.

4.5. ENFORCEMENT OF THE PROTECTION MEASURE

The enforcement of the protection measure adopted in the executing State on the basis of the EPO is left to the national law of the executing State.[85] In the event that the person causing the danger violates the protection measures, the executing State is allowed to take any non-criminal decisions, and to take any urgent and provisional measures, in order to put an end to the breach.[86] Further, the executing State is allowed to impose criminal penalties, given that a breach constitutes a criminal offence under its national law.[87] Germany, for example, has made use of this possibility: the Act implementing the Directive states that a breach of a measure taken in execution of an EPO is a criminal offence, and will be punished with a term of imprisonment of up to one year, or a fine.[88]

4.6. MODIFICATION AND WITHDRAWAL OF THE EPO AND THE DISCONTINUATION OF PROTECTION MEASURES TAKEN BY THE EXECUTING STATE

While the executing State has the exclusive competence to enforce the protection measures adopted on the basis of the EPO, the issuing State retains the competence to renew, review, modify, revoke and withdraw the original protection measure and, consequently, the EPO.[89] If the issuing State makes use of these rights, it has to inform the executing State of any decision it has taken in this regard, so that the executing State can address the consequences appropriately. If the executing State has revoked or withdrawn the EPO, the executing State will discontinue the measures that it has adopted in order to enforce the EPO[90] and, if the issuing State

85 Dir. 2011/99/EU, Art. 11(1).

86 Ibid., Art. 11(2)(b)(c).

87 Ibid., Art. 11(2)(a).

88 § 24 Gesetz zur Umsetzung der Richtlinie 2011/99/EU über die Europäische Schutzanordnung und zur Durchführung der Verordnung (EU) Nr. 606/2013 über die gegenseitige Anerkennung von Schutzmaßnahmen in Zivilsachen.

89 Dir. 2011/99/EU, Art. 13(1)(a).

90 Ibid., Art. 13(6). But still, the executing state retains the right to autonomously adopt any protection measure under its national law, in order to protect the person concerned: see Recital 23.

has modified the EPO, the executing State will also modify its protection measures.[91] In the latter case, the executing State has the right to refuse the modification if the new protection measure does not contain a prohibition or restriction listed in Article 5, or if the EPO is not complete.[92]

Even if the issuing State does not withdraw the EPO, the executing State may decide to discontinue the protection measure where there is a clear indication that the protected person does not reside or stay in the territory of the executing State, either because the victim has already left the Member State or, contrary to their initial intent, has never actually moved to that Member State.[93] In these cases, the victim is no longer in need of protection in the executing State and, thus, the protection measures can be terminated. Another ground on which the executing State can discontinue the protection measure is that the maximum term of duration has expired.[94] As the executing State applies its own law when adopting the protection measures on the basis of the EPO, it also applies its national rules on the duration of a protection measure. Thus, the protection measures adopted by the Member State may expire earlier than the original protection measure taken by the issuing State. In both cases, the executing State has to inform the issuing State and the protected person of the discontinuation.[95]

5. COMPARISON WITH THE REGULATION

The main difference[96] between the Directive and the Regulation is obvious: the different recognition mechanism. As the Directive requires an extra step, i.e. the adoption of similar measures that are available under the national law of the executing State, the whole process is potentially more time-consuming than automatic recognition under the Regulation. Further, the Directive offers more possibilities to refuse the cross-border recognition. Firstly, the issuing State has discretion whether to issue an EPO, having taken into account the length of the stay, and the need for the

91 Ibid., Art. 13(7)(a).
92 Ibid., Art. 13(7)(b).
93 Ibid., Art. 14(1)(a).
94 Ibid., Art. 14(1)(b).
95 Ibid., Art. 14(2).
96 See, for details regarding the differences between the Regulation and the Directive, S. Van der Aa, et al., *Mapping the Legislation and Assessing the Impact of Protection Orders in the European Member States*, Wolf Legal Publishers, AH Oisterwijk 2015, pp. 211 et seq.

protection in the other Member State: a requirement that is not needed to request a certificate under the Regulation. Secondly, under the Regulation, the victim does not have to prove that they intend to move to another Member State; rather, the certificate will simply be issued on the request of the victim. Moreover, the grounds on which the executing State can refuse the recognition under the Directive are much more extensive than those under the Regulation. In particular, the principle of double criminality[97] only applies for the Directive. Notably, under the Regulation, the Member State addressed cannot refuse the recognition of the protection measure on the ground that its national law does not allow for such a measure, based on the same facts.[98] In comparison, under the Directive, where no protection measure is available in the executing State in a similar case, the executing State does not have to adopt an equivalent measure, but only has to report any breach of the original protection measure. Finally, the Directive does not apply to all criminal protection measures but, rather, the scope of the Directive is limited to protection measures that aim specifically to protect a person against a criminal act in order to prevent new criminal acts. The Regulation, in comparison, does not exclude any civil protection measures from its scope. Such an exclusion would not make any sense, as civil protection measures always serve the victim's interests.[99] The only advantage of the Directive over the Regulation is that the EPO has no expiry date, while the Regulation limits the effects of recognition to one year from the issuing of the certificate.[100] However, this advantage is limited by the fact that the executing State can discontinue the measures taken on the basis of an EPO, in cases where the maximum duration provided by its national law has expired.

To conclude, the cross-border recognition procedure under the Regulation is clearly more attractive than the procedure under the Directive. Against this background, victims are better off applying for a civil protection measure to ensure cross-border recognition.

---

97 I.e. that both states must recognise the underlying behaviour as a crime: compare S. van der Aa and J. Ouwerkerk, 'The European Protection Order: No time to waste or a waste of time?' (2011) 19 *European Journal of Crime, Criminal Law and Criminal Justice* 267, s. 6.

98 Regulation 606/2013, Art. 13(3).

99 S. Van der Aa, et al., *Mapping the Legislation and Assessing the Impact of Protection Orders in the European Member States*, Wolf Legal Publishers, AH Oisterwijk 2015, p. 213.

100 Regulation 606/2013, Art. 4(4). Even if the protection measure has a longer duration, the protection measure can only be enforced in the other Member State for one year; after that date, the protected person would have to apply for a new certificate in the Member State of origin. See, for more details, A. Dutta, 'Cross-border protection measures in the European Union' (2016) 12 *Journal of Private International Law* 169, 177.

6. CONCLUSION

It is no surprise that the Directive has received so little attention so far. One reason for this is probably that the case for which the Directive was introduced, i.e. the protection of victims across the Union, is rare.[101] Especially in cases of domestic violence, the danger will often be eliminated when the victim leaves the offender and moves to another Member State. Hence, cross-border enforcement of such a protection measure will not be necessary. Another reason for the lack of practical use might also be the lack of awareness of the instruments among practitioners – this is at least the Commission's assumption in its 2020 report.[102]

However, the main reason for the lack of practical significance lies, most likely, in the Directive itself. As seen above, the Directive has many weak points[103] that make its application, in the few relevant cases, unattractive. In addition, it is likely that the cross-border recognition and enforcement procedure will actually take longer than simply applying for new protection measures in the other Member State. Theoretically, the Directive obliges the Member States to recognise the EPO with the same priority that would be applicable in a similar national case. Yet, it is more than doubtful whether this will actually be the case, as the competent authorities are not as familiar with either the issuing or the recognition of the EPO as they are with their own national procedures.[104] Against this background, it would not be surprising if victims would rather apply for a new protection measure when moving to another Member State than request an EPO for cross-border recognition of the original protection measure.

---

101 Compare the evaluation of S. van der Aa and J. Ouwerkerk, 'The European Protection Order: No time to waste or a waste of time?' (2011) 19 *European Journal of Crime, Criminal Law and Criminal Justice* 267, s. 11 ('The EPO would probably only be useful to a very limited number of victims and to a quite limited number of situations.').

102 Report from the Commission to the European Parliament and the Council on the implementation of Directive 2011/99/EU of the European Parliament and of the Council of 13 December 2011 on the European protection order, COM(2020) 187 final.

103 The main weak points are: (1) the limited scope of the Directive, as it applies only to criminal protection measures that are specifically issued to protect the victim; (2) the recognition process itself, as the issuing state has considerable discretion whether to issue an EPO, and the executing state can refuse the recognition on a number of grounds; and (3) the fact that the executing state is not obliged to adopt a protection measure if no such measure is available under its national law.

104 The Directive recommends provision of appropriate training to judges, prosecutors, police and judicial staff: Directive 2011/99/EU, Recital 31. Still, our perception in the project was that most practitioners were not familiar at all with either instrument.

PART II

PROTECTIVE MEASURES IN THE CONTEXT OF INTERNATIONAL PARENTAL CHILD ABDUCTION

DOMESTIC VIOLENCE AS AN ASPECT OF 1980 HAGUE CHILD ABDUCTION CONVENTION RETURN PROCEEDINGS

Marilyn FREEMAN and Nicola TAYLOR

1. INTRODUCTION

The Hague Convention of 25 October 1980 on the Civil Aspects of International Child Abduction (hereafter 'the Convention') provides for cooperation between its 101 signatory States to ensure that a child abducted from their State of habitual residence in breach of rights of custody is returned forthwith, unless one of the limited Convention exceptions to return applies. The return will usually, but not always, be to the child's State of habitual residence. Dyer discusses the Convention's intrusion upon the jurisdiction of the courts in the country to which the child has been taken, even if that is the country of the child's nationality, and the insistence that the child be returned, so that the courts of another country can exercise jurisdiction over the merits of custody.[1] This is because the Convention is premised on the assumption that it is best for children not to be abducted and, if they are, for them to be returned promptly, so their future can be decided by a court in the country with the closest connection to the child.

The Convention's emphasis on prompt return is designed to protect children internationally from the harmful effects of their wrongful removal or retention.[2] Unlike most other family law matters, the focus in the Convention is on the jurisdiction, not the child's welfare, unless one of the limited exceptions to return applies. It is important to note, given the subject of this contribution, that these exceptions do not include a provision specifically providing for the non-return of a child because of domestic violence or abuse suffered by the abducting parent.

The Convention applies when a child under the age of 16 years, at the time the tribunal hears the application for return, has been wrongfully taken to, or retained in, another Contracting State, in breach of rights of custody under the law of the State in which the child was habitually resident, and those rights were actually being exercised (either jointly or alone) at the time, or would have been, but for the removal or retention.[3] The Convention provides an internationally agreed mechanism for dealing with child abduction, yet its interpretation and implementation is a matter for each individual Contracting State, since there is no supranational body controlling its application.[4] This creates a number of challenges, as the ways in which international child abductions are approached, and how they are resolved, can differ widely in practice between Contracting States, including in relation to domestic violence.

Special Commission meetings to review the operation of the Convention are held approximately every four years by The Permanent Bureau of the Hague Conference on Private International Law (hereafter 'the HCCH'). To provide reliable data to inform discussions at the four most recent meetings of the Special Commission in 2001, 2006, 2011 and 2017, and to track trends over time, surveys have been undertaken of all

---

1 A. Dyer, 'The Hague Convention on the Civil Aspects of International Child Abduction – Towards Global Cooperation: Its Successes and Failures' (1993) 1(3–4) *International Journal of Children's Rights* 273–92, 273–74.

2 The Hague Convention of 25 October 1980 on the Civil Aspects of International Child Abduction (hereafter 'Convention'), Preamble.

3 Convention, Arts. 3 and 4.

4 M. Freeman and N.J. Taylor, 'Domestic Violence and Child Participation: Contemporary Challenges to the 1980 Hague Child Abduction Convention' (2020) 42(2) *Journal of Social Welfare and Family Law* 154–75, 154.

the applications received by participating Central Authorities in 1999,[5] 2003,[6] 2008[7] and 2015.[8] The longitudinal, comparative findings produced over this 16-year period provide important information on the general operation of the Convention and abducting family characteristics, as well as insights into the statistical trends apparent in the workings of Central Authorities and courts in Convention proceedings internationally.[9]

These statistical analyses show that international child abduction is a global and growing phenomenon, as the number of incoming applications and the number of Contracting States have both increased steadily during the period over which this data has been collected.[10] Several key trends have been identified and tracked that have a significant bearing on the international child abduction landscape and the Convention's operation. This contribution considers how return proceedings have evolved over the decades as a result of the change in the profile of the typical abductor, the growth in joint parenting, and our increased understanding of the intersection between international child abduction and domestic violence. The return-focused approach versus protection of individual interests in relation to domestic violence and gender equality is also discussed. Finally, two decisions of the UK Supreme Court, in 2011[11] and 2012,[12] are analysed, as they highlight a shift away from a pure return-focused approach.

---

5 N. Lowe, S. Armstrong and A. Mathias, *A Statistical Analysis of Applications Made in 1999 under the Hague Convention of 25 October 1980 on the Civil Aspects of International Child Abduction – Project Report*, Permanent Bureau of the Hague Conference on Private International Law, The Hague 2001.

6 N. Lowe, *A Statistical Analysis of Applications Made in 2003 under the Hague Convention of 25 October 1980 on the Civil Aspects of International Child Adoption (2007 Update)*, Hague Conference on Private International Law, The Hague 2008.

7 N. Lowe and V. Stephens, *A Statistical Analysis of Applications Made in 2008 under the Hague Convention of 25 October 1980 on the Civil Aspects of International Child Abduction, Preliminary Doc. Nos. 8A–8C*, Permanent Bureau of the Hague Conference, The Hague 2011.

8 N. Lowe and V. Stephens, *Part I: A Statistical Analysis of Applications Made in 2015 under the Hague Convention of 25 October 1980 on the Civil Aspects of International Child Abduction – Global Report*, Permanent Bureau of the Hague Conference on Private International Law, The Hague 2017.

9 N.J. Taylor and M. Freeman, 'International Child Abduction' in R. Treloar and M. Maclean (eds), *Family Justice Systems*, Edward Elgar Research Handbooks in Law and Society Series, Cambridge, forthcoming.

10 N. Lowe and V. Stephens, 'Global Trends in the Operation of the 1980 Hague Abduction Convention: The 2015 Statistics' (2018) 52(2) *Family Law Quarterly* 349–84.

11 *Re E (Children)* [2011] UKSC 27.

12 *In the Matter of S (A Child)* [2012] UKSC 10.

2. CHANGE IN PROFILE OF THE TYPICAL ABDUCTOR

The gender of the typical abductor envisaged at the time the Convention was drafted has generated much discussion, including whether, and how, that might differ from the profile that has developed since 1980. Debate has centred around whether the Convention was drafted in anticipation of non-custodial parents (usually fathers), or custodial parents (usually mothers), or both, being the taking parents. The Dyer Report, written by the First Secretary of the HCCH when work began on developing the Convention, specifically mentioned the non-custodial parent in the context of the frustration that may lead to an abduction:

> as an important factor in the incidence of international abduction of children by parents, one must mention frustration: frustration on the part of the non-custodial parent when unjustifiably deprived of the right of visitation with the child, frustration with the slowness, expense and inefficacy of legal proceedings concerning custody of the child (which often contributes to the re-kidnapping of the kidnapped child – self-help engendering self-help).[13]

Schuz regards this statement as envisaging 'the typical abduction situation as one in which the non-custodial parent abducted the child, either in order to pre-empt a non-favourable custody determination or out of frustration caused by the reduction in contact with the child as a result of losing custody'.[14] While she acknowledges that the Dyer Report does not refer specifically to fathers as abductors, she says there is no mention of factors that might cause a custodial parent to abduct a child, and that the belief that only non-custodial parents abducted, combined with the fact that mothers were usually granted custody, must have led the drafters to assume that most abductors were fathers.[15]

Support for this view may be found in the Explanatory Report on the Convention by Professor Pérez-Vera.[16] In the section discussing

---

13 A. Dyer, *Report on International Abduction by One Parent ('Legal Kidnapping')*, Preliminary Doc. 1, Actes et Documents of the XIVth Session, Hague Conference on Private International Law 1978, at p. 19.

14 R. Schuz, *The Hague Child Abduction Convention: A Critical Analysis*, Hart Publishing, Oxford and Portland, OR 2013, p. 8.

15 Ibid., p. 55.

16 E. Pérez-Vera, *Explanatory Report on the 1980 HCCH Child Abduction Convention*, Acts and Documents of the XIVth Session, Hague Conference on Private International Law, The Hague 1981 <http://www.hcch.net/upload/expl28.pdf> accessed 27.08.2021.

the Convention's subject-matter, she explained that one of the elements invariably present in all of the abduction cases examined was the outcome that the child was taken out of the family and social environment in which its life had developed.[17] That may be considered to provide implicit recognition of the usual abductor being thought of as the non-custodial parent who has removed the child from their primary carer, home and community.

Other commentators have also made observations on the profile of the typical abductor since the adoption of the Convention. For example, McEleavy stated:

> The removal or retention of children was largely viewed as an action by frustrated fathers who did not exercise a primary care role. Thereby in promoting return children would not only be going back to their home environment but to their primary carer. In such circumstances the drafters' use of the expression the restoration of the *status quo ante* can be fully understood.[18]

Lowe and Stephens commented that:

> At the time that the Convention was being negotiated, it was assumed that abductors were commonly noncustodial fathers.[19]

Baroness Hale, former President of the UK Supreme Court, also discussed the factual assumption underlying the Convention with respect to fathers as abductors, but highlighted how the statistical evidence had revealed it to be mistaken:

> As is well known, when the Convention was negotiated, there were two assumptions made, one factual and one legal, which have since proved unfounded. The factual assumption was that most abductors were not primary carers – rather they were disappointed non-primary carers, usually fathers, upset at the breakdown of their marriage and the loss of easy day to day contact with their children which this brings or dissatisfied with the contact they were having after separation. So the stereotypical abductor was taking or keeping

17 Ibid., para. 11.

18 P. McEleavy, 'The European Court of Human Rights and the Hague Child Abduction Convention: Prioritising Return or Reflection?' (2015) (62)(3) *Netherlands International Law Review* 365–405, 370.

19 N. Lowe and V. Stephens, 'Global Trends in the Operation of the 1980 Hague Abduction Convention: The 2015 Statistics' (2018) 52(2) *Family Law Quarterly* 349–84, 353.

> the children away from their home and the person who was looking after them, either by spiriting them away (there was much talk of the school gates) or by keeping them back after a visit. Many of the cases examined by Professor Marilyn Freeman in her research into the long-term effects of international child abduction fell into this category. Sending the children back home as soon as possible would restore the status quo and protect their stability. And so it could be assumed to be in the best interests of the individual child as well as of children generally. … However, as is well known, the conventional paradigm soon turned out to be mistaken. In 2008, in this country, 81 per cent of taking parents were mothers, and only 16 per cent were fathers; globally the averages were 69 per cent mothers and 28 per cent fathers.[20]

The Conclusions and Recommendations of the Fifth Special Commission confirmed that the trend of approximately two-thirds of the taking persons being primary carers, mostly mothers, gave rise 'to issues which had not been foreseen by the drafters of the Convention'.[21] Schuz, too, has recently noted that the Convention 'is invoked in types of cases which were not envisioned by the drafters and which might not naturally be classified as abduction cases'.[22] This had been reflected in case law, notably in the UK Supreme Court case of *Re E* [2011], where the Court stated:

> All parties recognise that the context in which these cases arise has changed in many ways from the context in which the Hague Convention was originally drafted. There is every indication that the paradigm case which the original begetters of the Convention had in mind was a dissatisfied parent who did not have the primary care of the child snatching the child away from her primary carer. … Nowadays, however, the most common case is a primary carer whose relationship with the other parent has broken down and who leaves with the children, usually to go back to her own family.[23]

While a primary carer might not, originally, have been regarded as the most likely parent to abduct a child, or the most common category of abductor, it does not follow that it was not within the contemplation of

---

20 B. Hale, 'Taking Flight – Domestic Violence and Child Abduction' (2017) 70(1) *Current Legal Problems* 3–16, 4.

21 HCCH, *Fifth Meeting of the Special Commission to Review the Operation of the 1980 and 1996 Hague Conventions (30 October–9 November 2006): Conclusions and Recommendations*, Hague Conference on Private International Law, The Hague 2006, Introduction.

22 R. Schuz, 'The Hague Child Abduction Convention and Re-Relocation Disputes' (2021) 35(1) *International Journal of Law, Policy and The Family* 1–36, 1.

23 *Re E (Children)* [2011] UKSC 27, para. 6.

the Convention's drafters that primary carers might abduct their children, and that the Convention might be used by the non-primary carer, left-behind parent to secure the return of the abducted child. The broad scope of the Convention's definition of 'rights of custody' in Article 5 should be considered in this context, as Article 3 sets out that the child's removal or retention will be wrongful when 'it is in breach of rights of custody'. Article 5 states that 'rights of custody' include 'rights relating to the care of the person of the child and, in particular, the right to determine the child's place of residence'. Had it not been envisaged that a child could be abducted by their custodial parent, the rationale is unclear for the Convention including, within the Article 5 definition of 'rights of custody', the right to determine the child's place of residence.[24]

Holliday and Baruffi agree that both mothers and fathers were contemplated as abductors:

> From the wording of the negotiations in the 14th Proceedings, the drafters worked from the premise that either parent could be the abductor and designed the Convention accordingly.[25]

In relation to the statistical trends, a change in the profile of abducting parents over time is evident. Lowe and Perry compared the British figures in 1987, a year after the coming into force of the Convention in the UK, with those in 1996.[26] In 1987, the Child Abduction Unit dealt with 40 applications, of which the mother was the abductor in 45% of applications, and the father in 48%. A considerable shift then occurred in the ratio of mother to father abductors between 1987 and 1996, from about 1:1 in 1987 to more than 2.5:1 in 1996. Lowe and Perry attributed this changing

---

24 M. Freeman, 'Primary Carers and the Hague Child Abduction Convention' (2001) *International Family Law Journal* 140–50, 140.

25 J. Holliday and M.C. Baruffi, 'Child Abduction' in P. Beaumont and J. Holliday (eds), *Guide to Global Private International Law*, Private International Law Series, Hart 2022, p. 2. The authors reference this statement, in fn. 14, as follows: 'Hague Conference on Private International Law, *Actes et documents de la quatorziéme session*, example in the foundational Dyer Report, Prel. Doc. No. 1 August 1978 (19–23) available at <https://assets.hcch.net/docs/05998e0c-af56-4977-839a-e7db3f0ea6a9.pdf> (electronic pages 17–21 in the *Actes*). See also the sociological findings by International Social Services showing "that fathers were abducting more than mothers" (electronic page 134 in the *Actes*) but giving examples of abductions by both (ibid., 137–141). See also para. 13 of the Explanatory Report' where Professor Pérez-Vera talks of how, in the majority of cases, the person concerned is the father or mother.

26 N. Lowe and A. Perry, 'International Child Abduction – The English Experience' (1999) 48(1) *International and Comparative Law Quarterly* 127–55.

pattern to their theory that the Convention had acted as a deterrent to the envisaged abductors (men contemplating kidnapping their children), while the deterrent effect had not been so strong among women because they were motivated by the need to escape violent or abusive relationships.[27] This raised the prospect of a direct link between gender, domestic violence and international child abduction.

This trend of mothers as the typical abductors has been confirmed by the statistical evidence collated globally from 1999 to 2015 for the Special Commission meetings. Of the applications received in 2015 by Central Authorities in 76 of the then 93 Contracting States, Lowe and Stephens found that 73% of taking persons were the mothers of the children involved in the return applications.[28] This represented an increase on the 69% of mothers recorded in 1999 and 2008, and the 68% recorded in 2003. While the abductor profile has been firmly consolidated, the reason(s) for the shift may be a matter for debate, but Lowe and Perry's suggestion of fleeing from domestic violence as a possible cause should not be discounted.

3. JOINT/SHARED PARENTING AND GOING HOME

There was rapid expansion during the 1980s of the idea of joint custody after divorce and/or separation.[29] This has, unsurprisingly, been reflected in the international child abduction field, with the profile of abductors as joint primary carers emerging as one of the standout trends in the 2015 statistical survey: 63% of the taking persons were joint primary carers, 20% were the child's sole primary carer, and 16% non-primary carers.[30] Overall, in 2015, 83% of taking persons were the primary or joint primary carers of the children involved, compared with 72% in 2008 and 68% in 2003.[31] Lowe and Stephens suggest that this 'goes some way at least to dispel the

27 Ibid., 133.

28 N. Lowe and V. Stephens, *Part I: A Statistical Analysis of Applications Made in 2015 under the Hague Convention of 25 October 1980 on the Civil Aspects of International Child Abduction – Global Report*, Permanent Bureau of the Hague Conference on Private International Law, The Hague 2017.

29 A. Dyer, 'The Hague Convention on the Civil Aspects of International Child Abduction – Towards Global Cooperation: Its Successes and Failures' (1993) 1(3–4) *International Journal of Children's Rights* 273–92, 281.

30 N. Lowe and V. Stephens, *Part I: A Statistical Analysis of Applications Made in 2015 under the Hague Convention of 25 October 1980 on the Civil Aspects of International Child Abduction – Global Report*, Permanent Bureau of the Hague Conference on Private International Law, The Hague 2017, p. 3.

31 Ibid., p. 8.

notion that most abducting mothers are sole primary carers'.[32] However, they also warn that these findings need to be treated with some caution, not least because the question of what a primary carer or joint primary carer is remains relatively open. Furthermore, the response rate to this survey question was relatively low, the information being available in only 976 of the 2,262 return applications in 2015, and in only 17% of applications in 2008 and 24% in 2003.[33] Notwithstanding their note of caution, Lowe and Stephens's intuitive belief is that the finding is consistent with the general trend towards joint parenting.

The incidence and impact of shared custody arrangements on children have been recognised by Baroness Hale:

> There are now many more shared custody arrangements following parental separation – children who genuinely have a home with each of their parents, so that both of them are primary carers.[34]

The trend towards most taking persons 'going home' to the State in which they had been brought up, or in which they had family ties, was also confirmed in 2015.[35] Lowe and Stephens found that 58% of applications involved a taking person who was 'going home', compared with 60% in 2008, 55% in 2003 and 52% in 1999.[36]

The reason these trends are important is that, whereas abductions were initially thought to be more likely to be carried out by a non-custodial father, keeping the child away from their home with their primary carer mother, they are now more likely to be undertaken by a primary or joint primary carer parent, who may well be returning home. Where the abducting parent is a joint primary carer, this means that the left-behind parent shares a right of custody to the child with the abducting parent.

Baroness Hale has noted that, 'in many parts of the world, the sharp distinction between custody and access no longer holds good'.[37]

---

32 N. Lowe and V. Stephens, 'Global Trends in the Operation of the 1980 Hague Abduction Convention: The 2015 Statistics' (2018) 52(2) *Family Law Quarterly* 349–84, 353.

33 Ibid., pp. 352–53.

34 B. Hale, 'Taking Flight – Domestic Violence and Child Abduction' (2017) 70(1) *Current Legal Problems* 3–16, 5.

35 N. Lowe and V. Stephens, *Part I: A Statistical Analysis of Applications Made in 2015 under the Hague Convention of 25 October 1980 on the Civil Aspects of International Child Abduction – Global Report*, Permanent Bureau of the Hague Conference on Private International Law, The Hague 2017.

36 Ibid., p. 9.

37 B. Hale, 'Taking Flight – Domestic Violence and Child Abduction' (2017) 70(1) *Current Legal Problems* 3–16, 5.

She attributes this, firstly, to the many more shared custody arrangements now in existence, where a child genuinely has a home with each of their parents, meaning that both adults are primary carers. Secondly, a left-behind parent who, in reality, only has a right of contact with the child, may acquire what amounts to 'rights of custody' under the Convention because:

> [E]ven sole custody orders tend to come with prohibitions [*ne exeat* clauses] on taking the child abroad, at least for more than a short holiday. ... And increasingly such prohibitions are recognized as giving 'rights of custody' because they effectively give the other parent the right to decide where the child is to live.[38]

This may have substantial impacts, since, in order to secure the return of the abducted child under the Convention, the left-behind parent must have 'rights of custody' in the child. While *ne exeat* clauses may, increasingly, be found to amount to 'rights of custody' under the Convention, the day-to-day reality for the child may be quite different to genuine shared custody, since the left-behind parent may have had little actual involvement in the child's life. However, that left-behind parent, due to their 'rights of custody', can utilise the beneficial provisions of the Convention to secure the return of the child. The joint primary carer mother who, with her child, has escaped from domestic violence in the home country, thus becomes thwarted by the use of the Convention in these circumstances.[39] Almost certainly, these situations will also involve the abducting mother's return, as she will wish to accompany her child back to the State of habitual residence, as many mothers do, even if this compromises her own safety.[40]

4. DOMESTIC VIOLENCE AND THE CONVENTION

Both domestic violence and international child abduction began to be recognised as serious social problems during the 1970s, as attention turned

---

38 Ibid., 5.

39 A mother would not, of course, need to raise Art. 13(1)(b) if the left-behind parent was unable to use the Convention because he lacked, or did not acquire, 'rights of custody'. However, once the left-behind parent is able to rely upon the Convention, the question of whether the Art. 13(1)(b) exception is successful will depend on other factors, including whether the court of the requested State considers that violence against the parent equates with harm to the child.

40 K. Trimmings and O. Momoh, 'Intersection between Domestic Violence and International Parental Child Abduction: Protection of Abducting Mothers in Return Proceedings' (2021) 35(1) *International Journal of Law, Policy and the Family* 1–19, 4.

to the intrafamilial dynamics that posed risks for the safety and well-being of family members. In relation to intimate partner violence (IPV):

> There was little recognition of IPV 50 years ago. IPV was viewed as a private family matter, a squabble between spouses behind closed doors. Virtually no social science research on IPV was available. Shelters, advocates, and victim services were nonexistent. Calls to police yielded little or no help, or police cajoled, scolded and bargained away victims' valid complaints in the presence of the abuser. … Few criminal sanctions were imposed and protective orders were rare (obtainable only after criminal conviction) and mostly not enforced. Physical abuse had to be heinous, extreme, or fatal, with victims seen as clearly nonprovocative to get the attention of the criminal justice system.[41]

Similarly, international child abduction was emerging as an issue of immense social importance, heightened by its cross-border context, and the law's inability to provide satisfactory remedies in the absence of mutual enforcement mechanisms between States:

> The risk of harm to the child and the certainty of distress to the parent from whom the child had been taken both suggest that lawyers, and indeed Governments, cannot remain entirely aloof.[42]

Thus, both domestic violence and international child abduction, in their own separate spheres, began to capture the attention of lawmakers, politicians and the public, and to generate responses to afford greater protection to, and redress for, their victims. While the tenor of domestic violence laws and the provision of related services have evolved significantly over past decades,[43] the 1980 Hague Convention has remained intact and steadfast across its 42-year history. Nevertheless, the novel features that marked out its distinctive approach to cross-border family dispute resolution have been critical to its remarkable success and increasing international reach.[44]

---

41 J. Johnston and N. Ver Steegh, 'Historical Trends in Family Court Response to Intimate Partner Violence: Perspectives of Critics and Proponents of Current Practices' (2013) 51(1) *Family Court Review* 63–73, 63.

42 A.E. Anton, 'The Hague Convention on International Child Abduction' (1981) 30(3) *International and Comparative Law Quarterly* 537–67, 537.

43 J. Johnston and N. Ver Steegh, 'Historical Trends in Family Court Response to Intimate Partner Violence: Perspectives of Critics and Proponents of Current Practices' (2013) 51(1) *Family Court Review* 63–73.

44 D. Bryant, 'The 1980 Child Abduction Convention – The Status Quo and Future Challenges' in T. John, R. Gulati and B. Köhler (eds), *The Elgar Companion to the Hague Conference on Private International Law*, Edward Elgar Publishing, Cheltenham 2020, pp. 181–95.

International, regional and jurisdictional initiatives, developed by the HCCH Permanent Bureau and the 101 Contracting Parties to the Convention, have helped to foster its continuing applicability over time.[45]

Research on domestic violence in private law contexts,[46] and on international child abduction,[47] has also flourished. However, in recent years, the intersection between both social issues has started to be examined more closely.[48] The growing recognition of the significance of domestic violence in abduction cases has, in part, been driven by the profile of the typical abductor discussed above:

> In practical terms this means that many taking parents are mothers, who may be returning to their country of origin, often citing flight from family violence by the other parent as the reason for leaving the country of habitual residence with the child.[49]

---

45 N.J. Taylor and M. Freeman, 'International Child Abduction' in R. Treloar and M. Maclean (eds), *Family Justice Systems*, Edward Elgar Research Handbooks in Law and Society Series, Cambridge, forthcoming.

46 A. Barnett, *Domestic Abuse and Private Law Children Cases: A Literature Review*, Ministry of Justice Analytical Series, London 2020; P. Jaffe, J. Johnston and C. Crooks, 'Custody Disputes Involving Allegations of Domestic Violence: Toward a Differentiated Approach to Parenting Plans' (2008) 46(3) *Family Court Review* 500–22.

47 N.J. Taylor and M. Freeman, 'Using Research to Improve Outcomes for Abducted Children' in G. Douglas, M. Murch and V. Stephens (eds), *International and National Perspectives on Child and Family Law: Essays in Honour of Nigel Lowe*, Intersentia, Cambridge 2018, pp. 329–42.

48 C.S. Bruch, 'The Unmet Needs of Domestic Violence Victims and Their Children in Hague Child Abduction Convention Cases' (2004) 38 *Family Law Quarterly* 529–45; M. Freeman and N.J. Taylor, 'Domestic Violence and Child Participation: Contemporary Challenges to the 1980 Hague Child Abduction Convention' (2020) 42(2) *Journal of Social Welfare and Family Law* 154–75; M. Kaye, 'The Hague Convention and the Flight from Domestic Violence: How Women and Children are Being Returned by Coach and Four' (1999) 12(2) *International Journal of Law, Policy and the Family* 191–212; B. Quillen, 'The New Face of International Child Abduction: Domestic-Violence Victims and Their Treatment Under the Hague Convention on the Civil Aspects of International Child Abduction' (2014) 49(3) *Texas International Law Journal* 621–43; S. Shetty and J.L. Edleson, 'Adult Domestic Violence in Cases of International Parental Child Abduction' 11(1) *Violence Against Women* 115–38; M.R. Weiner, 'International Child Abduction and the Escape from Domestic Violence' (2000) 69(2) *Fordham Law Review* 593–706; K. Trimmings and O. Momoh, 'Intersection between Domestic Violence and International Parental Child Abduction: Protection of Abducting Mothers in Return Proceedings' (2021) 35(1) *International Journal of Law, Policy and the Family* 1–19.

49 D. Bryant, 'The 1980 Child Abduction Convention – The Status Quo and Future Challenges' in T. John, R. Gulati and B. Köhler (eds), *The Elgar Companion to the Hague Conference on Private International Law*, Edward Elgar Publishing, Cheltenham 2020, p. 192.

The statistical analyses of return applications have also revealed another trend of critical relevance, given the number of judicial refusals to return, on the basis of Article 13(1)(b).[50] A grave risk of harm has always been the most commonly relied upon exception to the prompt return of a child under the Convention when the sole and multiple reasons for refusal are calculated, accounting for 26% of refusals in 1999 and 2003, 34% in 2008 and 25% in 2015.[51]

It is, therefore, unsurprising that considerable international attention has been devoted to Article 13(1)(b) and the safety of an abducted child on return to the country of habitual residence, and, where appropriate, the use of protective measures to ensure this.

> The Article 13(1)(b) exception is often cited as being one of the most difficult issues faced in the application of the Convention. It involves the challenge for courts in protecting children from harm without violating the integrity of the Convention.[52]

The Sixth Special Commission, prompted by concerns about jurisdictional differences of approach, particularly where there were allegations of domestic violence, recommended the establishment of a Working Group to develop a Guide to Good Practice on the implementation and application of Article 13(1)(b).[53] The Working Group commenced in 2013, and encountered many challenges during its seven-year role. For example, the 2017 draft of the Guide was criticised by prominent academics, domestic violence service providers, and a taking (protective) parent, for failing to give sufficient weight to domestic violence, and for setting the threshold to successfully trigger Article 13(1)(b) too high.[54] Similarly, a petition crafted in January 2020 by Professors Rhona Schuz and Merle Weiner, and signed

---

50 N. Lowe and V. Stephens, *Part I: A Statistical Analysis of Applications Made in 2015 under the Hague Convention of 25 October 1980 on the Civil Aspects of International Child Abduction – Global Report*, Permanent Bureau of the Hague Conference on Private International Law, The Hague 2017.

51 Ibid., p. 16.

52 D. Bryant, 'The 1980 Child Abduction Convention – The Status Quo and Future Challenges' in T. John, R. Gulati and B. Köhler (eds), *The Elgar Companion to the Hague Conference on Private International Law*, Edward Elgar Publishing, Cheltenham 2020, p. 193.

53 Ibid., p. 192.

54 Eight letters submitted to the US Department of State and the HCCH Permanent Bureau about a Draft Guide for Article 13(1)(b) and Related Draft Documents that were circulated for comment prior to the 2017 meeting of the Seventh Special Commission on the 1980 Hague Child Abduction Convention, The Hague 2017.

by 150 law professors, family justice professionals and other concerned individuals, asked the Council on General Affairs of the Hague Conference and the Hague Permanent Bureau:

> to make a small but crucial change before the *Guide* is released, although the finalized version has been silently approved by the Member States. The amendment attempts to clarify language in the proposed *Guide* which, as it stands, undermines the scientifically supported proposition that domestic violence perpetrated against a parent can harm that parent's child, even when the child is not a direct target of the violence.[55]

The Guide to Good Practice was published, unchanged, shortly thereafter, in March 2020, to provide practical guidance to judges, Central Authorities, lawyers and other practitioners faced with the application of Article 13(1)(b).[56] The Hon. Diana Bryant, Chair of the Working Group, considered that the petitioners had focused 'too rigidly on one sentence with the risk of taking it out of context'.[57] She did not agree that the sentence in contention would be misunderstood, and stated that 'the *Guide* provides plenty of support for the notion that a child's exposure to domestic violence can constitute a grave risk of harm'.[58]

Other key initiatives to tackle domestic violence and international child abduction have included an Experts' Meeting on Issues of Domestic/Family Violence and the Convention, jointly hosted in London in 2017 by the HCCH and Professor Marilyn Freeman, University of Westminster.[59] The report from this Experts' Meeting became an Information Document for the 2017 Seventh Special Commission, and canvassed a wide range of issues including:

> the challenge of striking the correct balance between resolving and properly investigating cases involving domestic and family violence (to the extent

---

55 R. Schuz and M. Weiner, 'A Small Change That Matters: The Article 13(1)(b) Guide to Good Practice' <https://www.familylaw.co.uk/news_and_comment/a-small-change-that-matters-the-article-13(1)(b)-guide-to-good-practice> accessed 27.08.2021.

56 Hague Conference on Private International Law, *Guide to Good Practice under the HCCH Convention of 25 October 1980 on the Civil Aspects of International Child Abduction – Part VI – Article 13(1)(b)*, The Hague 2020.

57 D. Bryant, 'Response to Professors Rhona Schuz and Merle H Weiner ("the authors"), A Mistake Waiting to Happen: The Failure to Correct the *Guide to Good Practice on Article 13(1)(b)*' (2020) *International Family Law Journal* 207–08, 207.

58 Ibid., 208.

59 University of Westminster and The Hague Conference on Private International Law, *Report on the Experts' Meeting on Issues of Domestic/Family*

required by the grave risk exception under the Convention) whilst maintaining the expedition necessary to return abducted children without undue delay.[60]

Finally, the POAM Project, launched in 2019, is exploring the intersection between domestic violence and international parental child abduction within the European Union.[61] It is primarily concerned with the protection of abducting mothers who have been involved in return proceedings where the background is one of violence and/or abuse by the left-behind father. A *Best Practice Guide* has recently been published on the protection of abducting mothers involved in return proceedings under the Convention, where the child's abduction had been motivated by acts of domestic violence from the left-behind father.[62]

5. A RETURN-FOCUSED APPROACH vs PROTECTION OF INDIVIDUAL INTERESTS

McEleavy discusses the desire, seen through the provisions of the Convention, of turning the clock back to the child's previous situation as quickly as possible so the child can, at least in theory, resume their pre-existing life with as little interruption as possible.[63] The Brussels ll bis Regulation[64] created an even stricter return structure, entitling the State of

Violence and the 1980 Hague Child Abduction Convention, London (Information Document No. 6), Seventh Special Commission on the Practical Operation of the 1980 Hague Child Abduction Convention and the 1996 Hague Child Protection Convention, The Hague 2017.

60 M. Freeman and N.J. Taylor, 'Domestic Violence and Child Participation: Contemporary Challenges to the 1980 Hague Child Abduction Convention' (2020) 42(2) *Journal of Social Welfare and Family Law* 154–75, 161.

61 See <https://research.abdn.ac.uk/poam/project/overview/> accessed 27.08.2021. POAM focuses on the utility of Regulation 606/2013 on mutual recognition of protection measures in civil matters, and Directive 2011/99/EU on the European Protection Order, in the context of parental child abductions motivated by acts of domestic violence.

62 K. Trimmings, O. Momoh, C. Honorati, A. Dutta and M. Župan, *Best Practice Guide – Protection of Abducting Mothers in Return Proceedings* (hereafter 'POAM Best Practice Guide'), reprinted in this volume.

63 P. McEleavy, 'The European Court of Human Rights and the Hague Child Abduction Convention: Prioritising Return or Reflection?' (2015) (62)(3) *Netherlands International Law Review* 365–405.

64 Council Regulation (EC) No 2201/2003 of 27 November 2003 concerning jurisdiction and the recognition and enforcement of judgments in matrimonial matters and the matters of parental responsibility, repealing Regulation (EC) No 1347/2000 [2003] OJ L338/1.

habitual residence to remain in control of the child's future, thus protecting the interests of Member States. One of the main reasons for this was expressed in *Rinau v. Rinau*:

> The Regulation seeks, in particular, to deter child abductions between member states and, in cases of abduction, to obtain the child's return without delay.[65]

However, McEleavy questions whether a summary return mechanism can continue to accord with twenty-first-century expectations and norms.[66] The European Court of Human Rights has shown support for the Convention's return regime,[67] which McEleavy describes as 'the high water mark for the Court's unrestricted prioritization of return'.[68] He states:

> The challenge for courts in abduction situations is how to align the objectives of the Convention with the contemporary profile of abduction cases, where it is the actions of primary carer mothers which are most often at issue, where a return will not be restoring the *status quo ante* in a literal sense, and where the mother may not have strong connections to the child's State of habitual residence and may face financial challenges there.[69]

The altered position of the European Court of Human Rights can be seen in the Grand Chamber's ruling in *Neulinger*, which focused on the rights of the child under Article 8 of the European Convention of Human Rights.[70] These rights would, it was held, be breached by a return to the State of habitual residence after the five years in which the child had been in the requested State. The Court also stated that the child's best interests were to be assessed, in each individual case, by an in-depth examination of the entire family situation.

McEleavy recounts how the appellate courts in England and Wales 'acted promptly in curtailing any potential *Neulinger* effect in the interpretation

---

65 Case C-195/08, PPU *Rinau v. Rinau* [2008] ECR I-5271, ECLI:EU:C:2008:406, at para. 52.

66 P. McEleavy, 'The European Court of Human Rights and the Hague Child Abduction Convention: Prioritising Return or Reflection?' (2015) (62)(3) *Netherlands International Law Review* 365–405, 365.

67 *Maumousseau and Washington v. France*, no. 39388/05, (2010) 51 EHRR 822, at para. 69.

68 P. McEleavy, 'The European Court of Human Rights and the Hague Child Abduction Convention: Prioritising Return or Reflection?' (2015) (62)(3) *Netherlands International Law Review* 365–405, 374.

69 Ibid., 375.

70 *Neulinger and Shuruk v. Switzerland* [GC], no. 41615/07, [2011] 1 FLR 122, ECHR; (2012) 54 EHRR 1087.

and application of the Hague Convention'.[71] He contends that primary carer abduction fits less easily into the summary return mechanism created in 1980, and observes, however, that 'greater sensitivity to such issues also opens the door to exploitation'.[72]

Schuz considers that it is important not to regard the Convention simply as a procedural venue-selecting mechanism because, firstly, decisions as to forum may become determinative; secondly, because the decision determines where the child will live pending determination; and, thirdly, the objective of protecting children from harm must be borne firmly in mind.[73]

There are two distinct approaches regarding how a requested court deals with cases where factual allegations of domestic violence have been made under the grave risk of harm defence:

> (1) 'the assessment of allegations approach' where the asserted facts relevant to the disputed allegations of domestic violence are tested by the court, considering all available documentary evidence and at times oral accounts, and (2) 'the protective measures approach' where the court assumes the allegations of domestic violence to be true and without any assessment of the veracity of the claims decides whether there are adequate protective measures to ameliorate the grave risk. The latter approach focuses on assessing the adequacy of protective measures as a substitute for investigating the disputed facts.[74]

A problem with using the Convention to protect a child, where the abducting parent makes claims about domestic violence being perpetrated against her, is that Article 13(1)(b) only relates to a grave risk to the child caused by their return, and not to any risk that might exist in relation to the returning abducting parent. The grave risk of harm defence may also be relevant where the abducting mother does not return with the child because of a fear of domestic violence against her. However, it has been recognised that the circumstances of the abducting mother and the child

---

71 P. McEleavy, 'The European Court of Human Rights and the Hague Child Abduction Convention: Prioritising Return or Reflection?' (2015) (62)(3) *Netherlands International Law Review* 365–405, 389; See also *X v. Latvia* [GC], no. 27853/09, (2014) 59 EHRR 100.

72 P. McEleavy, 'The European Court of Human Rights and the Hague Child Abduction Convention: Prioritising Return or Reflection?' (2015) (62)(3) *Netherlands International Law Review* 365–405, 401.

73 R. Schuz, *The Hague Child Abduction Convention: A Critical Analysis*, Hart Publishing, Oxford and Portland, OR 2013, p. 443.

74 POAM Best Practice Guide, s. 5.1.2.

may be interlinked, so that violence against the mother alone may warrant the non-return of the child under Article 13(1)(b) of the Convention.[75]

6. PROTECTIVE MEASURES APPROACH

6.1. *IN RE E* [2011] UKSC 27

This case concerned a primary carer mother who abducted her children to England from Norway. She argued that Article 13(1)(b) applied on the basis of the serious psychological abuse she had suffered at the hands of the father, as well as incidents of his physical violence towards other people, property, and the family pets. She stated that she, and the children, were frightened of the father, and there was evidence that the mental disorder from which she suffered would deteriorate if she had to return to Norway with the children.

Stephens and Lowe state that *Re E* was concerned with three key issues: (1) the weight that should be placed on the child's welfare in a 1980 Convention application and the compatibility with Article 3(1) of the United Nations Convention on the Rights of the Child (UNCRC); (2) the impact of the European Court of Human Rights ruling in *Neulinger*; and (3) the interpretation of Article 13(1)(b).[76]

The Supreme Court stated the fact that the best interests of the child are not expressly made a primary consideration in Hague Convention return proceedings 'does not mean that they are not at the forefront of the whole exercise'.[77] It further stated that the Convention also aims to serve the best interests of the individual child by making certain rebuttable assumptions about what will best achieve this.[78]

When considering Article 3(1) of the UNCRC, the Supreme Court stated that, if the Court faithfully applies the provisions of the Convention (and Brussels lla Regulation), it will also be complying with Article 3(1). The Court said that, in virtually all cases, the European Convention on Human Rights and the Convention march hand in hand.[79] There is no

---

75 See *In the Matter of S (A Child)* [2012] UKSC 10, para. 35 (the text of which appears as a quotation in section 6.2).

76 V. Stephens and N. Lowe, 'Children's Welfare and Human Rights under the 1980 Hague Abduction Convention – The Ruling in *Re E*' (2012) 34(1) *Journal of Social Welfare and Family Law* 125–35, 125.

77 *Re E (Children)* [2011] UKSC 27, para. 14.

78 Ibid., para. 14.

79 Ibid., para. 27.

need for Article 13(1)(b) to be narrowly construed as, by its very terms, it is of restricted application. The words are quite plain, and need no further elaboration or 'gloss'.[80] While the words 'physical or psychological harm' are not qualified, the Supreme Court found that:

> they do gain colour from the alternative 'or otherwise' placed 'in an intolerable situation' (emphasis supplied). As was said in *Re D*, at para 52, '"Intolerable" is a strong word, but when applied to a child must mean "a situation which this particular child in these particular circumstances should not be expected to tolerate"'. Those words were carefully considered and can be applied just as sensibly to physical or psychological harm as to any other situation. Every child has to put up with a certain amount of rough and tumble, discomfort and distress. It is part of growing up. But there are some things which it is not reasonable to expect a child to tolerate. Among these, of course, are physical or psychological abuse or neglect of the child herself. Among these also, we now understand, can be exposure to the harmful effects of seeing and hearing the physical or psychological abuse of her own parent.[81]

This case emphasised the role of protective measures whereby the Court asks first whether, taking the case at its highest, in accordance with Article 13(1)(b) of the Convention, there is a grave risk of harm to the child if returned. If the Court decides that there is, it will go on to consider whether there are sufficient protective measures available in the requesting State to deal with the grave risk of harm that would otherwise occur. If the Court believes this is the case, the child will be returned. If the Court does not believe there are sufficient protective measures available, it may then have to do the best it can to resolve the disputed allegations.[82] The reason the Court does not engage with the facts, under this approach, is that this is a matter for the Court in the requesting State to determine if the child is returned there. The Court found there was no reason to doubt that the risk to the mother's mental health, whether it was the result of objective reality or of the mother's subjective perception of reality, or a combination of the two, was very real.[83]

The Supreme Court concluded that the whole of the Hague Convention is designed for the benefit of children, not adults. The best interests, not only of children generally, but also of any individual child involved, are a primary concern in the Hague Convention process. The Court agreed

[80] Ibid., para. 31.
[81] Ibid., para. 34.
[82] Ibid., para. 36.
[83] Ibid., para. 49.

with the Strasbourg Court that, in this connection, their best interests have two aspects: to be reunited with their parents as soon as possible, so that one parent does not gain an unfair advantage over the other through the passage of time; and to be brought up in a 'sound environment', in which they are not at risk of harm. The Hague Convention is designed to strike a fair balance between those two interests. If it is applied correctly, it is most unlikely that there will be any breach of Article 8 or other Convention rights unless other factors supervene. *Neulinger* does not require a departure from the normal summary process, provided that the decision is not arbitrary or mechanical. The exceptions to the obligation to return are, by their very nature, restricted in their scope. They do not need any extra interpretation or gloss. It is now recognised that violence and abuse between parents may constitute a grave risk to the children. Where there are disputed allegations that can neither be tried nor objectively verified, the focus of the inquiry is bound to be on the sufficiency of any protective measures that can be put in place to reduce the risk. The clearer the need for protection, the more effective the measures will have to be.[84]

Stephens and Lowe state that, in *Re E*, 'the Supreme Court tackled *Neulinger* head on, rejecting the notion that it had introduced a free-standing merits assessment of the overall situation'.[85] They also noted the extrajudicial comments of Judge Costa, President of the Strasbourg Court (given at the Franco-British-Irish Colloque on Family Law on 14 May 2011), supporting this interpretation. They further explained that:

> In the Supreme Court's opinion, *Neulinger* rightly acknowledged that a return should not be ordered automatically and mechanically and that there needed to be an examination of the individual circumstances to ascertain whether such a return would be in accordance with the Convention, but this did not require a full merits examination. The guarantees in Article 8 ECHR must be interpreted and applied in the light of both the 1980 Convention and the UNCRC, but it was unnecessary to go further than the swift, summary approach envisaged in the Convention.[86]

While important observations were made on Article 13(1)(b) in *Re D* [2007][87] and *Re M* [2008],[88] *Re E* was the first Supreme Court or House of

84 Ibid., para. 52.

85 V. Stephens and N. Lowe, 'Children's Welfare and Human Rights under the 1980 Hague Abduction Convention – The Ruling in *Re E*' (2012) 34(1) *Journal of Social Welfare and Family Law* 125–35, 129.

86 Ibid.

87 *Re D (A Child) (Abduction: Rights of Custody)* [2007] 1 AC 619.

88 *Re M (Children) (Abduction: Rights of Custody)* [2007] UKHL 55, [2008] 1 AC 1288.

Lords case in which Article 13(1)(b) was directly in issue.[89] The Supreme Court rejected any narrow construction of Article 13(1)(b), as it needed 'no further elaboration or "gloss"'.[90] At first sight, this construction may appear to lower the threshold required for Article 13(1)(b) to be made out, but the supporting arguments rest on the idea that any guide to construction is unnecessary due to its already restricted scope, as opposed to any widening of the exception.[91]

Stephens and Lowe recognise that *Re E* helpfully clarified the interrelationship between the UNCRC, the ECHR and the 1980 Convention, and state that, with regard to the UNCRC, it is useful to have UK confirmation that the 1980 Convention is compatible with Article 3(1) (although they point out that this reflects well-established global jurisprudence, notably that of the senior courts of Argentina, Australia, Canada and Germany).[92] They suggest that it also provides useful authoritative guidance on the application of Article 13(1)(b), and that, although the rejection of a 'narrow interpretation' of Article 13(1)(b) looks, prima facie, to be signalling a new direction, in practice it is unlikely to make any significant difference to its application, as the literal interpretation adopted by the Court relies on Article 13(1)(b) being a tight exception anyway.[93] They conclude that the central importance of *Re E* lies in laying the spectre of *Neulinger*.

6.2. *IN THE MATTER OF S (A CHILD)* [2012] UKSC 10

Reardon describes how, just nine months after dealing with its last Hague Convention case in *Re E*, the Supreme Court once again revisited the Article 13(1)(b) defence in *In the Matter of S (A Child)*, because it took the view that the Court of Appeal in the instant case:

> had misinterpreted *Re E* and had itself imposed an 'impermissible gloss' on the wording of the Convention, and had wrongly overturned the first instance

89 V. Stephens and N. Lowe, 'Children's Welfare and Human Rights under the 1980 Hague Abduction Convention – The Ruling in *Re E*' (2012) 34(1) *Journal of Social Welfare and Family Law* 125–35, 131.

90 *Re E, (Children)* [2011] UKSC 27, para. 31.

91 V. Stephens and N. Lowe, 'Children's Welfare and Human Rights under the 1980 Hague Abduction Convention – The Ruling in *Re E*' (2012) 34(1) *Journal of Social Welfare and Family Law* 125–35, 131.

92 Ibid.

93 Ibid., 133.

> decision of Charles J. who had found the Article 13(b) defence to be made out and had exercised his discretion not to order a return.[94]

In *In the Matter of S (A Child)*, the mother suffered mental health problems, including anxiety and depression, for which she had undergone extensive psychotherapy. She removed the two-year-old child from Australia to England, and raised an Article 13(1)(b) defence under the Convention against return. She also alleged serious domestic abuse by the father, who had a history of significant drug and alcohol addiction. The mother's psychologist gave evidence that the mother was likely to suffer clinical depression if the child had to return, and if she returned with the child. The Court of Appeal had focused on what it considered to be the mother's subjective perception of risk, 'and in what circumstances (likely to be very rare, thought the Court of Appeal) such a subjective perception could ground an order for non-return'.[95]

The Supreme Court considered the written evidence and emphasised that:

> given the objective evidence before Charles J, it was unnecessary for him to go on to consider, as he then did, the issue of the mother's subjective perception; and that in their consideration of this issue the Court of Appeal wrongly interpreted what the Supreme Court said in *Re E*.[96]

The Supreme Court, notwithstanding its finding that the mother in this case had established an Article 13(1)(b) defence on objective grounds, emphatically rejected the Court of Appeal's 'crucial question' approach in an Article 13(1)(b) case:[97]

> In *In re E* this court considered the situation in which the anxieties of a respondent mother about a return with the child to the state of habitual residence were not based upon objective risk to her but nevertheless were of such intensity as to be likely, in the event of a return, to destabilise her parenting of the child to the point at which the child's situation would

[94] M. Reardon, 'Case Comment: *Re S* [2012, March 19] UKSC 10' UK Supreme Court Blog, at para. 2 <http://ukscblog.com/case-comment-re-s-2012-uksc-10/> accessed 27.08.2021.

[95] Ibid., para. 5.

[96] Ibid., para. 6.

[97] *In the Matter of S (A Child)* [2012] UKSC 10, para. 33, quoting Thorpe LJ's judgment in the Court of Appeal at para 43: 'The crucial question for the judge remained: were these asserted risk[s], insecurities and anxieties realistically and reasonably held in the face of the protective package the extent of which would commonly be defined not by the applicant but by the court?'.

> become intolerable. No doubt a court will look very critically at an assertion of intense anxieties not based upon objective risk; and will, among other things, ask itself whether they can be dispelled. But in *In re E* it was this court's clear view that such anxieties could in principle found the defence. Thus, at para 34, it recorded, with approval, a concession by Mr Turner QC, who was counsel for the father in that case, that, if there was a grave risk that the child would be placed in an intolerable situation, 'the source of it is irrelevant: eg, where a mother's subjective perception of events lead to a mental illness which could have intolerable consequences for the child'.[98]

The Supreme Court further stated:

> In the light of these passages we must make clear the effect of what this court said in *In re E*. The critical question is what will happen if, with the mother, the child is returned. If the court concludes that, on return, the mother will suffer such anxieties that their effect on her mental health will create a situation that is intolerable for the child, then the child should not be returned. It matters not whether the mother's anxieties will be reasonable or unreasonable. The extent to which there will, objectively, be good cause for the mother to be anxious on return will nevertheless be relevant to the court's assessment of the mother's mental state if the child is returned.[99]

Reardon observes that this 'may not prove to be straightforward in application', as it is clear that objective risk is not a *sine qua non* for an Article 13(1)(b) defence if the abductor's state of mind is such that this, itself, will put the child at risk of harm:[100]

> On the other hand, judges are encouraged to make an objective assessment of risk when considering the abductor's likely mental health if a return is ordered. The decision in *Re S* itself offers little guidance on this because the Court there was so plainly concerned to demonstrate that the mother's concerns *were* objectively justified, and so the vexed question of objective versus subjective perception of risk did not need to be addressed.[101]

Schuz states that the Supreme Court refused return on the basis of the unusually powerful medical evidence that proved the devastating effect of

98 Ibid., para. 27.
99 Ibid., para. 34.
100 M. Reardon, 'Case Comment: *Re S* [2012, March 19] UKSC 10' UK Supreme Court Blog, at para. 2 <http://ukscblog.com/case-comment-re-s-2012-uksc-10/> accessed 27.08.2021, para. 8.
101 Ibid., para. 8.

the father's behaviour on the mother's mental health.[102] The importance of the decision lies in its express recognition that the mother's subjective perceptions are relevant in determining the consequences of return on both her and the child.

7. ASSESSMENT OF ALLEGATIONS APPROACH

An example of the alternative approach, where the Court first considers the merits of the case, and then whether a grave risk of harm exists, may be found in the Court of Appeal case of *Re K* [2015].[103] This demonstrates how the Court considers the disputed allegations within the confines of the summary process, in order to evaluate the risk.[104]

Trimmings and Momoh strongly suggest that the assessment of allegations approach exemplified in *Re K* is more appropriate, and should be endorsed for application within the Contracting States to the Convention.[105] They accept this may lengthen the proceedings, but consider this inevitable:

> Speed should not take priority over the proper assessment of risk and consideration of the safety of the child and the abducting parent. Indeed, the emphasis on speed may encourage courts to minimise or ignore allegations of domestic violence rather than determining them, leaving thus an unassessed risk of harm.[106]

The *POAM Best Practice Guide* endorses the assessment of allegations approach over the protective measures approach, which, it states, seems also to correspond with the relevant proposal in the *HCCH Guide to Good Practice*.[107] The *Best Practice Guide* argues that it is difficult to see how 'grave risk' could be reliably assessed, and effective protective measures determined, without first deciding whether domestic violence has occurred.

---

102 R. Schuz, *The Hague Child Abduction Convention: A Critical Analysis*, Hart Publishing, Oxford and Portland, OR 2013, p. 284.

103 *Re K (1980 Hague Convention) (Lithuania)* [2015] EWCA Civ 720.

104 Ibid., per Black L.J., para. 53.

105 K. Trimmings and O. Momoh, 'Intersection between Domestic Violence and International Parental Child Abduction: Protection of Abducting Mothers in Return Proceedings' (2021) 35(1) *International Journal of Law, Policy and the Family* 1–19.

106 Ibid., p. 9.

107 POAM Best Practice Guide.

It contends that the protective measures approach appears illogical – 'putting the cart before the horse' – as it 'involves the consideration of protective measures to mitigate risk before that risk has been established and assessed'.[108] The *Best Practice Guide* continues by arguing powerfully that courts should not be tempted to avoid undertaking an evaluation of the merits of the allegations of domestic violence by simply proceeding to consideration of protective measures. Where documentary evidence is not available, the *Best Practice Guide* suggests that the court should hear limited oral evidence to determine the merits of the disputed allegations of domestic violence, as the authors consider that 'it is possible to undertake a limited finding of fact hearing to determine disputed allegations of domestic violence, well within the confines of the summary nature of return proceedings'.[109]

8. CONCLUSIONS AND FUTURE DIRECTIONS

The drafters of the Convention contemplated that either custodial or non-custodial fathers or mothers might abduct their children, but the applications for return over the past 42 years have firmly established primary, or joint primary, carer mothers as the majority of the taking parents (73% in 2015).[110] The 2015 statistical trends have also confirmed the rise in taking parents as joint primary carers (63%), and in taking parents 'going home' (58%).[111] Furthermore, Article 13(1)(b) remained the most commonly relied upon exception to the prompt return of a child under the Convention.[112] This statistical evidence, and postulations on its implications, indicate both the possible plight of mothers motivated to abduct by the desire, or necessity, to escape domestic violence, to protect themselves and/or their child(ren),[113] and the confounding influences that

108 Ibid., s. 5.1.2.

109 Ibid, s. 5.1.3.1.

110 N. Lowe and V. Stephens, *Part I: A Statistical Analysis of Applications Made in 2015 under the Hague Convention of 25 October 1980 on the Civil Aspects of International Child Abduction – Global Report*, Permanent Bureau of the Hague Conference on Private International Law, The Hague 2017, 8.

111 Ibid.

112 Ibid.

113 C.S. Bruch, 'The Unmet Needs of Domestic Violence Victims and Their Children in Hague Child Abduction Convention Cases' (2004) 38 *Family Law Quarterly* 529–45; D. Bryant, 'The 1980 Child Abduction Convention – The Status Quo and Future Challenges' in T. John, R. Gulati and B. Köhler (eds), *The Elgar Companion to the Hague Conference on Private International Law*, Edward Elgar Publishing,

may arise when 'rights of custody' under the Convention are extended to left-behind fathers by joint custody or *ne exeat* clauses.[114] While protective mechanisms are available to address the grave risk of harm faced by a child on return, doubt is sometimes cast on their efficacy and enforceability once the child, and often the mother, are back in the State of habitual residence.[115]

Considerable international attention has been devoted to better understanding domestic violence and international child abduction, and the intersection between them. Since the 1970s, the widening knowledge base on domestic violence and abuse has allowed laws and services to continually evolve to become more responsive to adult and child victims. However, the Convention, by its very nature as an international treaty, currently with 101 Contracting State parties and still growing in membership, is subject to constraints that mean it cannot be so easily amended. Instead, shifts in response to new knowledge about the intersection between abduction and domestic violence must come about through guidance to Contracting States by the HCCH, Special Commissions and Working Groups, as well as initiatives in individual States or regions. Article 13(1)(b) has clearly been a focus of concern, both by those who are anxious that the Convention's summary return mechanism is not undermined, and those who emphasise the Convention's aim to protect children, internationally, from harm which, they argue, includes harm to a child as a result of violence against his or her abducting mother. The decisions in *Re E*, *In the Matter of S (A Child)* and *Re K* all go some way to recognition of this latter view.

Cheltenham 2020; M. Kaye, The Hague Convention and the Flight from Domestic Violence: How Women and Children are Being Returned by Coach and Four' (1999) 12(2) *International Journal of Law, Policy and the Family* 191–212; N. Lowe and V. Stephens, 'Global Trends in the Operation of the 1980 Hague Abduction Convention: The 2015 Statistics' (2018) 52(2) *Family Law Quarterly* 349–84; N. Lowe and A. Perry, 'International Child Abduction – The English Experience' (1999) 48(1) *International and Comparative Law Quarterly* 127–55. B. Quillen, 'The New Face of International Child Abduction: Domestic-Violence Victims and Their Treatment Under the Hague Convention on the Civil Aspects of International Child Abduction' (2014) 49(3) *Texas International Law Journal* 621–43; S. Shetty and J.L. Edleson, 'Adult Domestic Violence in Cases of International Parental Child Abduction' 11(1) *Violence Against Women* 115–38; K. Trimmings and O. Momoh, 'Intersection between Domestic Violence and International Parental Child Abduction: Protection of Abducting Mothers in Return Proceedings' (2021) 35(1) *International Journal of Law, Policy and the Family* 1–19; M.R. Weiner, 'International Child Abduction and the Escape from Domestic Violence' (2000) 69(2) *Fordham Law Review* 593–706.

114 B. Hale, 'Taking Flight – Domestic Violence and Child Abduction' (2017) 70(1) *Current Legal Problems* 3–16.

115 POAM Best Practice Guide.

As discussed in this contribution, debate remains lively about the best approach for courts to adopt to allegations of domestic violence in abduction return proceedings. However, the aim, succinctly encapsulated in Professor Weiner's observation, is that the Convention must not be:

> another obstacle for women seeking to escape abusive situations, that women are not compelled to litigate custody in an unsafe venue, and that women are not required to litigate in a forum that was chosen solely by their batterers and imposed upon them by force. These goals must be accomplished without undermining the important framework of the Hague Convention.[116]

Finally, as the Convention is now approaching 42 years of age, it may be useful to keep in mind the prescient observation of Adair Dyer, one of the acknowledged fathers of the Convention, when he said more than 20 years ago that:

> The useful life of a law-making treaty should be at least 30 years, in my opinion. Flexibility and continuous nurturing can give it a much longer lifespan.[117]

---

116 M.R. Weiner, 'International Child Abduction and the Escape from Domestic Violence' (2000) 69(2) *Fordham Law Review* 593–706, 600.

117 A. Dyer, 'To Celebrate a Score of Years' (2000) 33(1) *New York University Journal of International Law and Politics* 1–16, at 15, fn 60. Our thanks are expressed to Professor Nigel Lowe for pointing us towards this quotation, in one of the many helpful discussions we have shared.

THE NEED FOR CROSS-BORDER PROTECTIVE MEASURES IN RETURN PROCEEDINGS

Onyója Momoh

1. INTRODUCTION

Cross-border measures for the protection of children and their parents in private international law situations have become an essential part of judicial decision-making, especially in Hague return proceedings. Not least important in that consideration is the need to ensure adequate international cooperation and implementation on a case-by-case basis. Protective measures may be put in place with the intention of addressing the grave risk of harm posed by the domestic violence alleged or established in a Hague Convention case. Examples may include non-molestation orders, occupation orders, restraining orders, non-harassment orders, exclusion orders, ouster orders, domestic abuse interdicts, eviction orders, prohibition of access orders, or prohibitive steps orders and other protection orders against (former) spouses, partners and cohabitants, as well as orders to protect children whose well-being is at risk.

The need for cross-border protective measures in return proceedings is an important subject matter that lent itself to scrutiny when, in 2011, the Hague Conference on Private International Law (hereafter 'the HCCH') published a Reflection Paper[1] on domestic and family violence and the Article 13(1)(b) exception in 1980 Hague Convention cases. This eventually led to the publication of the Guide to Good Practice on Article 13(1)(b) in 2020.[2] Parental child abduction cases committed against the backdrop of domestic violence have raised difficult questions regarding judicial practices, the conflict of national legislations, other governmental approaches, and cross-border cooperation, recognition and implementation. Notwithstanding this, the need for cross-border protective measures is evident in their role of empowering courts in different jurisdictions to protect and secure the welfare of children and their parents in complex familial circumstances, while furthering the aims of the 1980 Hague Convention in a child-focused manner, whether it be to combat the grave risk of harm (Article 13(1)(b)), the protection of human rights and fundamental freedoms (Article 20), or spurious applications designed to cause further harm (Article 13(1)(a)). In doing so, the key private international law instruments relied upon include Regulation 606/2013,[3] the European Protection Order Directive[4] and the 1996 Hague Convention.[5]

---

1 Permanent Bureau of the Hague Conference on Private International Law, 'Domestic and Family Violence and the Article 13 "Grave Risk" Exception on the Operation of the Hague Convention of 25 October 1980 on the Civil Aspects of International Child Abduction: A Reflection Paper' (HCCH, The Hague 2011), available at <https://assets.hcch.net/upload/wop/abduct2011pd09e.pdf> accessed 25 February 2022.

2 Hague Conference on Private International Law, 'Guide to Good Practice under the HCCH Convention of 25 October 1980 on the Civil Aspects of International Child Abduction – Part VI – Article 13(1)(b)', 2020 (hereafter 'HCCH Guide'), available at <https://assets.hcch.net/docs/225b44d3-5c6b-4a14-8f5b-57cb370c497f.pdf> accessed 25 February 2022.

3 Regulation (EU) No 606/2013 of the European Parliament and of the Council of 12 June 2013 on mutual recognition of protection measures in civil matters [2013] OJ L181/4.

4 Directive 2011/99/EU of the European Parliament and of the Council of 13 December 2011 on the European protection order [2011] OJ L338/2.

5 The 1996 Hague Convention on Jurisdiction, Applicable Law, Recognition, Enforcement and Co-operation in Respect of Parental Responsibility and Measures

2. THE GAP

It is widely understood that 'domestic violence directed towards a parent can be seriously harmful to the children who witness it or who depend upon the psychological health and strength of their primary carer for their well-being'.[6] Yet, neither the 1980 Hague Convention nor the Brussels IIa Regulation[7] have explicit regard to the safety of the abducting parent upon the return. Indeed, while the 2019 Brussels IIb Regulation has expanded the ambit of adequate protective measures to include 'allowing the child to stay with the abducting parent who is the primary carer until a decision on the substance of rights of custody has been made',[8] it does not directly address the need for *protective* measures for the parent. And so, although the Hague Conference has recognised that, '[i]n some situations, the grave risk to the child may also be based on potential harm to the taking parent by the left-behind parent',[9] and that 'the protection of the child may also sometimes require steps to be taken to protect an accompanying parent',[10] a gap remains as to the enforceability of protective measures intended to safeguard the abducting mother upon the return, with inconsistent practices in place resulting in varying levels of protection across jurisdictions. The POAM Best Practice Guide[11] has sought to address this gap.

---

for the Protection of Children. See also the Practical Handbook on the operation of the Hague Convention of 19 October 1996 on Jurisdiction, Applicable Law, Recognition, Enforcement and Co-operation in Respect of Parental Responsibility and Measures for the Protection of Children (hereafter '1996 Hague Convention Practical Operation Handbook').

6 B. Hale, 'Taking Flight – Domestic Violence and Child Abduction' (2017) 70 *Current Legal Problems* 3, 7.

7 Council Regulation (EC) No 2201/2003 of 27 November 2003 concerning jurisdiction and the recognition and enforcement of judgments in matrimonial matters and the matters of parental responsibility, repealing Regulation (EC) No 1347/2000 [2003] OJ L338/1.

8 Council Regulation (EU) 2019/1111 of 25 June 2019 on jurisdiction, the recognition and enforcement of decisions in matrimonial matters and the matters of parental responsibility, and on international child abduction (hereafter 'Brussels IIb'), para. 45.

9 HCCH Guide, para. 57.

10 Hague Conference on Private International Law, Conclusions and Recommendations of the Fifth Meeting of the Special Commission (2006), para 1.1.12, available at <https://assets.hcch.net/upload/concl28sc5_e.pdf> accessed 25 February 2022.

11 The Best Practice Guide – Protection of Abducting Mothers in Return Proceedings (hereafter 'POAM Best Practice Guide'), reprinted in this volume.

3. VULNERABILITIES OF TAKING PARENTS

There are many vulnerabilities for parents caught up in child abductions motivated by domestic violence. To begin with, it is of note that latest statistical information on the operation of the 1980 Hague Abduction Convention shows that 73% of parental child abductions are committed by mothers.[12] Alarmingly, many of these mothers are fleeing domestic violence. Although there are no comprehensive statistics on how many 1980 Convention cases involve allegations or findings of domestic violence, empirical research has confirmed that this phenomenon frequently plays a major role in parental child abduction cases. The grave risk of harm exception to return, under Article 13(1)(b), is pertinent to abductions committed against the background of domestic violence. Indeed, it is the most prevalent exception raised, often by mothers opposing the return, based either on the allegations involving the child as the 'direct victim', or as an 'indirect victim', where the child is exposed to the effects of domestic violence directed towards the mother. Among such effects are reduced or impaired parenting capacities of the mother, resulting from the impact of the violence on her physical and/or psychological health. The grave risk of harm may also be raised where the abducting mother is unable to return with the child, due to a fear of the child's father; the subsequent separation from the primary carer mother may be argued to create a grave risk for the child. It has, therefore, been recognised that the circumstances of the abducting mother and the child may be intertwined to the extent that domestic violence perpetrated solely against the mother may justify the finding that the return would expose the child to a grave risk of psychological harm or otherwise place the child in an intolerable situation, pursuant to Article 13(1)(b). In addition to this, the United Nations Committee on the Rights of the Child (UNCRC),[13] and the

12 N. Lowe and V. Stephens, 'A Statistical Analysis of Applications Made in 2015 under the Hague Convention of 25 October 1980 on the Civil Aspects of International Child Abduction', Part I – Regional (revised) (September 2017), Permanent Bureau of the Hague Conference on Private International Law, The Hague 2017; Part II – Global Report (September 2017), Permanent Bureau of the Hague Conference on Private International Law, The Hague 2017; Part III – National Reports (July 2018), Permanent Bureau of the Hague Conference on Private International Law, The Hague 2018. See also S. De Silva, 'The International Parental Child Abduction Service of the International Social Service Australian Branch' (2006) 11 *The Judges' Newsletter* 61; and M. Župan, M. Drventić and T. Kruger, 'Cross-Border Removal and Retention of a Child – Croatian Practice and European Expectation' (2020) 34 *International Journal of Family Law and Policy* 60.

13 United Nations Committee on the Rights of the Child, General Comment No. 13, 2011.

Istanbul Convention,[14] echo the recognition that a child's exposure to domestic violence suffered by their parent can constitute a grave risk of harm and, therefore, protecting the mother will indirectly protect the child and ameliorate the grave risk of harm.

The vulnerabilities of returning parents and the subject child(ren) go beyond the physical or emotional abuse that has occurred, to the effects of a lack of financial and emotional support in the State of habitual residence, plus probable financial dependence on the left-behind parent. After all, families have very different financial means and structures. Indeed, the English courts have given a broad interpretation to the term 'protective measures', and have held that the expression was not limited to specific measures, but extended, for example, to 'general features' of the requesting State.[15] In particular, the Court of Appeal has held that 'the general right to seek the assistance of the court or other state authorities might in some cases be sufficient to persuade a court that there was not a grave risk within Article 13(b)'.[16] This type of protective measure includes, for example, access to courts and other legal services, state assistance and support, including financial assistance, housing assistance, health services, women's shelters and other means of support for victims of domestic violence; responses by police and the criminal justice system more generally; and availability of protective measures to victims of domestic violence in the requesting State, such as non-molestation injunctions.[17]

In addition, a taking parent returning to their country of habitual residence sometimes builds a picture of lack of credibility as a respondent in return proceedings, due to the failure to report the incidents of domestic violence in the State of habitual residence prior to the abduction. This becomes an uphill struggle to prove the need for ongoing protection upon return. It is important to note that, as domestic violence, by its very

---

14 Council of Europe Convention on preventing and combating violence against women and domestic violence, CETS No. 210, Istanbul 11.5.2011, entry into force 01.08.2014.

15 *Re C (Children) (Abduction Article 13(B))* [2018] EWCA Civ 2834, para. 41. See also *Re S (A Child) (Hague Convention 1980: Return to Third State)* [2019] EWCA Civ 352, paras. 50 and 51, where Moylan LJ referred to his judgment in *Re C*, and reiterated that the 'expression "protective measures" has a wide meaning'.

16 *Re C (Children) (Abduction Article 13(B))* [2018] EWCA Civ 2834, para. 41. See, e.g. *Re M (Children)* [2016] EWCA Civ 942, where the Court of Appeal stated that the police force and justice system of other jurisdictions were part of the protective measures. This passage was recently quoted with approval in *CH v. GLS* [2019] EWHC 3842 (Fam).

17 *In the Matter of A (A Child) (Hague Abduction; Art 13(b): Protective Measures)* [2019] EWHC 649 (Fam), para. 24.

nature, usually occurs behind closed doors, supporting or corroborative documentary evidence can be limited. Indeed, the absence of police or other authority intervention is not untypical of a disempowered victim of domestic violence, demonstrated by psychological conditions such as battered woman syndrome.

4. THE CHILD: HARMFUL EFFECTS OF WITNESSING DOMESTIC VIOLENCE

The harmful effects on a child of witnessing domestic violence perpetrated on a parent are serious, and can constitute a grave risk of harm. There is an obvious intersection between protective measures for the child and measures for the mother. Case law from various jurisdictions dictates that protective measures for the mother are, by extension, measures that protect the child. Where a court is assessing the grave risk of harm, i.e. psychological harm on a child on the basis of domestic violence perpetrated primarily on the abducting mother, in protecting the well-being of the child from this impact, the court is compelled to protect the abducting mother, so that the child may benefit from the safeguards afforded to that mother.

At the HCCH Sixth Special Commission Meeting, it was acknowledged that protective orders under the 1996 Hague Convention were not only capable of having regard to 'the impact on a child of violence committed by one parent against the other', but that, when looking at what protective orders should be made to safeguard the child, 'there was nothing to prevent judges from considering harm to parents'.[18] It follows that, to protect the child from harm, one has to protect the parent who has suffered that harm, to stop the violence and end what the child is seeing. In assessing the level of harm, the POAM Best Practice Guide[19] adopts case law interpretation that: (1) the risk must be real, and of a level of seriousness to constitute 'grave';[20] and (2) the level of harm must be one that a child should not be expected to tolerate.[21]

---

18 Permanent Bureau of the Hague Conference, 'Conclusions and Recommendations and Report of Part I of the Sixth Meeting of the Special Commission on the Practical Operation of the 1980 Hague Child Abduction Convention and the 1996 Hague Child Protection Convention' (June 2011), Permanent Bureau of the Hague Conference on Private International Law, The Hague 2011, paras. 35–38, available at <https://www.hcch.net/en/publications-and-studies/details4/?pid=6224&dtid=57> last accessed 25 February 2022.

19 POAM Best Practice Guide, reprinted in this volume, s. 5.1.3.3.

20 HCCH Guide, p. 26.

21 Ibid.

4.1. PSYCHOLOGICAL HARM

Children exposed to domestic violence can be psychologically harmed. Article 13(1)(b) cases[22] have demonstrated a recognition of the psychological impact on a child occasioned by witnessing physical harm to a parent, or experiencing the deteriorating mental health of that parent from the abuse suffered. Indeed, the HCCH Guide provides ample support for the notion that a child's exposure to domestic violence can constitute a grave risk of harm.[23] And so, where there is compelling and substantial evidence to show that a child has witnessed domestic violence, '[t]he harm caused by witnessing domestic abuse is recognised to be substantial and can have long-term effects on the welfare and development of children',[24] leading to post-traumatic stress disorder,[25] a 'fixed and immutable subjective fear',[26] and behavioural issues.[27]

Where case law is concerned, courts in many jurisdictions appear equipped to recognise that the grave risk of harm may exist. The UK Supreme Court case of *Re E (Children)*[28] summarised that 'it is now recognised that violence and abuse between parents may constitute a grave risk to the children'.[29] This case reiterated that a child should not reasonably be expected to tolerate 'exposure to the harmful effects of seeing and hearing the physical or psychological abuse of her own parent'.[30]

---

22 E.g., *S v. S* [1999] NZFLR 625; *Khan v. Fatima* (2012) 680 F.3d 781 (7th Cir. 2012); *Hernandez v. Cardoso* (2016) 844 F.3d 692; *Gomez v. Fuenmayor*, 812 F.3d 1005 (11th Cir. 2016); *Abbott v. Abbott*, 130 S.Ct. 1983, 1997 (2010); and *Walsh v. Walsh* 221 F.3d 204, 220 (1st Cir. 2000), where a child witnessing a parent's 'severe abuse' constituted a grave risk of harm.

23 D. Bryant AO, QC, 'Response to Professors Rhona Schuz and Merle H Weiner' ('the authors'), 'A Mistake Waiting to Happen: The Failure to Correct the Guide to Good Practice on Article 13(1)(b)' (2020) IFL 207.

24 *DM v. KM* [2016] EWHC 1282 (Fam), para. 26; In *Miltiadous v. Tetervak* 686 F. Supp. 2d 544 (2010), the court heard evidence that one of the children had suffered from post-traumatic stress disorder ('PTSD') from witnessing domestic violence between the parents.

25 PTSD is a type of anxiety disorder that may develop after being involved in, or witnessing, traumatic events.

26 *Re S (A Child) (Hague Convention 1980: Return to Third State)* [2019] EWCA Civ 352, paras. 27 and 34.

27 *In DM v. KM* [2016] EWHC 1282 (Fam), Cafcass found that one of the behaviours exhibited by the child was revealing of a child 'learning to blame the victim for the abuser's actions and would have long term consequences for his emotional and social development were it to continue' (para. 17).

28 *Re E (Children)* [2011] UKSC 27.

29 *Re E (Children)* [2011] UKSC 27, para. 52.

30 *Re E (Children)* [2011] UKSC 27, para. 34. In addition, it was stated that the determination of the risk of harm should include an assessment far beyond the child's 'immediate future', as the need for 'effective protection may persist' (para. 35).

It is important to note that the harm to the mother need not be physical, with *Re E* highlighting that a child may continue to suffer, placing the child in an intolerable situation, as a consequence of the mother being a victim of domestic violence and the impact of the return on her mental health. *Re S (a Child)* also considered the mother's psychological health, and how that, too, would impact on the child. This recognition in the UK jurisdiction is not recent, as in the case of *TB v. JB (Abduction: Grave Risk of Harm)*,[31] Hale L.J. (as she then was), in dissent, noted that primary carers who had fled from abuse and maltreatment, and for whom a return to such an environment would have a seriously detrimental effect upon the children, should not be expected to return.[32] *TB v. JB* was referred to in the Australian case of *Mander*,[33] adopting Baroness Hale's observations in respect of spousal abuse. In this case, it was found that the Article 13(1)(b) threshold had been proved, given the acts of violence, 'uncontrollable … bloody and severe',[34] which the mother had suffered, and the children had witnessed. The court also referred to social science literature, at the time, emphasising that 'serial spousal abusers are also likely to be child abusers',[35] and that, in this case, the father's violence knew no bounds between parent and child, or husband and wife, to cause any restraint.[36] Further, in the case of *Khan v. Fatima*, the court accepted the findings of psychologists and social scientists that 'the repeated physical and psychological abuse of a child's mother by the child's father, in the presence of the child … is likely to create a risk of psychological harm to the child'.[37] In *Walsh v. Walsh*[38] the United States Court of Appeal for the Fifth Circuit determined that spousal abuse amounted to a grave risk to the child who had observed repetitive abuse towards the mother. Similarly, in *Baran v. Beaty*,[39] the court refused a return order on the basis that the child would be exposed to a grave risk of physical or psychological harm, even though the violence and verbal

---

31 *TB v. JB (Abduction: Grave Risk of Harm)* [2001] 2 FLR 515.

32 Ibid.

33 *State Central Authority, Secretary to the Department of Human Services v. Mander*, No. (P)MLF1179 of 2003.

34 Ibid.

35 Ibid.

36 Ibid.

37 *Khan v. Fatima* (2012) 680 F.3d 781 (7th Cir. 2012), para. 783. See also the US cases of *Hernandez v. Cardoso* (2016) 844 F.3d 692, *Gomez v. Fuenmayor*, 812 F.3d 1005 (11th Cir. 2016), *Abbott v. Abbott*, 130 S.Ct. 1983, 1997 (2010), and *Walsh v. Walsh* 221 F.3d 204, 220 (1st Cir. 2000), where a child witnessing a parent's 'severe abuse' constituted a grave risk of harm.

38 *Walsh v. Walsh* 221 F.3d 204, 220 (1st Cir. 2000).

39 *Baran v. Beaty*, 526 F.3d 1340 (11th Cir. 2008).

abuse was directed primarily at the mother.[40] In *Van De Sande*[41] the court also found that there was a grave risk of harm to the child, even when the violence was directed solely at the abducting mother, and threats only had been made towards the child.[42]

Therefore, identifying the harmful effects to the child would enable a court to properly examine and assess measures of protection that may be available, and whether, in fact, those measures can adequately ameliorate the harm exemplified in the above cases. As is explored below, protective measures contribute to the overall physical, psychological and emotional well-being of the victim/survivor parent, which will directly benefit the child.

The abuse may persist even with distance between the parties. For example, in *Ermini v. Vittori*[43] the United States Court of Appeal found that the father's propensity for violence, and danger towards the mother and child, would persist upon return, in view of the father's threatening phone calls, which reflected a 'continuing inability'[44] to control his temper outbursts or hostility. In this case, protective measures could not ameliorate the ongoing 'hostility, irresponsibility and irrational behaviour'[45] of the father, and the court concluded that the potential for violence was overwhelming.

4.2. REDUCED PARENTING CAPACITIES OF THE PARENT

Domestic violence suffered by a parent may affect their physical and mental health to the extent of destabilising the parenting of their children. When assessing the adequacy of protective measures, it is also important to take into account the risk of the child being placed in an intolerable situation as a result of the impairment of the parent's ability to parent the child.[46] Key recent developments, including the Brussels IIb Regulation and HCCH Guide, acknowledge the need to protect that primary carer relationship.[47]

---

40 *Van De Sande v. Van De Sande*, 431 F.3d 567 (7th Cir. 2005).
41 Ibid.
42 Ibid.
43 *Ermini v. Vittori*, 2014 WL 3056360 (C.A.2) (2nd Cir. 2014).
44 Ibid., p. 7.
45 Ibid.
46 POAM Best Practice Guide, reprinted in this volume, s. 5.1.3.3.
47 Brussels IIb, p. 45–46; HCCH Guide, para. 57.

4.3. SEPARATION FROM THE PRIMARY CAREGIVER

A child's interests and security have been found to be inextricably linked to his/her primary carer's interests and security, and therefore a return order separating them would impact on the child to the extent of constituting a grave risk of harm.[48] As noted, the Brussels IIb Regulation takes into account the need to consider adequate protective measures that will enable the child to remain with the taking parent until welfare decisions have been made.[49]

5. THE NEED FOR PROTECTIVE MEASURES

The underlying philosophy of the 1980 Convention is that international child abduction is harmful to children, and should, therefore, be discouraged. The Convention also seeks to prevent the abducting parent from establishing 'artificial jurisdictional links' with the requested State, with the intention of obtaining an advantage in custody proceedings, and thus benefiting from his/her own wrongdoing. Accordingly, the Convention sets out a legal mechanism designed to ensure the prompt return of a wrongfully removed or retained child to the country of his/her habitual residence. In line with this policy, the narrowness of the interpretation means that there are only a limited number of exceptions available to the abducting parent, including Article 13(1)(b), while these exceptions are to be interpreted in a narrow fashion. Therefore, protective measures, in the context of cases involving allegations of abuse, are useful tools in tackling domestic violence, and in the appraisal of Article 13(1)(b) the court should take into account all relevant matters, including all available protective measures.[50] Moreover, Article 11(4) of the Brussels IIa Regulation provides that a court shall not refuse a return order on the basis of Article 13(1)(b) if it is established that there are 'adequate arrangements' to secure the child's protection after his or her return. Article 27(3) of the Brussels IIb Regulation[51] reflects similar expectations. The appropriate protective measures, and their effectiveness, will differ from case to case, and from jurisdiction to jurisdiction.[52] Therefore, where the evaluation

---

48 *Pollastro v. Pollastro* [1999] 45 R.F.L. (4th) 404 (Ont. C.A.).
49 Brussels IIb, para. 45.
50 *Re C (Children) (Abduction Article 13(B))* [2018] EWCA Civ 2834, paras. 40–41.
51 Brussels IIb, Art. 27(3).
52 *Re E (Children)* [2011] UKSC 27, para. 36.

of the merits[53] of the allegations of domestic violence has led the court to the conclusion that the effects of domestic violence on the child upon his/her return to the State of habitual residence meet the high standard of the grave risk of harm exception, the court must consider 'the availability, adequacy and effectiveness' of protective measures.[54] In addition, when assessing whether or not protective measures have been taken in the State of habitual residence, and whether they will adequately safeguard the protection of the child upon his or her return, it is always a helpful exercise to utilise the assistance of the Central Authority of the State of habitual residence[55] and/or the international cooperation arrangements between Hague network judges.[56]

In emphasising the importance of determining the adequacy and effectiveness of protective measures, the POAM Best Practice Guide highlights the Practice Guide for the Application of the Brussels IIa Regulation, which states that '[i]t is not sufficient that procedures exist in the Member State of origin for the protection of the child, but it must be established that the authorities in the Member State of origin have taken concrete measures to protect the child in question'.[57]

The types of protective measures that may be available in the context of return proceedings include measures akin to non-molestation/non-harassment orders (for example, 'not to use violence or threats towards the mother, nor to instruct anybody else to do so', or 'not to communicate with the mother directly'), orders related to the occupation of the family home (for example, 'to vacate the family home and make it available for a sole occupancy by the mother and the child'), orders related to financial support (for example, 'to pay for the return tickets for the mother and the child', or 'to provide financial support/maintenance to the mother and the child upon their return'), and orders related to residence or access to the child (for example, 'not to seek to separate the mother from the child',[58]

---

53 *X v. Latvia* (App. no. 27853/09) Grand Chamber [2013]: effective examination – 'thorough, limited and expeditious' investigation.

54 HCCH Guide, para. 59.

55 European Commission, 'Practice Guide for the Application of the Brussels IIa Regulation', p. 55 (hereafter 'EC Practice Guide'), available at <https://op.europa.eu/en/publication-detail/-/publication/f7d39509-3f10-4ae2-b993-53ac6b9f93ed> accessed 25 February 2022.

56 *Re E (Children)* [2011] UKSC 27, para. 36.

57 EC Practice Guide, p. 55.

58 The Brussels IIb Regulation acknowledges that adequate arrangements to secure the return of the child may include 'allowing the child to stay with the abducting parent who is the primary carer until a decision on the substance of rights of custody has been made in the Member State following the return' (Brussels IIb, para. 45).

or 'not to seek contact with the child unless awarded by the court or agreed'). Further, the availability of any such protective measures should be considered against the background of access to courts and other legal services, and state assistance and support, including financial assistance, housing assistance, health services, women's shelters, and other means of support to victims of domestic violence, and responses by police and the criminal justice system more generally.

In addition, the courts have, in many circumstances, endorsed, or even made, orders giving effect to 'soft landing' measures within return[59] proceedings: measures that encompass 'more light-touch' practical arrangements to facilitate and implement the child's return, and enable a 'soft-landing' of the child in the State of habitual residence. These measures are distinguishable from protective measures against specific and identifiable grave risks of, for example, domestic violence. Soft-landing measures may comprise the left-behind parent purchasing return flight tickets for the mother and children, to enable them to journey to the country of habitual residence; the provision of a home, or financial measures such as paying maintenance, or a down payment for a home; or money to obtain legal advice, and to instigate proceedings relating, for example, to the custody of the children. It is of note that soft-landing measures and protective measures may overlap. For example, measures akin to the provision of a home, or money for separate accommodation for the mother and children, share a commonality with non-occupation orders that constitute an injunctive relief, and a means of prohibiting the father from living in the same home, in order that the grave risk of harm is ameliorated. Interestingly, the HCCH Guide makes the point that the court of the State of refuge cannot make orders that are not required to mitigate an established grave risk.[60] However, the HCCH Guide also observes that there are additional measures that, although not directly relevant to the issue of domestic violence, are nevertheless 'practical arrangements'[61] to assist in the implementation of a return order; in order words, soft-landing measures.

The benefits of protective measures can be described as per the following sections.

---

59 HCCH Guide, p. 49. See also *Re S (A Child) (Hague Convention 1980: Return to Third State)* [2019] EWCA Civ 352, para. 55.

60 HCCH Guide, para. 47.

61 Ibid., para 49.

5.1. DETERRING FUTURE ABUSE

Protective measures are designed to deter and mitigate the harm that has been identified by the court in Hague return proceedings. To deter future abuse effectively, or perhaps even end ongoing abuse (see intimidatory litigation),[62] one relies on the adequacy and efficacy of protective measures. As reflected on by Baroness Hale, 'one of the principal reasons' for the HCCH Guide was to protect 'victims of domestic violence and abuse from the hard choice of returning to a place where they do not feel safe and losing their children'.[63]

5.2. HALTING UNDESIRABLE CONTACT

Even though protection orders are sometimes breached, and satisfactory follow-up measures by relevant authorities may be lacking, in many cases protection orders do halt the undesirable contact.

5.3. IMPROVING OVERALL PHYSICAL, PSYCHOLOGICAL AND EMOTIONAL WELL-BEING OF THE VICTIM/SURVIVOR

When protective measures are effective, they can improve the overall physical, psychological and emotional well-being of the victim/survivor. It is important to recognise that the cessation of physical abuse does not necessarily ameliorate other harmful behaviours, including coercive or controlling behaviour within or outside return proceedings. An example of this is the exposure to 'intimidatory litigation', whereby the left-behind father uses the return proceedings abusively, as a means of further harassment, rather than from a genuine desire to secure the return of the child, and to pursue their parental relationship. On this basis, one may find that the left-behind parent was not actually exercising their custody rights when the removal or retention occurred, or that they had perhaps initially consented to the removal, but subsequently sought to withdraw consent. Thus, intimidatory tactics may qualify, under Article 13(1)(a), as a

62 POAM Best Practice Guide, reprinted in this volume, s. 2.1.2.

63 B. Hale, 'Taking Flight – Domestic Violence and Child Abduction' (2017) 70 *Current Legal Problems* 3.

ground for refusal. Such 'intimidatory litigation' adds greatly to the anxiety suffered by the mother, who, as a survivor of an abusive relationship, is likely to already be overwhelmed with the effects of that relationship. If this abuse is identified at an early stage, especially during proceedings, interim measures can be put in place to protect the victim/survivor from ongoing harm.

5.4. REDUCING THE FREQUENCY AND INTENSITY OF VIOLENCE

In circumstances where the perpetrator is still able to circumvent some measures, and where the contact does not stop completely, the overall frequency and intensity of violence tends to decrease.

5.5. EMPOWERING THE VICTIM/SURVIVOR

There is a risk that a victim or survivor of domestic violence may, potentially, be at risk of revictimisation at the hands of their partner. Protection orders are said to psychologically empower the victim/survivor, while sending a clear message to the offender that domestic violence is a public concern, and will not be tolerated.

6. CONCLUSION

The efficacy of protective measures to secure and enhance the safety of parents and children caught in private international law disputes should not be hampered by their cross-border characteristics. Moreover, it is because of these characteristics that there lies a higher sense of responsibility and due diligence in ensuring that such measures can be recognised and implemented adequately. In Hague return proceedings, in particular in cases where domestic violence is alleged to have been perpetrated on the taking parent, a return can be ordered, knowing that when the parent travels back with the child, she is being protected by means of all available legal avenues, as appropriate in the circumstances of the case. Indeed, in line with the POAM project findings, it is reiterated that protective measures, when issued with confidence, knowing that they will be recognised and enforced, strengthen the effectiveness of the 1980 Hague Convention and its return policy.[64]

Further, in parental child abduction cases committed against the backdrop of allegations of domestic violence, the consideration of protective measures gives substance and insight into the type of harm, the seriousness of the harm, an assessment of the needs, and careful consideration of whether any future risks can be avoided. Nevertheless, given the concerns over the effectiveness of protective measures, the POAM Best Practice Guide recommends that the employment of protection orders in return proceedings is not considered in cases where there is a risk of severe future violence: in essence, in cases where the risk of harm is 'clearly grave', and where protective measures would not ameliorate the risk, i.e. grave physical, sexual or psychological abuse, significant, severe, and repeated violence, with a disregard for the law, including breaches of previous protection orders.

Finally, protective measures may facilitate the 'safe return of the child',[65] but must not preclude the safe return of the accompanying parent whose protection would serve as protection of the child(ren) from the grave risk of psychological harm, or some other intolerable situation. The need for cross-border protective measures in return orders has become an essential part of the fabric of 1980 Convention proceedings, and ensuring that we have the right tools for recognition and enforcement is key.

64 POAM Best Practice Guide, reprinted in this volume, s. 5.2.
65 1996 Hague Convention Practical Operation Handbook, p. 70.

THE LAW APPLICABLE TO CROSS-BORDER PROTECTIVE MEASURES IN AND OUTSIDE OF RETURN PROCEEDINGS

Do All Roads Lead to the *Lex Fori*?

Jan von Hein

1. INTRODUCTION

The Hague Convention of 25 October 1980 on the Civil Aspects of International Child Abduction (hereafter 'Hague Child Abduction

Convention' or 'Convention')[1] is generally regarded as 'one of the most successful private international law conventions'.[2] As stated in Article 1 of the Convention, the principal aims of this instrument are: 'a) to secure the prompt return of children wrongfully removed to or retained in any Contracting State; and b) to ensure that rights of custody and of access under the law of one Contracting State are effectively respected in the other Contracting States'. To achieve the purpose of ensuring an expeditious return of the abducted child to the State of his or her former habitual residence, Article 13 of the Convention strictly limits the grounds for refusing to grant a return order. In particular, Article 13(1)(b) provides that a court of the requested Contracting State may reject an application to return the child, if 'there is a grave risk that his or her return would expose the child to physical or psychological harm or otherwise place the child in an intolerable situation'. This 'grave risk' exception has turned out to be the main legal battleground for parents in many abduction cases.[3]

Observers noticed more than two decades ago that the drafters of the Convention had made an implicit assumption about the typical sociological fact pattern underlying child abduction cases: an assumption that did not fit with the majority of cases actually decided by the courts of the Contracting States:

> Contrary to what was believed to be the profile of the abducting parent when the Convention was drafted (namely a father removing a child to another jurisdiction and from the primary carer), for many years the statistics have shown that international parental child abduction cases involving a sole or joint primary carer as the taking parent are most prevalent. In practical terms, this means that many taking parents are mothers, who may be returning to their country of origin, often citing flight from family violence by the other parent as the reason for leaving the country of habitual residence with the child.[4]

---

1 Hague Convention of 25 October 1980 on the Civil Aspects of International Child Abduction (Hague Convention no. 28) <https://assets.hcch.net/docs/e86d9f72-dc8d-46f3-b3bf-e102911c8532.pdf> accessed 26.08.2021.

2 D. Bryant, 'The 1980 Child Abduction Convention – the status quo and future challenges' in T. John, R. Gulati and B. Köhler (eds), *The Elgar Companion to the Hague Conference on Private International Law*, Edward Elgar, Cheltenham 2020, pp. 183–197, p. 183.

3 For a general survey of case law related to this provision, see Hague Conference on Private International Law, *Guide to Good Practice under the HCCH Convention of 25 October 1980 on the Civil Child Abduction – Part VI, Article 13(1)(b)*, 2020 (hereafter 'HCCH Guide') <https://www.hcch.net/en/publications-and-studies/details4/?pid=6740&dtid=3> accessed 26.08.2021.

4 D. Bryant, 'The 1980 Child Abduction Convention – the status quo and future challenges' in T. John, R. Gulati and B. Köhler (eds), *The Elgar Companion to the*

For courts in the requested State, this typical scenario raises the question as to whether a threat of violence against the abducting mother may also constitute a 'grave risk' to the abducted child, within the meaning of Article 13(1)(b) of the Convention.[5] In particular, judges have to consider whether, and on which grounds of jurisdiction, they may take protective measures in respect of the abducting mother, in order to alleviate concerns regarding the child's well-being.[6] Furthermore, the choice-of-law issue, i.e. the determination of the law applicable to such measures of protection, must be addressed.[7]

Apart from the court that has to decide on the application for a return order filed by the father of the abducted child under the Convention, other courts may have to address the issue of protective measures against domestic violence, following a pertinent application by the abducting mother herself.[8] Such proceedings outside of the framework of the Convention may be related, inter alia, to issues like parental responsibility (see section 3.2 below), or claims concerning trespass, approaching and contact, in particular pertaining to the marital home (see section 3.3.2), or – finally, but importantly – tortious claims in general (see section 3.4). In addition, intricate legal questions regarding jurisdiction for protective measures, and the law applicable to those measures, may arise as well.

Hague Conference on Private International Law, Edward Elgar, Cheltenham 2020, pp. 183–197, p. 194 (footnote omitted); Best Practice Guide – Protection of Abducting Mothers in Return Proceedings (hereafter 'POAM Best Practice Guide'), reprinted in this volume, s. 2.1.1; K. Trimmings and O. Momoh, 'Intersection between Domestic Violence and International Parental Child Abduction: Protection of Abducting Mothers in Return Proceedings' (2021) 35 *International Journal of Law, Policy and The Family* 1, 2.

5 See the HCCH Guide, paras. 57–59; O. Momoh, 'The interpretation and application of Article 13(1) b) of the Hague Child Abduction Convention in cases involving domestic violence: Revisiting *X v Latvia* and the principle of "effective examination"' (2019) 15 *Journal of Private International Law* 626–57; POAM Best Practice Guide, s. 2.2; K. Trimmings and O. Momoh, 'Intersection between Domestic Violence and International Parental Child Abduction: Protection of Abducting Mothers in Return Proceedings' (2021) 35 *International Journal of Law, Policy and The Family* 1, 5 et seq.

6 POAM Best Practice Guide, s. 5.2.1.1; K. Trimmings and O. Momoh, 'Intersection between Domestic Violence and International Parental Child Abduction: Protection of Abducting Mothers in Return Proceedings' (2021) 35 *International Journal of Law, Policy and The Family* 1, 15–19; on cross-border protection measures in the EU, see A. Dutta, 'Cross-border protection measures in the European Union' (2016) 12 *Journal of Private International Law* 169–84.

7 See POAM Best Practice Guide, s. 5.2.1.1; A. Dutta, 'Cross-border protection measures in the European Union' (2016) 12 *Journal of Private International Law* 169–84, 171 et seq.

8 POAM Best Practice Guide, s. 5.2.1.1.

The following parts of this contribution will take a closer look at the law applicable to protective measures in the two scenarios just mentioned, i.e., first, protective measures ordered by the return court, and, second, protective measures taken by other courts in proceedings related to the issues enumerated above. Since jurisdiction and applicable law are often closely intertwined in this area of family law, the contribution will also analyse questions of jurisdiction, in so far as these are also relevant to choice-of-law issues. The contribution will not deal with the circulation, i.e. the recognition and enforcement, of cross-border protective measures, because these problems will be analysed in detail by Katarina Trimmings, Onyója Momoh and Michael Wilderspin, in their contributions to this volume.

2. PROTECTIVE MEASURES ISSUED BY THE RETURN COURT

2.1. JURISDICTION

The recently released guide on Article 13(1)(b) of the Convention contains several paragraphs devoted to the issue of protective measures issued by the court hearing the return application.[9] As a starting point, the mere existence of incidences involving domestic violence directed against the abducting mother is, 'in and of itself', not considered sufficient to constitute a grave risk to the child in every case.[10] However, courts do frequently reach the conclusion that severe potential harm to the taking parent may be characterised as a 'grave risk' to the abducted child as well, particularly when the parent threatened by serious violence is also the primary carer.[11] Thus, protective measures issued by the return court may mitigate pertinent risks to the abducting mother and, thus, also alleviate concerns related to the 'grave risk' exception (Art. 13(1)(b) Hague Child Abduction Convention).

Although this interplay between protective measures and the 'grave risk' exception is, in principle, generally accepted nowadays,[12] the

9 HCCH Guide, paras. 46–59.

10 HCCH Guide, para. 58, citing *Souratgar v. Fair*, 720 F.3d 96 (2nd Cir. 2013).

11 See HCCH Guide, para. 57 et seq., citing *Taylor v. Taylor*, 502 Fed.Appx. 854, 2012 WL 6631395 (C.A.11 (Fla.)) (11th Cir. 2012).

12 HCCH Guide, para. 59; K. Trimmings and O. Momoh, 'Intersection between Domestic Violence and International Parental Child Abduction: Protection of

Convention itself does not contain any provision determining which court is competent, and which law should be applied to protective measures. The Hague Conference, in its guide to Article 13(1)(b) of the Convention, tacitly admits these lacunae, stating that:

> In some States, the court hearing the return application may have internal jurisdiction *under national law* to order measures of protection as part of its return order. In other States, the court may not have such jurisdiction.[13]

Since the Convention is silent on this issue, the jurisdiction of the return court to order protective measures must be derived from other legal sources. Among the Member States of the European Union,[14] the Brussels IIb Regulation,[15] which will be applicable from 1 August 2022 (Art. 105(2) Brussels IIb Regulation), seems to provide for a clear solution to this problem. Article 27(5) of the Brussels IIb Regulation explicitly envisages protective measures in order to mitigate a 'grave risk':

> Where the court orders the return of the child, the court may, where appropriate, take provisional, including protective, measures in accordance with Article 15 of this Regulation in order to protect the child from the grave risk referred to in point (b) of Article 13(1) of the 1980 Hague Convention, provided that the examining and taking of such measures would not unduly delay the return proceedings.

The fact that Article 15 of the Brussels IIb Regulation and the accompanying Recitals 45 and 46 of said Regulation only make an explicit reference to risks to the child has led some critics to draw the conclusion that 'the Regulation is concerned solely with the protection of the child', and not of the abducting mother.[16] Yet, this literal reading seems to be too narrow. Since Article 27(5) of the Brussels IIb Regulation is meant to support and complement the application of Article 13(1)(b) of the Hague Abduction

---

Abducting Mothers in Return Proceedings' (2021) 35 *International Journal of Law, Policy and The Family* 1, 10–15.

13 HCCH Guide, para. 46 (emphasis added).

14 Except for Denmark.

15 Council Regulation (EU) 2019/1111 of 25 June 2019 on jurisdiction, the recognition and enforcement of decisions in matrimonial matters and the matters of parental responsibility, and on international child abduction (recast) [2019] OJ L178/1.

16 K. Trimmings and O. Momoh, 'Intersection between Domestic Violence and International Parental Child Abduction: Protection of Abducting Mothers in Return Proceedings' (2021) 35 *International Journal of Law, Policy and The Family* 1, 17.

Convention, the more generous interpretation of a 'grave risk' to the child, developed in the context of this Convention – i.e. that domestic violence is not only a direct threat against the primary carer, but may indirectly constitute a severe danger to the child's well-being, too[17] – should also be recognised within the framework of the Brussels IIb Regulation.

Recital 46 of Brussels IIb gives further guidance on the interpretation of this rule. In particular, this Recital emphasises that the return court should cooperate closely with the court and authorities of the Member State of origin:

> If necessary, the court seised with the return proceedings under the 1980 Hague Convention should consult with the court or competent authorities of the Member State of the habitual residence of the child, with the assistance of Central Authorities or network judges, in particular within the European Judicial Network in civil and commercial matters and the International Hague Network of Judges.

For cases in which, for intertemporal reasons, the former Brussels IIa Regulation[18] remains applicable, one may argue that the Hague return court has the competence to take protective measures pursuant to Article 11(4) of the Brussels IIa Regulation.[19] This provision, which roughly corresponds to Article 27(3) of the Brussels IIb Regulation, provides that 'a court cannot refuse to return a child on the basis of Article 13b of the 1980 Hague Convention if it is established that adequate arrangements have been made to secure the protection of the child after his or her return'.

While it may be possible to interpret this provision as granting the power to make 'adequate arrangements' to both the Hague return court and

---

17 See HCCH Guide, para. 57 et seq., citing *Taylor v. Taylor*, 502 Fed.Appx. 854, 2012 WL 6631395 (C.A.11 (Fla.)) (11th Cir. 2012).

18 Council Regulation (EC) No 2201/2003 of 27 November 2003 concerning jurisdiction and the recognition and enforcement of judgments in matrimonial matters and the matters of parental responsibility, repealing Regulation (EC) No 1347/2000 [2003] OJ L338/1.

19 See, for a cautious endorsement of this position, POAM Best Practice Guide, s. 5.2.1.1.; K. Trimmings and O. Momoh, 'Intersection between Domestic Violence and International Parental Child Abduction: Protection of Abducting Mothers in Return Proceedings' (2021) 35 *International Journal of Law, Policy and The Family* 1, 10; for a more sceptical assessment, see A. Dutta, 'Cross-border protection measures in the European Union' (2016) 12 *Journal of Private International Law* 169–84, 182; O. Momoh, 'The interpretation and application of Article 13(1) b) of the Hague Child Abduction Convention in cases involving domestic violence: Revisiting *X v Latvia* and the principle of "effective examination"' (2019) 15 *Journal of Private International Law* 626–57, 636 et seq.

the courts in the country of origin, the wording of this Article rather seems to assign a passive role to the Hague return court with regard to merely taking into account 'adequate arrangements' that already 'have been made', i.e. taken by another court or competent authority.[20] This reading is confirmed by the more elaborate formulation of the successor rule, Article 27(3) of the Brussels IIb Regulation, and Recital 45 of the same Regulation, which names only court orders or protective measures taken in the *country of origin* as examples of 'adequate arrangements':

> Where a court considers refusing to return a child solely on the basis of point (b) of Article 13(1) of the 1980 Hague Convention, it should not refuse to return the child if either the party seeking the return of the child satisfies the court, or the court is otherwise satisfied, that adequate arrangements have been made to secure the protection of the child after his or her return. Examples for such arrangements could include a court order from *that Member State* prohibiting the applicant to come close to the child, a provisional, including protective measure from *that Member State* allowing the child to stay with the abducting parent who is the primary carer until a decision on the substance of rights of custody has been made in *that Member State* following the return.[21]

In addition, even if one were inclined to endorse a more generous reading of which court is competent to make 'adequate arrangements', the systematic relationship between Articles 27(3) and 27(5) of the Brussels IIb Regulation would strongly suggest that the latter paragraph was conceived as a *lex specialis* governing protective measures taken by the Hague return court.

Thus, the proper approach consists in basing protective measures taken by the Hague return court on the approach taken in older cases on Article 20

---

20 See A. Frąckowiak-Adamska, 'No Deal Better than a Bad Deal – Child Abduction and the Brussels IIa Regulation' in P. Beaumont, M. Danov, K. Trimmings and B. Yüksel (eds), *Cross-Border Litigation in Europe*, Hart, Oxford 2017, pp. 755, 759, who interprets the provision as 'an expression of mutual trust between Member States – if one of them [i.e. the country of origin] puts in place adequate arrangements, another one [i.e. the requested State] cannot refuse the return' – but who concedes that the provision 'does not state who shall organise the arrangements'; see also E. Pataut, 'Art. 11 Brussels II*bis*', para. 46, in P. Mankowski and U. Magnus (eds), *Brussels IIbis Regulation*, Sellier European Law Publishers, Munich 2012; U. Spellenberg, 'Vorbemerkungen C zu Art. 19 EGBGB – Art. 11 Brüssel IIa-VO', para. C 67, in J. von Staudinger (ed), *Kommentar zum Bürgerlichen Gesetzbuch mit Einführungsgesetz und Nebengesetzen*, Sellier – De Gruyter, Berlin 2018.

21 Recital 45 Brussels IIb Regulation, emphasis added.

of the Brussels IIa Regulation.[22] In cases that fall within the scope of neither the Brussels IIa nor the Brussels IIb Regulations, Article 11 of the 1996 Hague Convention on the Protection of Children[23] provides a proper ground of jurisdiction.[24]

2.2. APPLICABLE LAW

Although the recently enacted Brussels IIb Regulation introduces a specific provision concerning the Hague return court's jurisdiction for protective measures (Art. 27(5) Brussels IIb Regulation), this Regulation still contains no rules on determining the applicable law. Thus, the legal situation is unchanged, compared with the previous Brussels IIa Regulation.[25] Pursuant to Article 98(1) of the Brussels IIb Regulation, which corresponds to the former Article 62(1) of the Brussels IIa Regulation, the 1996 Hague Convention on the Protection of Children shall continue to have effect in relation to matters not governed by the Brussels IIb Regulation. Since the Brussels IIb Regulation does not cover choice-of-law issues, the conflicts rule contained in Article 15(1) of the Hague Convention on the Protection of Children remains applicable.[26] This provision states that, '[i]n exercising their jurisdiction under the provisions of Chapter II [of the Convention], the authorities of the Contracting States shall apply their own law'. This rule encompasses provisional measures taken by a court that has jurisdiction pursuant to Article 11 of the Hague Convention on the Protection of Children. Providing for mutually

---

22 Cf. 'Pathway 4' described in POAM Best Practice Guide, s. 5.2.1.1; K. Trimmings and O. Momoh, 'Intersection between Domestic Violence and International Parental Child Abduction: Protection of Abducting Mothers in Return Proceedings' (2021) 35 *International Journal of Law, Policy and The Family* 1, 16.

23 Hague Convention of 19 October 1996 on Jurisdiction, Applicable Law, Recognition, Enforcement and Co-operation in Respect of Parental Responsibility and Measures for the Protection of Children <https://assets.hcch.net/docs/f16ebd3d-f398-4891-bf47-110866e171d4.pdf> accessed 26.08.2021.

24 HCCH Guide, para. 48; POAM Best Practice Guide, s. 5.2.1.1; K. Trimmings and O. Momoh, 'Intersection between Domestic Violence and International Parental Child Abduction: Protection of Abducting Mothers in Return Proceedings' (2021) 35 *International Journal of Law, Policy and The Family* 1, 13 et seq.

25 For a short survey of the *status quaestionis*, see J. von Hein, 'Vorbemerkungen zu Art. 24 EGBGB', para. 8, in J. von Staudinger (ed), *Kommentar zum Bürgerlichen Gesetzbuch mit Einführungsgesetz und Nebengesetzen*, Sellier – De Gruyter, Berlin 2019, with further references.

26 J. Pirrung, 'Art. 61 Brüssel IIa', para. 3, in P. Mankowski and U. Magnus (eds), *Brussels IIbis Regulation*, Sellier European Law Publishers, Munich 2012.

fine-tuned rules on jurisdiction and choice of law ensures that, in most cases, courts will be able to adjudicate on protective measures for the benefit of a child without further delay.[27]

However, an intricate problem arises from the fact that, among the EU Member States (except for Denmark), the jurisdictional rules of the Brussels IIb Regulation take precedence over those of the 1996 Hague Convention on the Protection of Children. Applying the jurisdictional rules of the Brussels IIb Regulation, but determining the applicable law pursuant to the 1996 Hague Protection Convention, is not without problems, because the Brussels IIb Regulation contains a few heads of jurisdiction that are not found in the Convention itself. Thus, German courts have developed a test that focuses on whether a court that bases its jurisdiction on the Brussels IIa (now IIb) Regulation would also be competent by virtue of a hypothetical application of the rules found in Chapter II of the 1996 Hague Protection Convention.[28] Many academic writers favour a more generous approach that would extend the principle of parallelism between jurisdiction and applicable law to heads of jurisdiction that are found only in the Brussels IIa or IIb Regulations, but not in the 1996 Hague Protection Convention.[29]

With regard to Article 27(5) of the Brussels IIb Regulation, it is hard to deny that this provision was not modelled on a blueprint corresponding to the 1996 Hague Convention. Unlike the Brussels IIb Regulation, the 1996 Hague Protection Convention does not contain a specific rule dealing with protective measures taken by a court hearing an application under the 1980 Hague Abduction Convention (see above, section 2.1). Nevertheless, one must not leap to conclusion that, for want of an exact mirror image regarding this ground for jurisdiction, the *lex fori* principle found in Article 15(1) of the 1996 Hague Protection Convention should not apply. This is because Article 27(5) of the Brussels IIb Regulation is not a self-standing rule on jurisdiction, but explicitly refers to 'provisional, including protective, measures *in accordance with Article 15* of this Regulation'.[30] This means that Article 27(5) of the Brussels IIb Regulation

27 On the methodological underpinnings, see J. von Hein, 'The role of the HCCH in shaping private international law' in T. John, R. Gulati and B. Köhler (eds), *The Elgar Companion to the Hague Conference on Private International Law*, Edward Elgar, Cheltenham 2020, pp. 112, 116 et seq.

28 BGH 20 December 2017 – XII ZB 333/17, BGHZ 217, 165, para. 20.

29 See J. von Hein, Vorbemerkungen zu Art. 24 EGBGB', para. 8, in J. von Staudinger (ed), *Kommentar zum Bürgerlichen Gesetzbuch mit Einführungsgesetz und Nebengesetzen*, Sellier – De Gruyter, Berlin 2019, with comprehensive references.

30 Emphasis added.

merely has a clarifying function regarding the relationship between the 'grave risk' exception of Article 13(1)(b) of the Hague Abduction Convention and the taking of protective measures, while the true jurisdictional basis for a protective measure taken by the Hague return court remains anchored in Article 15 of the Brussels IIb Regulation (formerly Article 20, Brussels IIa Regulation). Since Article 15 is closely modelled on Article 11 of the Hague Convention on the Protection of Children, the Hague return court would also be competent by virtue of a hypothetical application of the latter Convention. Thus, at the end of the day, the Hague return court is on firm legal ground in applying its own substantive law to a protective measure.

3. PROTECTIVE MEASURES ISSUED BY ANOTHER COURT

3.1. A FALSE FRIEND: THE HAGUE CONVENTION ON THE INTERNATIONAL PROTECTION OF ADULTS

A lawyer representing an abducting mother threatened by her violent husband may be tempted to scroll through the list of conventions displayed on the website of the Hague Conference, in order to find a convention that would allow his or her client to apply for a measure of protection on her own initiative.[31] There, the lawyer may come across the 2000 Hague Convention on the International Protection of Adults.[32] Although the title of this Convention seems to suggest that it could be useful in the context at stake here, a closer look quickly reveals that the Hague Adults Convention is a 'false friend' in this regard. The Convention's substantive scope is defined in Articles 1(1), 3 and 4 thereof. According to Article 1(1) of the Hague Adults Convention, the Convention applies to the protection of adults who, by reason of an impairment or insufficiency of their personal faculties, are not in a position to protect their interests. The need for protection is determined on a factual basis; it is not a precondition for the Convention's applicability that a person suffers from incapacity in a legal sense.[33]

---

31 See the list at <https://www.hcch.net/en/instruments/conventions> accessed 26.08.2021.

32 Hague Convention of 13 January 2000 on the International Protection of Adults (Hague Convention no. 35) <https://assets.hcch.net/docs/c2b94b6b-c54e-4886-ae9f-c5bbef93b8f3.pdf> accessed 26.08.2021.

33 See the official report by P. Lagarde, *Protection of Adults Convention – Explanatory Report*, 2nd ed., HCCH, The Hague 2017, para. 9; in the literature, see also A. Ruck Keene, 'Hague 35 – Overview and Protective Measures' in R. Frimston, A. Ruck Keene,

However, the need for protection must have its cause in personal characteristics of the adult concerned.[34] Thus, if a person is in need of a protective measure because of external influences, as is the case with a wife beaten by her violent husband, or a victim pursued by a stalker, this may justify protective measures, but the notion of 'protection of adults' within the meaning of the Convention does not encompass such cases.[35]

3.2. PROCEEDINGS RELATED TO PARENTAL RESPONSIBILITY

An abducting mother is not compelled to wait for the father to file an application for a return order just to establish a ground for jurisdiction in the State where the child is present. Even if proceedings related to parental responsibility are pending in the country of origin, the mother may apply for a protective measure in the State of refuge by virtue of Article 15 of the Brussels IIb Regulation (formerly Art. 20, Brussels IIb Regulation).[36] However, it may be more difficult to convince a judge in self-standing proceedings that domestic violence threatening the mother should also be considered a grave risk to the child, than it is in proceedings before the Hague return court (see section 2.1 above). The applicable law is determined according to Article 15(1) of the Hague Convention on the Protection of Children in those cases as well.

C. van Overdijk and A.D. Ward (eds), *The International Protection of Adults*, Oxford University Press, Oxford 2015, para. 8.22; J. von Hein, 'Adults, protection of' in J. Basedow, G. Rühl, F. Ferrari and P. de Miguel Asensio (eds), *Encyclopedia of Private International Law*, Edward Elgar, Cheltenham 2017, pp. 21, 23.

34 P. Lagarde, *Protection of Adults Convention – Explanatory Report*, 2nd ed., HCCR, The Hague 2017, para. 9; A. Ruck Keene, 'Hague 35 – Overview and Protective Measures' in R. Frimston, A. Ruck Keene, C. van Overdijk and A.D. Ward (eds), *The International Protection of Adults*, Oxford University Press, Oxford 2015, para. 8.24; J. von Hein, 'Adults, protection of' in J. Basedow, G. Rühl, F. Ferrari and P. de Miguel Asensio (eds), *Encyclopedia of Private International Law*, Edward Elgar, Cheltenham 2017, p. 23.

35 P. Lagarde, *Protection of Adults Convention – Explanatory Report*, 2nd ed., HCCR, The Hague 2017, para. 9; A. Ruck Keene, 'Hague 35 – Overview and Protective Measures' in R. Frimston, A. Ruck Keene, C. van Overdijk and A.D. Ward (eds), *The International Protection of Adults*, Oxford University Press, Oxford 2015, para. 8.24; J. von Hein, 'Adults, protection of' in J. Basedow, G. Rühl, F. Ferrari and P. de Miguel Asensio (eds), *Encyclopedia of Private International Law*, Edward Elgar, Cheltenham 2017, pp. 23 et seq.

36 POAM Best Practice Guide, s. 5.2.1.1.

3.3. PROCEEDINGS RELATED TO THE MARITAL HOME

3.3.1. *The Right to Use the Marital Home*

In order to shield a wife from her violent husband, the allocation of the marital home for her sole use will frequently be a very effective protective measure. The German Civil Code (Bürgerliches Gesetzbuch – BGB),[37] for example, provides that, if the spouses are living apart, or if one of them wishes to live apart, one spouse may demand that the other permits him or her the sole use of the matrimonial home or part of the matrimonial home, to the extent that this is necessary, taking account of the concerns of the other spouse, in order to avoid an inequitable hardship (§ 1361b(1), 1st sentence BGB). If the spouse against whom the application is directed has unlawfully and intentionally injured the body, health or liberty of the other spouse, or unlawfully threatened such an injury or injury to life, then, as a general rule, sole use of the whole home is to be permitted (§ 1361b(2), 1st sentence BGB). The claim to permission for use of the home is excluded only if no further injuries or unlawful threats are to be feared, unless the injured spouse cannot be expected to continue living with the other spouse by reason of the severity of the act (§ 1361b(2), 2nd sentence BGB).

The allocation of the marital home may be considered part of the 'matrimonial property regime', within the meaning of Article 1(1) of the EU Matrimonial Property Regulation.[38] According to the definition in Article 3(a) of the EU Matrimonial Property Regulation, a 'matrimonial property regime' means, inter alia, a set of rules concerning the property relationships between the spouses as a result of marriage or its dissolution. This wide definition also covers the allocation of the marital home in cases where domestic violence is involved.[39] Thus, jurisdiction for such protective

---

37 Civil Code in the version promulgated on 2 January 2002 (Federal Law Gazette [Bundesgesetzblatt] I, p. 42, 2909; 2003 I, p. 738), last amended by Art. 4, para. 5 of the Act of 1 October 2013 (Federal Law Gazette I, p. 3719), trans. by C. von Schöningh, available at <https://www.gesetze-im-internet.de/englisch_bgb/englisch_bgb.html#p4872> accessed 26.08.2021.

38 Council Regulation (EU) 2016/1103 of 24 June 2016 implementing enhanced cooperation in the area of jurisdiction, applicable law and the recognition and enforcement of decisions in matters of matrimonial property regimes [2016] OJ L183/1.

39 German Federal Government, 'Entwurf eines Gesetzes zum Internationalen Güterrecht und zur Änderung von Vorschriften des Internationalen Privatrechts', *Bundestags-Drucksache* 19/4852, p. 39; S. Gössl, 'Art. 17a EGBGB', para. 1a, in K.H. Johannsen, D. Henrich and C. Althammer (eds), *Familienrecht*, 7th ed., CH Beck, Munich 2020;

measures may be derived from Article 19 of the EU Matrimonial Property Regulation.[40] Similar to the model found in Article 15 of the Brussels IIb Regulation, Article 19 of the EU Matrimonial Property Regulation provides that:

> Application may be made to the courts of a Member State for such provisional, including protective, measures as may be available under the law of that State, even if, under this Regulation, the courts of another Member State have jurisdiction as to the substance of the matter.

Usually, it will be the courts in the country of origin that have jurisdiction as to the substance of the matter, pursuant to Articles 5–9 of the EU Matrimonial Property Regulation; in special cases, where no other head of jurisdiction is available, the courts of a Member State shall have jurisdiction in so far as immovable property of one or both spouses is located in the territory of that Member State (Art. 10, EU Matrimonial Property Regulation). Moreover, in cases involving third States, the *forum necessitatis* found in Article 11 of the EU Matrimonial Property Regulation may come into play.

Even if a court of the State of refuge does not have jurisdiction as to the substance of the matter, under the EU Matrimonial Property Regulation, it may still order a provisional measure pursuant to Article 19 of the EU Matrimonial Property Regulation, if such a measure is available under the law of that Member State.[41] In this respect, the Regulation refers to the autonomous heads of jurisdiction found in Member State laws. In Germany, for example, jurisdiction for a provisional allocation of a marital home situated abroad would flow from §§ 50(1), 105, 111 No. 5, 200, and 201 No. 4 of the Act on proceedings in family matters and in matters of

B. Heiderhoff, 'Art. 17a EGBGB', para. 1, in W.J. Hau and R. Poseck (eds), *Beck-Onlinekommentar BGB*, CH Beck, Munich 2021; D. Looschelders, 'Art. 1 EuGüVO', para. 18, in F.J. Säcker, R. Rixecker, H. Oetker and B. Limperg (eds), *Münchener Kommentar zum Bürgerlichen Gesetzbuch*, vol. 12, 8th ed., CH Beck, Munich 2020.

40 R. Hausmann, *Internationales und Europäisches Familienrecht*, 2nd ed., CH Beck, Munich 2018, Ch. E, 'Ehewohnungs-, Haushalts- und Gewaltschutzsachen', para. 4; B. Heiderhoff, 'Art. 17a EGBGB', para. 8, in W.J. Hau and R. Poseck (eds), *Beck-Onlinekommentar BGB*, CH Beck, Munich 2021.

41 R. Hausmann, *Internationales und Europäisches Familienrecht*, 2nd ed., CH Beck, Munich 2018, Ch. B, 'Güterrechtssachen', para. 241; D. Looschelders, 'Art. 19 EuGüVO', para. 4, in F.J. Säcker, R. Rixecker, H. Oetker and B. Limperg (eds), Münchener Kommentar zum Bürgerlichen Gesetzbuch, vol. 12, 8th ed., CH Beck, Munich 2020.

non-contentious jurisdiction (FamFG).[42] This means, prima facie, that the court in the district in which the applicant has her habitual residence would have jurisdiction to enact a protective measure concerning the provisional allocation of a marital home situated abroad.[43] However, since Article 19 of the EU Matrimonial Property Regulation was modelled on Article 35 of the Brussels Ia Regulation,[44] one has to take into account the pertinent case law of the CJEU, according to which 'the granting of provisional or protective measures ... is conditional on, inter alia, the existence of a real connecting link between the subject-matter of the measures sought and the territorial jurisdiction of the ... State of the court before which those measures are sought'.[45] In the Brussels Ia context, the CJEU has deduced from the necessity of a 'real connecting link' that the provisional measure sought must relate 'to specific assets of the defendant located or to be located within the confines of the territorial jurisdiction of the court to which application is made'.[46] If one transposes this requirement to Article 19 of the EU Matrimonial Property Regulation,[47] it is doubtful whether a court in the State of refuge may grant a protective measure that is related to a marital home situated outside of the forum State, i.e. in the country of origin. However, it is not yet authoritatively settled to what extent the criterion of 'real connecting link' limits the jurisdiction for provisional measures, in the context of matrimonial property law.[48] The protective aim of a provisional measure related to the marital home

---

42 Act on Proceedings in Family Matters and in Matters of Non-contentious Jurisdiction of 17 December 2008 (BGBl. 2008 I, pp. 2586, 2587), as amended by Art. 2 of the Act of 22 June 2019 (Federal Law Gazette I, p. 866), trans. by K. Guida, available at <https://www.gesetze-im-internet.de/englisch_famfg> accessed 26.08.2021.

43 P. Winkler von Mohrenfels, 'Anhang zu Art. 17a EGBGB', paras. 76, 82, in F.J. Säcker, R. Rixecker, H. Oetker and B. Limperg (eds), *Münchener Kommentar zum Bürgerlichen Gesetzbuch*, vol. 12, 8th ed., CH Beck, Munich 2020.

44 Regulation (EU) No 1215/2012 of the European Parliament and of the Council of 12 December 2012 on jurisdiction and the recognition and enforcement of judgments in civil and commercial matters [2012] OJ L351/1.

45 Case C-391/95, *Van Uden Maritime BV v. Kommanditgesellschaft in Firma Deco-Line and Another*, ECLI:EU:C:1998:543, para. 40; for a closer doctrinal analysis of the legal situation in the Brussels Ia framework, see C. Heinze, 'Die Sicherung von Forderungen im europäischen Zivilprozessrecht' (2020) 119 *Zeitschrift für Vergleichende Rechtswissenschaft* 167, 175–77.

46 Case C-391/95, *Van Uden Maritime BV v. Kommanditgesellschaft in Firma Deco-Line and Another*, ECLI:EU:C:1998:543, para. 47.

47 D. Looschelders, 'Art. 19 EuGüVO', para. 5, in F.J. Säcker, R. Rixecker, H. Oetker and B. Limperg (eds), *Münchener Kommentar zum Bürgerlichen Gesetzbuch*, vol. 12, 8th ed., CH Beck, Munich 2020.

48 Cf. also on the particularities of family law in this regard, D. Looschelders, 'Art. 19 EuGüVO', para. 6 *in fine*, in F.J. Säcker, R. Rixecker, H. Oetker and B. Limperg (eds), *Münchener Kommentar zum Bürgerlichen Gesetzbuch*, vol. 12, 8th ed., CH Beck,

in cases of domestic violence, and the practical need to complement Article 27(5) of the Brussels IIb Regulation (see section 2.1 above) in this regard, arguably justify a more generous interpretation of the 'real connecting link', for the purposes of Article 19 of the EU Matrimonial Property Regulation, than that preferred in the Brussels Ia context.

With regard to choice of law, a court having jurisdiction pursuant to Article 19 of the EU Matrimonial Property Regulation may not simply apply its own law, but has to determine the applicable law according to Articles 20–35 of the EU Matrimonial Property Regulation. Because EU Regulations take precedence over autonomous private international law, the German legislature, for example, has deleted the allocation of the marital home from its autonomous choice-of-law rule governing the protection of one of the spouses from violent behaviour (Art. 17a Einführungsgesetz zum Bürgerlichen Gesetzbuch – EGBGB).[49] Where the spouses have not reached an agreement on the applicable law (Art. 22, EU Matrimonial Property Regulation), Article 26(1) of the EU Matrimonial Property Regulation contains a cascade of connecting factors, ranging from: (a) their first common habitual residence; to (b) their common nationality; and, finally, to (c) the State with which the spouses are most closely connected. In addition, Article 30 of the EU Matrimonial Property Regulation gives courts the possibility of applying exceptions based on overriding mandatory provisions. Recital 55, second sentence, of the EU Matrimonial Property Regulation specifies that 'the concept of "overriding mandatory provisions" should cover rules of an imperative nature such as rules for the protection of the family home'.[50] This surely covers mandatory rules on the allocation of a marital home situated within the forum State.[51] However, one has to doubt whether a court would be

Munich 2020; R. Hausmann, *Internationales und Europäisches Familienrecht*, 2nd ed., CH Beck, Munich 2018, Ch. B, 'Güterrechtssachen', B Rn. 244.

49 Introductory Act to the Civil Code of 21.09.1994, Federal Law Gazette I, p. 2494, as amended by the Gesetz zum Internationalen Güterrecht und zur Änderung von Vorschriften des Internationalen Privatrechts, Federal Law Gazette 2018 I, p. 2573, 2580, English trans. by J. Mörsdorf-Schulte available at <https://www.gesetze-im-internet.de/englisch_bgbeg/> accessed 26.08.2021; on the reasoning behind this change, see German Federal Government, 'Entwurf eines Gesetzes zum Internationalen Güterrecht und zur Änderung von Vorschriften des Internationalen Privatrechts', *Bundestags-Drucksache* 19/4852, p. 39.

50 For closer analysis, see D. Looschelders, 'Art. 30 EuGüVO', para. 5, in F.J. Säcker, R. Rixecker, H. Oetker and B. Limperg (eds), *Münchener Kommentar zum Bürgerlichen Gesetzbuch*, vol. 12, 8th ed., CH Beck, Munich 2020; see also J. von Hein, 'Conflicts between International Property, Family and Succession Law – Interfaces and Regulatory Techniques' (2017) 6 *European Property Law Journal* 142, 149.

51 See, on § 1361b BGB, C. von Bar and P. Mankowski, *Internationales Privatrecht, Besonderer Teil*, 2nd ed., CH Beck, Munich 2019, § 4, para. 342; S. Gössl, 'Art. 17a EGBGB',

well-advised to regard its own law on the allocation of a marital home as mandatory, in so far as immovable property situated outside of the forum State is concerned.[52]

3.3.2. *Prohibitions as to Trespass, Approaching and Contact Pertaining to the Marital Home*

3.3.2.1. Marital Home in the Forum State

Apart from being allocated the sole use of the marital home, an abducting mother may apply for measures that prohibit her violent husband from trespassing, approaching or otherwise contacting her. In so far as those measures are related to the marital home,[53] the question arises as to where the line should be drawn between the EU Matrimonial Property Regulation and other legal sources. Since the definition contained in Article 3(a) of the EU Matrimonial Property Regulation limits the notion of 'matrimonial property regimes' to 'rules concerning the property relationships between the spouses', it is commonly understood that rules not governing the allocation of the home as such, but merely related measures concerning issues such as trespass, approaching, and other forms of contact with the abused spouse, are not covered by the EU Matrimonial Property Regulation.[54] This restrictive reading of the EU Matrimonial Property Regulation motivated the German legislature to retain Article 17a EGBGB, which refers to the *lex fori* with regard to trespass, approaching and other

---

para. 1a, in K.H. Johannsen, D. Henrich and C. Althammer (eds), *Familienrecht*, 7th ed., CH Beck, Munich 2020; D. Looschelders, 'Art. 30 EuGüVO', para. 5, in F.J. Säcker, R. Rixecker, H. Oetker and B. Limperg (eds), *Münchener Kommentar zum Bürgerlichen Gesetzbuch*, vol. 12, 8th ed., CH Beck, Munich 2020.

52 Cf. D. Looschelders, 'Art. 30 EuGüVO', para. 5, in F.J. Säcker, R. Rixecker, H. Oetker and B. Limperg (eds), *Münchener Kommentar zum Bürgerlichen Gesetzbuch*, vol. 12, 8th ed., CH Beck, Munich 2020.

53 See, e.g. § 1361b(3), 1st sentence, BGB: 'If one spouse has been permitted the use of the matrimonial home in whole or in part, the other spouse must refrain from everything that is suitable to render more difficult or defeat the exercise of this right of use.'

54 German Federal Government, 'Entwurf eines Gesetzes zum Internationalen Güterrecht und zur Änderung von Vorschriften des Internationalen Privatrechts', *Bundestags-Drucksache* 19/4852, p. 39; S. Gössl, 'Art. 17a EGBGB', para. 1a, in K.H. Johannsen, D. Henrich and C. Althammer (eds), *Familienrecht*, 7th ed., CH Beck, Munich 2020; B. Heiderhoff, 'Art. 17a EGBGB', para. 1, in W.J. Hau and R. Poseck (eds), *Beck-Onlinekommentar BGB*, CH Beck, Munich 2021; P. Winkler von Mohrenfels, 'Art. 17a EGBGB', para. 1, in F.J. Säcker, R. Rixecker, H. Oetker and B. Limperg (eds), *Münchener Kommentar zum Bürgerlichen Gesetzbuch*, vol. 12, 8th ed., CH Beck, Munich 2020.

forms of contact, in so far as these are related to a marital home situated in the forum State.[55]

However, even after the EU Matrimonial Property Regulation is taken out of the equation, the question remains as to whether the national legislature is competent to pass or preserve choice-of-law rules on issues of trespass, approaching, and other forms of contact, or whether the applicable law must, rather, be determined by another EU Regulation, namely the Rome II Regulation on the law applicable to non-contractual obligations.[56] The law at the place of damage (Art. 4(1), Rome II Regulation), including damage that is likely to occur (Arts. 2(2) and (3), Rome II Regulation), or the law of the country where the spouses are habitually resident (Art. 4(2), Rome II Regulation), will usually coincide with the law of the State in which the marital home is situated. However, an accessory connection with a family relationship pursuant to Article 4(3) of the Rome II Regulation may lead to deviations from those connecting factors,[57] particularly in States where the general effects of marriage are still governed by the law of the common nationality of the spouses.[58]

Many writers argue that protective measures concerning trespass, approaching and other forms of contact related to a marital home should be characterised as 'non-contractual obligations arising out of family relationships' (Art. 1(2)(a), Rome II Regulation), and thus be excluded from the scope of the Rome II Regulation.[59] This interpretation would only leave room for an application of the Rome II Regulation to protective measures

---

55 Gesetz zum Internationalen Güterrecht und zur Änderung von Vorschriften des Internationalen Privatrechts, Federal Law Gazette 2018 I, p. 2573.

56 Regulation (EC) No. 864/2007 of the European Parliament and of the Council of 11 July 2007 on the law applicable to non-contractual obligations (Rome II), OJ 2007 L199/40.

57 Commission of the European Communities, *Proposal for a Regulation of the European Parliament and of the Council on the law applicable to non-contractual obligations ('Rome II')*, COM(2003) 427 final, p. 13; I. Bach, 'Art. 4 Rome II', para. 89, in P. Huber (ed), *Rome II Regulation – Pocket Commentary*, Sellier European Law Publishers, Munich 2011; U. Magnus, 'Article 4 Rome II', para. 155, in P. Mankowski and U. Magnus (eds), *European Commentaries on Private International Law – Rome II Regulation*, Sellier European Law Publishers, Munich 2019; J. von Hein, 'Article 4 Rome II', para. 63, in G.P. Calliess and M. Renner (eds), *Rome Regulations* – Commentary, 3rd ed., Wolters Kluwer, Alphen aan den Rijn 2020; for a critical analysis, see E. Rodríguez Pineau, 'The Law Applicable to Intra-Family Torts' (2012) 8 *Journal of Private International Law*, 113, 130 ('a rather inadequate legal framework for intra-family torts').

58 See, e.g., Art. 29(1) of the Italian Code on Private International Law, Legge 31.05.1995, n. 218, Riforma del sistema italiano di diritto internazionale privato, *Supplemento ordinario* n. 68 *alla Gazzetta Ufficiale* n. 128, 03.06.1995.

59 R. Repasi, 'Art. 17a EGBGB', para. 18, in B. Gsell, H. Krüger, S. Lorenz and C. Reymann (eds), *Beck-Online Großkommentar BGB*, CH Beck, Munich 2020;

not related to a marital home, for example because the partners were not married (see section 3.4 below). According to a different line of reasoning, the Rome II Regulation should be applied, in principle, to determining the law applicable to protective measures concerning trespass, approaching and other forms of contact related to a marital home.[60] However, specific substantive provisions on protecting a spouse from her violent husband might still be characterised as overriding mandatory rules within the meaning of Article 16 of the Rome II Regulation.[61]

In the context at stake here – protecting taking mothers from a threat of violence when they return to the country of origin – an autonomous choice-of-law rule such as Article 17a EGBGB is hardly ever relevant, because, in those scenarios, the marital home that is the pivotal point of orders concerning trespass, approaching and other forms of contact is typically located outside the forum State where the abducting mother has sought refuge. Thus, regardless of the proper interpretation of the Rome II Regulation, an autonomous choice of law rule such as Article 17a EGBGB, which only refers to a marital home situated in the forum State, cannot be applied in most of these cases anyway.

Jurisdiction for protective measures concerning trespass, approaching and other forms of contact related to a marital home situated inside the forum State may be based on Article 7(2) of the Brussels Ia Regulation.[62] Article 1 of the Brussels Ia Regulation does not contain an exception corresponding to Article 1(2)(a) of the Rome II Regulation.[63] The exception

P. Winkler von Mohrenfels, 'Art. 17a EGBGB', para. 4, in F.J. Säcker, R. Rixecker, H. Oetker and B. Limperg (eds), *Münchener Kommentar zum Bürgerlichen Gesetzbuch*, vol. 12, 8th ed., CH Beck, Munich 2020; see also R. Hausmann, *Internationales und Europäisches Familienrecht*, 2nd ed., CH Beck, Munich 2018, Ch. E, 'Ehewohnungs-, Haushalts- und Gewaltschutzsachen', para. 21; B. Heiderhoff, 'Art. 17a EGBGB', para. 8, in W.J. Hau and R. Poseck (eds), *Beck-Onlinekommentar BGB*, CH Beck, Munich 2021.

60 Cf. M. Breidenstein, 'Das anwendbare Recht bei Schutzanordnungen nach dem Gewaltschutzgesetz' (2012) *Familienrecht und Familienverfahrensrecht* 172, 175.

61 On the notion of overriding mandatory provisions within the meaning of Art. 16 Rome II Regulation, in general, see Case C-149/18, *Agostinho da Silva Martins v. Dekra Claims Services Portugal SA*, ECLI:EU:C:2019:84, paras. 23–35; on protective measures in the context of domestic violence, see M. Andrae, *Internationales Familienrecht*, 4th ed., Nomos, Baden-Baden 2019, § 4, para. 208 ('typische Eingriffsnorm'); however, see also the sceptical assessment by M. Breidenstein, 'Das anwendbare Recht bei Schutzanordnungen nach dem Gewaltschutzgesetz' (2012) *Familienrecht und Familienverfahrensrecht* 172, pp. 176 et seq.

62 R. Hausmann, *Internationales und Europäisches Familienrecht*, 2nd ed., CH Beck, Munich 2018, Ch. E, 'Ehewohnungs-, Haushalts- und Gewaltschutzsachen', para. 2.

63 B. Heiderhoff, 'Art. 17a EGBGB', para. 28, in W.J. Hau and R. Poseck (eds), *Beck-Onlinekommentar BGB*, CH Beck, Munich 2021.

for matrimonial property relations found in Article 1(2)(a) of the Brussels Ia Regulation must be interpreted in accordance with Article 3(a) of the EU Matrimonial Property Regulation.[64] Thus, if one excludes protective measures concerning trespass, approaching and other forms of contact related to a marital home from the scope of the EU Matrimonial Property Regulation, this characterisation paves the way for applying the Brussels Ia Regulation. Apart from Article 7(2) of the Brussels Ia Regulation, provisional measures concerning trespass, approaching and other forms of contact related to a marital home situated in the forum State may be based on Article 35 of the Brussels Ia Regulation, in conjunction with domestic laws, for example §§ 50(1), 105, 111 No. 5, 200(1) no. 1, and 201 No. 4 of the Act on proceedings in family matters and in matters of non-contentious jurisdiction (see section 3.3.1 above).

3.3.2.2. Marital Home Outside of the Forum State

The question remains as to how one must determine the law applicable to protective measures concerning trespass, approaching and other forms of contact related to a marital home located outside of the forum State, i.e. in the country of origin. Since autonomous provisions, such as Article 17a EGBGB, have deliberately been designed as unilateral choice-of-law rules, only referring to a marital home within the forum state, such rules must not be extended to a marital home situated outside of this country.[65] Thus, some writers approve of applying the Rome II Regulation.[66] Other voices argue for the application of the law that governs the general effects of

---

64 P. Mankowski, 'Art. 1 Brüssel Ia-VO', para. 89, in T. Rauscher (ed), *Europäisches Zivilprozess- und Kollisionsrecht – Brüssel Ia-VO*, 5th ed., Otto Schmidt, Cologne 2021.

65 M. Andrae, *Internationales Familienrecht*, 4th ed., Nomos, Baden-Baden 2019, § 4, para. 211; S. Gössl, 'Art. 17a EGBGB', para. 2, in K.H. Johannsen, D. Henrich and C. Althammer (eds), *Familienrecht*, 7th ed., CH Beck, Munich 2020; R. Hausmann, *Internationales und Europäisches Familienrecht*, 2nd ed., CH Beck, Munich 2018, Ch. E, 'Ehewohnungs-, Haushalts- und Gewaltschutzsachen', para. 37; B. Heiderhoff, 'Art. 17a EGBGB', para. 11, in W.J. Hau and R. Poseck (eds), *Beck-Onlinekommentar BGB*, CH Beck, Munich 2021; R. Repasi, 'Art. 17a EGBGB', para. 24, in B. Gsell, H. Krüger, S. Lorenz and C. Reymann (eds), *Beck-Online Großkommentar BGB*, CH Beck, Munich 2020.

66 S. Gössl, 'Art. 17a EGBGB' in K.H. Johannsen, D. Henrich and C. Althammer (eds), *Familienrecht*, 7th ed., CH Beck, Munich 2020, para. 4; B. Heiderhoff, 'Art. 17a EGBGB', para. 23, in W.J. Hau and R. Poseck (eds), *Beck-Onlinekommentar BGB*, CH Beck, Munich 2021; R. Repasi, 'Art. 17a EGBGB', para. 27, in B. Gsell, H. Krüger, S. Lorenz and C. Reymann (eds), *Beck-Online Großkommentar BGB*, CH Beck, Munich 2020.

marriage,[67] which, from the perspective of a German court, would usually lead to the law of the State where both spouses have (or last had) their common habitual residence (Art. 14(2), Nos. 1 and 2, EGBGB). If one follows the view that protective measures related to domestic violence among spouses are most closely connected with the law governing the general effects of marriage, pursuant to Article 4(3) of the Rome II Regulation,[68] the practical results of these two divergent approaches will converge in this case.

Jurisdiction for protective measures concerning trespass, approaching and other forms of contact related to a marital home outside of the forum state may be based, in theory, on Article 7(2) of the Brussels Ia Regulation.[69] However, it is difficult to imagine how such acts, related to a marital home situated in the country of origin, could result in localising either the place of acting, or the place of damage, in the State where the abducting mother has sought refuge.

Jurisdiction for provisional measures concerning trespass, approaching and other forms of contact related to a marital home situated outside of the forum state may also be derived from Article 35 of the Brussels Ia Regulation, in conjunction with domestic laws, for example §§ 50(1), 105, 111 No. 5, 200(1) no. 1, and 201 No. 4 of the Act on proceedings in family matters and in matters of non-contentious jurisdiction. Thus, the Member State where the applicant has her habitual residence would have jurisdiction as to the taking of a protective measure concerning trespass, approaching, or another form of contact related to a marital home situated abroad.

---

67 M. Andrae, *Internationales Familienrecht*, 4th ed., Nomos, Baden-Baden 2019, § 4, para. 211; R. Hausmann, *Internationales und Europäisches Familienrecht*, 2nd ed., CH Beck, Munich 2018, Ch. E, 'Ehewohnungs-, Haushalts- und Gewaltschutzsachen', para. 40; P. Winkler von Mohrenfels, 'Art. 17a EGBGB', para. 9, in F.J. Säcker, R. Rixecker, H. Oetker and B. Limperg (eds), *Münchener Kommentar zum Bürgerlichen Gesetzbuch*, vol. 12, 8th ed., CH Beck, Munich 2020.

68 See on the accessory connection of intrafamily torts in general, I. Bach, 'Art. 4 Rome II', para. 89, in P. Huber (ed), *Rome II Regulation – Pocket Commentary*, Sellier European Law Publishers, Munich 2011; U. Magnus, 'Article 4 Rome II', para. 155, in P. Mankowski and U. Magnus (eds), *European Commentaries on Private International Law – Rome II Regulation*, Sellier European Law Publishers, Munich 2019; J. von Hein, 'Article 4 Rome II', para. 63, in G.P. Calliess and M. Renner (eds), *Rome Regulations* – Commentary, 3rd ed., Wolters Kluwer, Alphen aan den Rijn 2020.

69 R. Hausmann, *Internationales und Europäisches Familienrecht*, 2nd ed., CH Beck, Munich 2018, Ch. E, 'Ehewohnungs-, Haushalts- und Gewaltschutzsachen', para. 2; cf. also B. Heiderhoff, 'Art. 17a EGBGB', para. 27, in W.J. Hau and R. Poseck (eds), *Beck-Onlinekommentar BGB*, CH Beck, Munich 2021; R. Repasi, 'Art. 17a EGBGB', para. 28, in B. Gsell, H. Krüger, S. Lorenz and C. Reymann (eds), *Beck-Online Großkommentar BGB*, CH Beck, Munich 2020.

However, the caveats already mentioned (see section 3.3.1 above) must be kept in mind. Protective measures may also be based on specific provisions on domestic violence that do not presuppose a family relationship between the partners, for example the German Act on Protection Against Violence (Gewaltschutzgesetz).[70] In this regard, the abducting mother may apply for a provisional measure concerning domestic violence either at the place where the offence was, or threatens to be, committed, the place where the joint residence of the applicant and the respondent is located, or the place where the respondent has his habitual residence (§§ 105, 111 No. 6, 210, 211, and 214 FamFG).[71] In practice, however, these points of attachment will usually be situated in the country of origin, and not in the country where the abducting mother has sought refuge.

3.4. PROCEEDINGS RELATED TO TORTS IN GENERAL

Finally, abducting mothers may be interested in other protective measures that are not in any way related to a marital home. First, the parents of a child may not be married to each other, therefore general tort laws or specific provisions on domestic violence that do not presuppose a family relationship between the partners, such as the German Act on Protection Against Violence (Gewaltschutzgesetz, see section 3.3.2.2 above), may be applied by virtue of the Rome II Regulation.[72] Jurisdiction in these cases

---

70 Act on Protection Against Violence (Gewaltschutzgesetz) of 11.12.2001 (Federal Law Gazette I, p. 3513), most recently amended by Art. 4 of the Act of 1 March 2017 (Federal Law Gazette I, p. 386); English translation in Federal Ministry for Family Affairs, Senior Citizen, Women and Youth and Federal Ministry of Justice and for Consumer Protection (eds), *Greater Protection in Cases of Domestic Violence*, 5th. ed., Bonifatius, Paderborn 2019, pp. 28–31.

71 Cf., on autonomous rules of jurisdiction under the German Act on Protection Against Violence, R. Hausmann, *Internationales und Europäisches Familienrecht*, 2nd ed., CH Beck, Munich 2018, Ch. E, 'Ehewohnungs-, Haushalts- und Gewaltschutzsachen', para. 20; B. Heiderhoff, 'Art. 17a EGBGB', para. 28, in W.J. Hau and R. Poseck (eds), *Beck-Onlinekommentar BGB*, CH Beck, Munich 2021; R. Repasi, 'Art. 17a EGBGB', para. 29, in B. Gsell, H. Krüger, S. Lorenz and C. Reymann (eds), *Beck-Online Großkommentar BGB*, CH Beck, Munich 2020; P. Winkler von Mohrenfels, 'Anhang zu Art. 17a EGBGB', para. 79, in F.J. Säcker, R. Rixecker, H. Oetker and B. Limperg (eds), *Münchener Kommentar zum Bürgerlichen Gesetzbuch*, vol. 12, 8th ed., CH Beck, Munich 2020.

72 R. Hausmann, *Internationales und Europäisches Familienrecht*, 2nd ed., CH Beck, Munich 2018, Ch. E, 'Ehewohnungs-, Haushalts- und Gewaltschutzsachen', para. 21; B. Heiderhoff, 'Art. 17a EGBGB', para. 7, in W.J. Hau and R. Poseck (eds), *Beck-Onlinekommentar BGB*, CH Beck, Munich 2021; R. Repasi, 'Art. 17a EGBGB', para. 19, in B. Gsell, H. Krüger, S. Lorenz and C. Reymann (eds), *Beck-Online*

may be based on Article 7(2) of the Brussels Ia Regulation,[73] provided that either a place of acting or a place of damage can be located within the forum State, a condition that will not be fulfilled in typical scenarios of international child abduction (see section 3.3.2 above). Likewise, autonomous rules that refer to either the place where the offence threatens to be committed, the place where the joint residence of the couple is located, or the place where the respondent has his habitual residence, will not usually suffice to establish (in conjunction with Art. 35, Brussels Ia Regulation)[74] a jurisdiction for provisional measures outside of the country of origin (see section 3.3.2 above).

Second, even between a married couple, claims may arise that are not in any way related to the marital home (for example, preventing an abusive husband from stalking his spouse at her place of work). In these cases, the Rome II Regulations will determine the applicable law, and Article 7(2) of the Brussels Ia Regulation may govern jurisdiction, with the caveats already mentioned.[75]

4. A HIDDEN CONFLICTS RULE IN THE EU PROTECTIVE MEASURES REGULATION?

As the preceding analysis has shown, determining the law of protective measures in cases of domestic violence can be a very complicated matter. The multitude of legal sources makes it very difficult for the average

Großkommentar BGB, CH Beck, Munich 2020; P. Winkler von Mohrenfels, 'Art. 17a EGBGB', para. 5, in F.J. Säcker, R. Rixecker, H. Oetker and B. Limperg (eds), *Münchener Kommentar zum Bürgerlichen Gesetzbuch*, vol. 12, 8th ed., CH Beck, Munich 2020.

73 M. Andrae, *Internationales Familienrecht*, 4th ed., Nomos, Baden-Baden 2019, § 4 para. 35; R. Hausmann, *Internationales und Europäisches Familienrecht*, 2nd ed., CH Beck, Munich 2018, Ch. E, 'Ehewohnungs-, Haushalts- und Gewaltschutzsachen', para. 2; B. Heiderhoff, 'Art. 17a EGBGB', para. 28, in W.J. Hau and R. Poseck (eds), *Beck-Onlinekommentar BGB*, CH Beck, Munich 2021; R. Repasi, 'Art. 17a EGBGB', para. 28, in B. Gsell, H. Krüger, S. Lorenz and C. Reymann (eds), *Beck-Online Großkommentar BGB*, CH Beck, Munich 2020; P. Winkler von Mohrenfels, 'Anhang zu Art. 17a EGBGB', para. 78, in F.J. Säcker, R. Rixecker, H. Oetker and B. Limperg (eds), *Münchener Kommentar zum Bürgerlichen Gesetzbuch*, vol. 12, 8th ed., CH Beck, Munich 2020.

74 M. Andrae, *Internationales Familienrecht*, 4th ed., Nomos, Baden-Baden 2019, § 4, para. 35.

75 See R. Repasi, 'Art. 17a EGBGB', para. 19, in B. Gsell, H. Krüger, S. Lorenz and C. Reymann (eds), *Beck-Online Großkommentar BGB*, CH Beck, Munich 2020.

practitioner to discern the applicable law with sufficient speed and clarity, particularly when one takes into account that, in cases of international child abduction, and with regard to provisional measures, time is of the essence. Thus, the POAM Best Practice Guide[76] proposes to derive a hidden conflicts rule from Article 3(1) of the EU Regulation on the mutual recognition of protection measures in civil matters (Regulation 606/2013).[77] According to the definition in Article 3(1):

> 'protection measure' means any decision, whatever it may be called, ordered by the issuing authority of the Member State of origin *in accordance with its national law* and imposing one or more of the following obligations on the person causing the risk with a view to protecting another person, when the latter person's physical or psychological integrity may be at risk.[78]

However, this proposal faces several objections. First, the EU Regulation on the mutual recognition of protection measures in civil matters provides only for rules on recognition, and not for rules of decision; in particular, the Commission failed to even include a provision on jurisdiction in the final text of the Regulation.[79] Furthermore, Recital 12 of Regulation 606/2013 indicates that the legislature was rather concerned with drawing the line between autonomous EU law and the questions that remain governed by the 'national' law of the Member States, i.e. with clarifying that the Regulation does not create a genuinely European kind of protection order. Therefore, it seems more plausible to consider choice-of-law issues as untouched by Regulation 606/2013.[80] Secondly, an extensive interpretation of Article 3(1) of Regulation 606/2013 would not solve the problem that courts in the

76 POAM Best Practice Guide, s. 4.3.3.g.

77 Regulation (EU) No 606/2013 of the European Parliament and of the Council of 12 June 2013 on mutual recognition of protection measures in civil matters [2013] OJ L181/4.

78 Emphasis added.

79 This is conceded by A. Dutta, 'Cross-border protection measures in the European Union' (2016) 12 *Journal of Private International Law* 169–84, 171 et seq.

80 R. Hausmann, *Internationales und Europäisches Familienrecht*, 2nd ed., CH Beck, Munich 2018, Ch. E, 'Ehewohnungs-, Haushalts- und Gewaltschutzsachen', para. 24; B. Heiderhoff, 'Art. 17a EGBGB', para. 6, in W.J. Hau and R. Poseck (eds), *Beck-Onlinekommentar BGB*, CH Beck, Munich 2021; see also R. Repasi, 'Art. 17a EGBGB', para. 13, in B. Gsell, H. Krüger, S. Lorenz and C. Reymann (eds), *Beck-Online Großkommentar BGB*, CH Beck, Munich 2020; P. Winkler von Mohrenfels, 'Anhang zu Art. 17a EGBGB', para. 130, in F.J. Säcker, R. Rixecker, H. Oetker and B. Limperg (eds), *Münchener Kommentar zum Bürgerlichen Gesetzbuch*, vol. 12, 8th ed., CH Beck, Munich 2020.

State of refuge frequently lack jurisdiction for protective measures to be implemented in the country of origin (see sections 3.3.2 and 3.4 above): a *lex fori* approach without a proper forum will not be of much help. On the other hand, there is a sizeable number of provisions that already govern jurisdiction and the law applicable to cross-border protective measures (see section 2 above, for protective measures issued by the court hearing the return application, and section 3.2, for proceedings related to parental responsibility). As the law currently stands, such explicit provisions must not be derogated by a hidden conflicts rule.

5. SUMMARY AND CONCLUSION

The preceding observations have shown that determining the law applicable to cross-border protective measures is a complex affair, involving several EU Regulations, Hague Conventions, and, finally yet importantly, autonomous rules on private international law. Thus, it remains a task for the European legislature to provide for a better, more coherent and comprehensive framework on the conflicts issues related to cross-border protective measures. One can only hope that the thorough study presented by the POAM project will help to pave the way for such improvements.

IMPLEMENTATION OF CROSS-BORDER PROTECTIVE MEASURES IN RETURN PROCEEDINGS

Problems of Evidence under National Procedural Law

Mirela Župan and Marin Mrčela

1. INTRODUCTION

Domestic violence is the most common defence raised by abducting mothers in child abduction proceedings. Mothers turn to this defence in an attempt to build an argument for applying the 'grave risk of harm' exception to the application of the child's rapid return mechanism under the 1980 Hague Convention. However, the Hague courts being forewarned of domestic violence does not lead to the immediate refusal of the return of the child. The allegations made must be evidenced in a way that will convince the court of the accuracy and truth of the risk that the child might face upon return. The burden of proof in relation to domestic violence is not an easy burden to fulfil, for the party opposing the return. The traditional approach to the above scenario is built on the assumption that application of Article 13(1)(b) is the 'Convention's Achilles heel'.[1] For the court, it is the 'most difficult and heart-rending task' to decide over return, faced with a parent's claims that the child would face risks upon return.[2] The assumption that the overuse of the grave risk of harm defence is the main problem has been challenged by academics, who argue that the actual problem is with the lack of efficient safeguards to secure the protection of the child, and the mother, upon their return.[3]

Though the POAM project was based on the above facts,[4] its research was not confined merely to the above default pattern. POAM takes the view that domestic violence allegations instigated by the mother must be evaluated to ensure an adequate assessment of future risk, and to establish whether protection measures will ensure the safe return of the child. Instead of instituting domestic violence committed against the mother and/or child as an exception to ordering a return, the court should perceive the argument, when raised, through another lens. If violence by the proxy is supported by sufficient evidence, the next question is whether it can be

---

1 M. Weiner, 'Navigating the Road between Uniformity and Progress: The Need for Purposive Analysis of the Hague Convention on the Civil Aspects of International Child Abduction' (2002) 33 *Columbia Human Rights Law Review* 337.

2 R. Schuz, *The Hague Child Abduction Convention: A Critical Analysis*, Hart Publishing, Oxford 2013, p. 271.

3 See more in K. Trimmings, *Child Abduction within the European Union*, Hart Publishing, Oxford 2013, p. 3, fn. 14.

4 Best Practice Guide – Protection of Abducting Mothers in Return Proceedings (hereafter 'POAM Best Practice Guide'), reprinted in this volume; K. Trimmings and O. Momoh, 'Intersection between Domestic Violence and International Parental Child Abduction: Protection of Abducting Mothers in Return Proceedings' (2021) 35 *International Journal of Law, Policy and The Family* 1–19.

mitigated by a measure of protection. This idea has already gained traction, inside and outside of Europe.[5] The major focus of the POAM research is on the applicability of the EU protection mechanism package[6] that has evolved for cross-border settings (EU protection measures package): Directive 2011/99/EU of the European Parliament and of the Council of 13 December 2011 on the European protection order (EPO),[7] and Regulation (EU) 606/2013 of the European Parliament and of the Council of 12 June 2013 on mutual recognition of protection measures in civil matters (EPO – civil),[8] within child abduction proceedings.

The above perception requires a holistic approach: full respect has to be given to a number of intertwined values, policies and legal sources. Child abduction should not be seen as an isolated legal problem, nor should its legal regulation be observed exclusively through the mechanism of swift return envisaged by the 1980 Hague Convention. Implementation of the EU protection measures package in child abduction proceedings should be guided by a balanced appreciation of contemporary policies relating to child protection,[9] and measures combating domestic violence.[10]

However, it should be borne in mind that the 1980 Hague Convention itself does not explicitly speak of the imposition of protection measures, nor do they arise, as such, from its system.[11] That is why, as a rule,

---

5 S.M. King, 'The Hague Convention and Domestic Violence: Proposals for Balancing the Policies of Discouraging Child Abduction and Protecting Children from Domestic Violence' (2013) 47 *Family Law Quarterly* 299 et seq.; L. Cleary, 'Disaggregating the Two Prongs of Article 13(b) of the Hague Convention to Cover Unsafe and Unstable Situations' (2020) 88 *Fordham Law Review* 2619; M. Hayman, 'Domestic Violence and International Child Abduction at the Border of Canadian Family and Refugee Law' (2018) 29 *Journal of Law and Social Policy* 114–32.

6 E.M. Garcia, *The Construction of Europe through Judicial Cooperation in Matters of Protection of Victims of Domestic Violence*, Tirant lo Blanch, Madrid 2019, pp. 10–24.

7 Directive 2011/99/EU of the European Parliament and of the Council of 13 December 2011 on the European protection order [2011] OJ L338/2.

8 Regulation (EU) No 606/2013 of the European Parliament and of the Council of 12 June 2013 on mutual recognition of protection measures in civil matters [2013] OJ L181/4.

9 *EU Strategy on the Rights of the Child*, Communication from the Commission to the European Parliament, the Council, the European Economic and Social Committee and the Committee of the Regions, COM(2021), 142 final, Brussels, 24 March 2021, p. 1.

10 The *Gender Equality Strategy 2020–2025* called on the Member States to work further on implementing, among other things, the EU protection measures package: *A Union of Equality: Gender Equality Strategy 2020–2025*, Communication from the Commission to the European Parliament, the Council, the European Economic and Social Committee and the Committee of the Regions, Brussels COM(2020) 152 final, 5 March 2020, p. 8.

11 M. Weiner, 'The Article 13(1)(b) Guide to Good Practice' in M. Weiner (ed), *Domestic Violence Report*, vol. 25/1, 2019, p. 21.

protection measures were not previously perceived as a tool to enhance the mechanism of child abduction proceedings or as an instrument that would ensure more returns in the context of child abduction proceedings. However, the evolution of law, especially European law, offers some new pathways, among these the intertwining of the legal regimes of abduction proceedings and protection measures. Protection against violence was introduced in child abduction regimes by the Brussels IIa Regulation,[12] and extended within the Recast procedure.[13] However, the complexity of this merger stems from the fact that the legal way of issuing European protection measures is regulated by the corresponding rules of European and national law, which, in combined application with the international and European rules on child abduction – also leaning on national law – opens numerous legal issues.

The primary task of this contribution is to examine the intersection between child abduction rules and protection measures rules, in the context of presenting evidence in support of allegations of domestic violence. In the context of abduction, the presentation of such evidence may find an exception of grave risk, while, in the context of protection measures, the imposition of such measures is justified if violence is properly evidenced. Despite this difference, it is necessary to establish 'proof of domestic violence' for both purposes. Grave risk of harm is, in principle, specific to the child, but the evidence of violence may also be specific to the abducting mother, and indirectly to a child that has witnessed violence or suffered from it.[14]

The focus of this contribution is on the procedures, and evidence presented, in the course of investigating allegations of domestic violence in child abduction cases, and on ameliorating the risks of such violence. The authors will seek to establish the middle path in proving allegations of domestic violence within strict abduction proceedings time-frames. This contribution is devoted to four aspects of the problem. The authors, first,

---

12 Council Regulation (EC) No 2201/2003 of 27 November 2003 concerning jurisdiction and the recognition and enforcement of judgments in matrimonial matters and the matters of parental responsibility, repealing Regulation (EC) No 1347/2000 [2003] OJ L338, pp. 1–29.

13 Council Regulation (EU) 2019/1111 of 25 June 2019 on jurisdiction, the recognition and enforcement of decisions in matrimonial matters and the matters of parental responsibility, and on international child abduction [2019] OJ L178/1.

14 O. Momoh, 'The interpretation and application of Article 13(1) b) of the Hague Child Abduction Convention in cases involving domestic violence: Revisiting *X v. Latvia* and the principle of "effective examination"' (2019) 15 *Journal of Private International Law* 627.

set out the basic step-by-step approach to assertion of domestic violence in child abductions. Thereafter, the procedures of assessing the grave risk of harm, and of issuing a protection measure, are evaluated. The authors will deal with issues pertaining to standard of proof, types of evidence that should be considered, and collecting evidence in a situation of cross-border child related violence matter as well as burden of proof. The procedure of issuing EU protection measures is, in particular, examined from the standpoint of various domestic procedural rules that may hinder application of the EU protection measures package, in the context of child abductions. The contribution, ultimately, addresses the burden of proof and evidence in relation to *ex officio* protective measures, to establish the different possible scenarios if protective measures are issued in return proceedings, or in proceedings separate from return proceedings.

2. A STEP-BY-STEP APPROACH TO THE ASSERTION OF DOMESTIC VIOLENCE IN CHILD ABDUCTIONS

Application of Article 13(1)(b) by assertions of grave risk may be triggered in a range of situations. One of these is the child's exposure to domestic violence by the left-behind parent towards the taking parent. The approaches of courts to allegations of domestic violence have been categorised in several ways. Schuz identifies four categories: (1) where the abduction court does not deal with the issue of domestic violence, as it is considered to be part of the decision on the merits; (2) where the court assesses the risk upon return, and considers implementing protective measures for severe risk situations; (3) where the court undertakes a thorough analysis of the veracity of the allegations on its own motion, usually by appointing an expert; (4) where the court wishes to take a stance on the allegations of domestic violence raised by the abduction, but invokes an adversarial process where the parties have to present evidence to support or refute the allegations.[15] Momoh simplifies the typology of approaches by: (1) developing a new category where a court assumes that allegations of domestic violence are true, and goes straight to protective measures; and (2) by merging the types 2 to 4 identified by Schuz into

15 R. Schuz, *The Hague Child Abduction Convention: A Critical Analysis*, Hart Publishing, Oxford 2013, pp. 272–73.

one category.[16] However, the case law collected during POAM research cancelled out category (1) of both typologies above: situations where the court either takes the allegations for granted with no examination of the evidence, or completely disregards the allegations with no examination of the evidence. The obligation to assess the alleged violence also stems from the ECtHR ruling in *X v Latvia*. The court should consider the disputed allegations of domestic violence, with the examination leading to a ruling on 'specific reasons [for the decision] in light of the circumstances of the case'.[17] POAM research confirms that UK, German, Italian, Croatian and Spanish courts are assessing the risk upon return, although they mainly do not consider implementing protective measures. Different approaches were identified, even among the courts of the same Member State.[18]

Consistency in the interpretation and application of the grave risk exception requires evaluation of any assertion of grave risk through a systematic step-by-step analysis.[19] A court has to embrace its obligation to investigate the veracity of allegations, and be able to establish if the assertions are of such a nature, and of sufficient detail and substance, that they could constitute a grave risk. At this stage, the court undoubtedly has to examine the evidence to establish either that the findings are confirmed, and that it may proceed to the second step, or that the allegations are broad, general and unfounded, and should hence be dismissed. It is questionable whether the court should instantly undertake an effort to collect information on available protective measures[20] in the State of habitual residence, or in the State of abduction. There are pros and cons to each approach. From one angle, it would not be logical for the court to go straight to protective measures at any earlier stage of the proceedings, as it may be seen as prejudging the existence of harm before the assessment on grave risk has been conducted.[21] Moreover, establishing the availability

---

16 O. Momoh, 'The interpretation and application of Article 13(1) b) of the Hague Child Abduction Convention in cases involving domestic violence: Revisiting *X v. Latvia* and the principle of "effective examination"' (2019) 15 *Journal of Private International Law* 627, 636.

17 *X v. Latvia*, no. 27853/09 Grand Chamber [2013], para. 107.

18 See POAM Project Reports at <https://research.abdn.ac.uk/poam/resources/reports/> accessed 25.02.2022.

19 Permanent Bureau of the Hague Conference, *Revised Draft Guide to Good Practice on Article 13(1)(b) of the 1980 Convention*, Preliminary Document No. 4, February 2019, hereafter 'Revised Guide', available at <https://assets.hcch.net/docs/1e6f828a-4120-47b7-83ac-a11852f77128.pdf> accessed 25.02.2022, para. 38 et. seq.

20 Advocated by the Revised Guide.

21 O. Momoh, 'The interpretation and application of Article 13(1) b) of the Hague Child Abduction Convention in cases involving domestic violence: Revisiting *X v. Latvia*

and appropriateness of protective measures may be a lengthy process, and may not be accomplished, due to insufficient cross-border cooperation and weak support from the authorities of the Member State of habitual residence.[22] But it must be borne in mind that Regulation 2019/1111 now requires a court in the State where the mother is seeking refuge to consider protective measures: not only that the court may impose a protection measure on its own, but that the court considering refusing the return of a child on the sole basis of the grave risk defence may not refuse the return if adequate arrangements may be imposed in the return State.[23] From this perspective, the court also has to act, at an early stage of proceedings, upon collection of evidence in support of issuing a protection measure. The abduction court should investigate both the measure of protection in the *lex fori* and the return State. If it is not satisfied that adequate arrangements are being offered by the State of habitual residence, or that State has indicated that they are not able to assure safeguarding measures, or, if upon request by a court of refugee, the court of the State of habitual residence has not responded timeously, or has not responded at all,[24] a second option is that such a court may issue its own measure, and secure the return.

It is advocated that the court primarily seeks evidence of the alleged violence, but it should also lend an ear to evidence required to issue protection measures, either in the State of habitual residence or the State of refuge. The court should make sure that the evidence regarding domestic violence collected in the grave risk context meets the threshold needed to issue the measure, if one should be needed. Having established that it

---

and the principle of "effective examination"' (2019) 15 *Journal of Private International Law* 627, 636–37.

22 A. Dutta, 'Cross-Border Protection Measures in the European Union' (2016) 12 *Journal of Private International Law*, 181.

23 The Recast Brussels II*bis* Regulation retains the predecessor of this rule within the provisions of Art. 27(3) (previously Art. 11(4)), indicating that protection upon return should be provided by the authorities of the State of habitual residence, upon a request of the authorities of a refugee State. The Recast Brussels II*bis* Regulation builds upon this rule, with Art. 27(5) empowering the court of abduction to issue its own measure of protection. The EU protection package should be able to fit neatly into the latter provision. See Arts. 27(3) and (5), Reg. 2019/1111.

24 Croatian practice has witnessed a case where a child was returned to an unsafe environment: the German court failed to respond to a request for a safeguard measure, while Croatian courts of all instances, up to the Supreme Court, dealt with a situation where a thorough analysis could not be properly carried out due to the lack of information from Germany: County Court of Zagreb (Županijski sud u Zagrebu), Gž Ob-803/17-2 of 14 July 2017. 43 Constitutional Court of the Republic of Croatia (Ustavni sud Republike Hrvatske), U-III/4419/2017 of 28 December 2017; POAM Project Report – Croatia, pp. 10–12.

holds sufficient evidence for the risk to qualify as grave, the court must proceed to reconsider how the available measures of protection should be used to protect the child from the grave risk of harm.

The court is expected to conduct effective examination within a set time-frame: '[a] thorough, limited and expeditious investigation is key'.[25] Hence, the evidence the court takes into consideration must be well-chosen and properly evaluated, in order to provide specific reasons for the ruling.

3. EVIDENCING ALLEGED DOMESTIC VIOLENCE IN ABDUCTION PROCEEDINGS

3.1. THE POLICY PERSPECTIVE OF EVIDENCING ALLEGED DOMESTIC VIOLENCE IN ABDUCTION PROCEEDINGS

The implementation of protective measures in child abduction proceedings is a complex, multilayered matter. It requires combined application, not only of the set of rules pertaining to child abduction and related protective measures, but also of a broad vision of related underlying general policies. If we were to limit interpretation only to the 1980 Hague Convention, we would be guided by the basic purpose of the Convention, provided in Article 1: swift return of the child. Such an isolated approach could be counterproductive to efforts made by the international community, EU and nation States to safeguard the best interest of the child,[26] and to punish those who commit domestic violence.[27]

The general policy objectives affect the attitude towards the evidence needed to construct the 'grave risk of harm' defence, in the event of domestic violence. It has already been established that the Article 13(1)(b) defence equally entails a situation of domestic violence committed towards

---

25 O. Momoh, 'The interpretation and application of Article 13(1) b) of the Hague Child Abduction Convention in cases involving domestic violence: Revisiting *X v. Latvia* and the principle of "effective examination"' (2019) 15 *Journal of Private International Law* 627, 656.

26 M. Freeman, *The Child Perspective in the Context of the 1980 Hague Convention*, Policy Department for Citizens' Rights and Constitutional Affairs European Parliament, Brussels 2020.

27 O. Momoh, 'The interpretation and application of Article 13(1) b) of the Hague Child Abduction Convention in cases involving domestic violence: Revisiting *X v. Latvia* and the principle of "effective examination"' (2019) 15 *Journal of Private International Law* 627, 626–57.

a child, and the understanding that violence towards a parent is a violence towards a child.[28] However, it is up to the national authorities to establish the threshold of evidence necessary to establish that the risk is grave. It is the same threshold that can justify the issuance of the protective measure. In the light of Article 1 of the 1980 Hague Convention, the grave risk should be evidenced by convincing and strong proof, to safeguard the exceptional nature of this defence to the basic mechanism of the prompt return of a child. However, courts are struggling to meet the requirements of other equally relevant principles and policies. A court may face a dilemma as to whether the ultimate purpose of the Convention is to prevent forum shopping in parental responsibility matters, to protect the safety and best interests of the child, or to protect the child and mother from violence. The court may, thus, be split as to the appropriate enquiry, when deciding whether the application of the Article 13(1)(b) defence is merited.[29] Evidence required by the court depends on the perception of the court as to whether the exception in Article 13(1)(b) should be construed narrowly or widely.

The traditional approach[30] to the exception has the potential to turn the court's decision into one based on the merits of custody, or a 'best interest' analysis.[31] A narrow perception can lead to a superficial court investigation of the violence, where the return of the child is ordered if the abductor fails to bring forward straightforward and convincing evidence that violence is an immediate and serious harm. It has to be borne in mind that domestic violence is often not reported, or, if it is reported, in abduction cases the evidence would most likely be in another State. In these circumstances, the high evidentiary standard that needs to be proved to the degree necessary to utilise the 'grave risk of harm' defence is impossible to meet.[32]

---

28 Hague Conference on Private International Law, *Conclusions and Recommendations and Report of Part I of the Sixth Meeting of the Special Commission on the Practical Operation of the 1980 Hague Child Abduction Convention and the 1996 Hague Child Protection Convention*, Prel. Do. No. 14, The Hague 2011, at p. 32.

29 K. Simpson, 'What Constitutes a "Grave Risk of Harm?": Lowering the Hague Child Abduction Convention's Article 13(b) Evidentiary Burden to Protect Domestic Violence Victims' (2017) 24 *George Mason University Law Review* 841, 862.

30 Although this approach was advocated by the Explanatory Report, the circumstances of abduction patterns have completely changed since 1980: E. Pérez-Vera, *Explanatory Report on the 1980 Hague Child Abduction Convention*, Hague Conference on International Private Law, The Hague 1982, para. 34.

31 L. Silberman, 'Interpreting the Hague Convention: In Search of a Global Jurisprudence' (2005) 38 *UC Davis Law Review* 1049.

32 K. Simpson, 'What Constitutes a "Grave Risk of Harm?": Lowering the Hague Child Abduction Convention's Article 13(b) Evidentiary Burden to Protect Domestic Violence Victims' (2017) 24 *George Mason University Law Review* 841, 862.

If the exception in Article 13(1)(b) is viewed from a wider perspective of the overall need to assure the best interest of a child, and to combat domestic violence, this evidential standard should be lowered from the 'straightforward and convincing' evidentiary standard to the 'preponderance of the evidence' standard. To mitigate the risk of fraudulent claims, the court of abduction could mirror the 'well-founded fear' standard used in international migration law.[33] It could be advocated that the court should collect both subjective and objective evidence. Objective evidence could include police reports, photographs of injuries or witness testimony, while subjective evidence could relate to how fearful the abductor is of the perpetrator, and whether there is a belief the perpetrator will abuse again, if given the opportunity.

3.2. DOMESTIC PROCEDURAL RULES IMPLEMENTING THE 1980 HAGUE CONVENTION PROCEEDINGS

The rising rate of parental child abductions being triggered by violence brought to the attention of global actors that allegations of domestic and family violence, and the risks to the children, were not always being adequately and promptly examined.[34] However, for decades, the returns of children to 'possibly uncertain fates'[35] remained controversial. The *via media* is between two opposing considerations: the court needs sufficient information to determine whether allegations of grave risk are unfounded, or whether the defence is established, but this has to be done

33 Such a burden of proof, in the context of refugee status procedures, entails that the applicant must establish the case by showing, on the evidence, that he or she has a well-founded fear of persecution: R. Perruchoud and J. Redpath-Cross (eds), *Glossary on Migration*, International Organization for Migration, 2011, p. 16.

34 Permanent Bureau of the Hague Conference, 'Conclusions and Recommendations and Report of Part I of the Sixth Meeting of the Special Commission on the Practical Operation of the 1980 Hague Child Abduction Convention and the 1996 Hague Child Protection Convention' (June 2011), paras. 35–38 <https://assets.hcch.net/upload/wop/abduct2012pd14e.pdf> last accesssed 25.02.2022; Permanent Bureau of the Hague Conference, 'Conclusions and Recommendations of Part I and Part II of the Special Commission on the Practical Operation of the 1980 Child Abduction Convention and the 1996 Child Protection Convention and a Report of Part II of the Meeting' (April 2012) <https://assets.hcch.net/upload/wop/concl28-34sc6en.pdf> accessed 25.02.2022.

35 P. Beaumont and P.E. McEleavy, *Anton's Private International Law*, 3rd ed., W. Green, Edinburgh 2011, p. 816.

within the strict time-frame of child abduction proceedings.[36] This implies the gathering of evidence in a reduced form.

In child abduction proceedings, it is left to the contracting State to 'place' the Convention proceedings within its own national legal system. Contracting States are not obliged to introduce new procedures into their national laws, but they must use the most expeditious procedures available.[37] Hague return cases lend themselves to determination by means of summary proceedings. Thus, the most advantageous existing procedure assures that Convention proceedings are peremptory. The 1980 Hague Convention indirectly imposes that such proceedings should be guided by this *ratio*. A full trial, consisting of an evidentiary hearing, will not normally be necessary or desirable. The Judge should make his or her decision without detailed examination of the facts, as proceedings could, potentially, become submerged under copious quantities of factual submissions.[38]

3.2.1. *Scope of Investigation*

Article 13(1)(b) of the 1980 Hague Convention clearly states that, in considering the circumstances relevant to establishing, inter alia, the grave risk of harm defence, 'the judicial and administrative authorities shall take into account the information relating to the social background of the child provided by the Central Authority or other competent authority of the child's habitual residence'.[39] The Convention, however, does not go into detail on the evidence that the authorities should seek to establish in return proceedings.

Domestic rules and practices concerning the taking and admission of evidence should be applied in return proceedings. However, the necessity for speed should be taken into account when domestic rules are being applied. It is, thus, important to limit the enquiry to the matters in dispute that are directly relevant to the issue of return. The approach to the evidence considered, in cases involving the application of Article 13(1)(b), varies among Contracting States, though some typical common denominators may be identified.

---

36 R. Schuz, *The Hague Child Abduction Convention: A Critical Analysis*, Hart Publishing, Oxford 2013, p. 271.

37 Art. 2 of the 1980 Hague Convention.

38 P.R. Beaumont and P.E. McEleavy, *The Hague Convention on International Child Abduction*, Oxford University Press, Oxford 1999, p. 258.

39 Art. 13(3) of the 1980 Hague Convention.

3.2.2. *Type of Evidence*

The traditional approach to grave risk of harm resembles that of the 1993 Special Commission Report, which argued that the abduction procedure could be concluded *solely* on the documentary and written evidence.[40] Although this is an evidentiary basis, other evidence types should not, a priori, be excluded.

Violence by a proxy usually happens in a closed private area, with no witnesses to confirm the abuse. Victims of domestic violence often do not utilise the legal system. Gender-based violence has the highest rate of non-reported violence.[41] If violence is not reported to legal authorities, the incident is left with no documentary evidence. The absence of police or other authority intervention is not untypical of a disempowered victim of domestic violence. The authorities must undertake additional efforts to properly assess the risk, as the non-reporting of a violent act may be a measure of self-protection by the victim: disclosure of the abuse often results in retribution by the perpetrator and increased 'punishment', which the victim seeks to avoid.[42] The court is, hence, obliged to take into account the allegations of domestic violence, and consider other appropriate evidence. The court may establish the facts by observation, by hearing the witnesses, by reading the documentation, and via the use of technical recordings.[43] Today, in theory and in practice, the system of so-called legal assessment of evidence, whereby the law provides in advance the values of certain evidence, has been abolished. Instead, judges have to determine the facts by discretionary assessment of evidence, applying a reasonable and logical approach to their evaluations of available evidence.[44]

---

40 'Courts in a number of countries normally decide on requests for return of a child on the basis only of the application and any documents or statements in writing submitted by the parties, without taking oral testimony or requiring the presence of the parties in person.': 'Report of the Second Special Commission Meeting to Review the Operation of the Hague Convention on the Civil Aspects of International Child Abduction Held 18–21 January 1993', conclusion 7, p. 5, available at <https://assets.hcch.net/docs/432981e4-238b-4ed4-a41e-bb239d5acdac.pdf> accessed 25.02.2022.

41 R. Manjoo and J. Jones (eds), *The Legal Protection of Women from Violence: Normative Gaps in International Law*, Routledge, London 2018; R. Shreeves and M. Prpic, *Violence against Women in the EU: State of Play*, European Parliamentary Research Service, 2019, p. 3.

42 European Institute for Gender Equality, *Risk assessment and management of intimate partner violence in the EU*, EIGE, Luxembourg 2019, p. 27.

43 M. Mrčela and D. Delost, 'Dokazni standardi u kaznenom postupku' (2019) 28 *Policijska sigurnost (Zagreb)* 418.

44 M. Mrčela and D. Delost, 'Dokazni standardi u kaznenom postupku' (2019) 28 *Policijska sigurnost (Zagreb)*, 419.

When it comes to domestic violence, the allegations can be corroborated by documentary or oral evidence. The evidence roadmap developed by the Best Practice Guide may serve as a useful practical tool.[45]

Legislation may provide that affidavit evidence, transcripts of oral evidence, and legal arguments from the requesting State are admissible as evidence of fact. The 1980 Hague Convention introduced a relaxation of domestic evidentiary rules, via a provision that any application submitted to the Central Authority or petition submitted to a court, along with any documents or information appended thereto, is admissible in court.[46] This provision encourages Contracting States to ensure that such documentary evidence can be given due weight under their national evidence rules.[47]

3.2.3. *Documentary Evidence and Written Submissions*

Usually the supporting or corroborative documentary evidence of domestic violence is scarce. If the victim has utilised the legal system, the typical documentary evidence usually relates to previous proceedings in the State of habitual residence, seeking protection from domestic violence. Such evidence may take the form of police and/or medical reports, previous non-molestation orders, ouster orders, non-harassment orders, child arrangements orders, or even criminal proceedings relating to specific acts of violence.[48]

Hague return proceedings are conducted primarily on the basis of written submissions and evidence. Contemporaneous evidence that captures some or all aspects of the allegations, if available, could be the most desirable and expeditious type of evidence. Such evidence may be the court's first choice, if available. The documentary evidence that a court may take into consideration can vary, depending on the individual facts of the case. The value or weight of a particular piece of evidence will depend on its nature and source.

Such evidence might include documentation from previous court proceedings, such as judgments or court orders; evidence from authorities or relevant organisations, such as police disclosure, local authority disclosure (children services), women's shelters, or medical reports; or

45 POAM Best Practice Guide, s. 5.1.3.1.
46 Art. 30 of the 1980 Hague Convention.
47 Permanent Bureau of the Hague Conference, Guide on the Application of the 1980 Hague Child Abduction Convention, Part II – Implementing Measures, The Hague 2003, p. 31.
48 POAM Best Practice Guide, s. 5.1.3.1.

other corroborative evidence, such as text messages, emails, social media posts or photographs.[49] This evidence could demonstrate that allegations, or proof, of domestic violence existed prior to the child abduction, and prior to the return proceedings. A concrete example is the practice of a German court that disregarded allegations of domestic violence on the basis of contemporaneous evidence that, in the State of habitual residence, allegations of sexual abuse of a child, raised by the mother, had been dismissed in court proceedings.[50]

The court could also take into account written statements.[51] This might be the statement of the abducting mother who claims to be the victim, presented in written form, or in the form of an affidavit, or the response of the left-behind father. This type of evidence could also include the written statements of supporting witnesses. The credibility of these witness statements should be assessed, having in mind the circumstances of each individual case.

A third form of documentary evidence is a written expert report, which can be commissioned by the court, in order to establish the level of risk of harm that domestic violence could have on the child, in a particular case. These may be used in order to establish the impact of the violence on the mental health of the mother, as well as its consequences for the child, determining the level of risk of harm connected with the possible return to the State of habitual residence. These are usually joint psychiatric or psychological reports, or social worker reports, where experts give their findings on the influence of domestic violence on the mental health of the mother and/or child. An expert report could also be used to assess the risks of separation of the child from the mother, in the event of a return. The commissioning of expert witness reports could be a lengthy process that may jeopardise the ability of the court to finish the return proceedings within the specific time limits.[52] In order to obey these time-related rules, judges commissioning expert reports should set achievable timescales for expert witnesses. An expert witness has to be attuned to the

---

49 Ibid.

50 OLG Karlsruhe 25 June 2020 – 2 UF 200/13, INCADAT reference HC/E/DE 1470.

51 M. Mrčela and D. Delost, 'Dokazni standardi u kaznenom postupku', (2019) 28 *Policijska sigurnost (Zagreb)*, 4, 33.

52 In the case of *Adžić v. Croatia*, in which the overall length of return proceedings was more than three years, the forensic expert in psychiatry submitted their report two months after the court commissioned it. Thus, the time to submit the report exceeded, in itself, the time-frame set by the Hague Convention: *Adžić v. Croatia*, no. 22643/14, 12 March 2015.

nature and requirements of the 1980 Hague Convention return procedure. A well-versed expert will have a specific focus on the grave risk to a child, instead of going into the merits of custody. An expert witness is able to establish the risk of exposure of the child to domestic violence, and the risk of disruption to the child's development. A well-versed expert witness is able to help a judge understand the impact of grave risk to a child's development; successful assertions of grave risk are often associated with an expert testimony supporting a diagnosis of post-traumatic stress disorder (PTSD). A witness must be able to communicate clearly to a judge the future risk upon return.[53] In order to facilitate this process, some countries have identified pools of court experts who are familiar with the Hague Convention proceedings, and are able to provide their expertise within the given time-frame.[54]

Considering the summary nature of abduction proceedings, as well as the return procedure time-frame, welfare reports are not the most appropriate evidentiary method. Welfare reports may lead a court towards the edge of deciding on the merits, which should be discouraged. However, in some jurisdictions, welfare reports are requested by the abduction court, in particular as a mode of hearing the views of the child. POAM research indicates that welfare reports are sometimes requested by the Member States' courts, as well. If the court seeks a welfare report, it should be assessed in conjunction with other evidence in the case. Fundamental flaws may be found in decision-making based solely on welfare reports, if these are based only on the mother's account of events.[55]

3.2.4. Oral Hearings

In general terms, oral hearings are used on a restricted basis in child abduction proceedings.[56] This is because elaborate hearings may slip easily into determination of the merits. Thus, consideration on evidence must constantly be guided by the underlying basic principles that the Convention proceedings are just a precursor to the substantive hearing, in

---

53 J.L. Edleson, 'The Role of Expert Witness in Proving Grave Risk to Children' in M. Weiner (ed), *Domestic Violence Report*, vol. 25/1, 2019, p. 17.

54 POAM Best Practice Guide, s. 5.1.3.1.

55 *Karrer v. Romania*, no. 16965/10, 21 February 2012.

56 Report of the Second Special Commission Meeting to Review the Operation of the Hague Convention on the Civil Aspects of International Child Abduction Held 18–21 January 1993, conclusion 7, p. 5.

the State of habitual residence of the child.[57] Some Contracting States even adopt rules on 'expedited hearings', or limit the circumstances in which oral hearings may be held. Some Contracting States, thus, introduced rules to define and limit the circumstances in which oral evidence may be admitted. The concept of finding-of-fact hearings, or fact-finding hearings, enables the England and Wales courts to undertake a limited form of hearing, to determine disputed allegations of domestic violence.[58] Domestic legislation in some EU Member States has also been adapted. For instance, in Austria, the procedural law enables rather informal hearings; Belgian law requires that parties are summoned to appear within eight days of the registration of the request to the court, at the hearing set by the judge; and, in the Czech Republic, special provisions on return proceedings in sections 478–91 of the Act on Special Court Proceedings provide that the court has to schedule the hearing within three days of the initiation of the return.[59] In Croatia, courts are empowered with tools that distinguish abduction procedures from ordinary family law procedures: parties may be summoned by phone call, fax, or email; the court does not have to hold an oral hearing.[60]

Oral hearings do not, necessarily, need to cause undue delay. If they are performed under strict judicial control, they can be highly focused and time-limited. A judge should have the benefit of oral testimony, depending on the issue at hand. Oral hearings are justified where documentary evidence is unavailable, either because it does not exist, or it cannot be obtained from the State of habitual residence in a timely manner. They may also be justified in situations where parties submit conflicting documentary evidence, and the matter can only be resolved through cross-examination or oral evidence. Oral evidence may also be appropriate where there is an unresolvable clash in affidavit evidence on a crucial point.

As the aim of these hearings is not to determine the existence of violence beyond reasonable doubt, as in criminal proceedings,[61] these fact-findings should have a limited scope, in order to assess the allegations of

---

57 P.R. Beaumont and P.E. McEleavy, *The Hague Convention on International Child Abduction*, Oxford University Press, Oxford 1999, p. 139.

58 *Klentzeris v. Klentzeris* [2007] EWCA Civ 533; POAM Best Practice Guide, s. 5.1.3.1.

59 Responses to the Questionnaire concerning the practical operation of the 1980 Child Abduction Convention (Prel. Doc. No. 2 of January 2017) <https://www.hcch.net/en/instruments/conventions/publications1/?dtid=33&cid=24> accessed 27.01.2022.

60 M. Župan, M. Drventić and T. Kruger, 'Cross-Border Removal and Retention of a Child – Croatian Practice and European Expectation' (2020) 34 *International Journal of Law, Policy and the Family* 60, 65.

61 M. Mrčela and D. Delost, 'Dokazni standardi u kaznenom postupku', (2019) 28 *Policijska sigurnost (Zagreb)*, 4, 427.

domestic violence in line with the time constraints attached to the return proceedings. Oral evidence could also be used to verify the reliability of the existing documentary evidence. The first option for the court is to hear the parties, in order to weigh their allegations of domestic violence, allowing the cross-examination of each party.[62] The parties may propose to hear witnesses. Having in mind the nature and purpose of return proceedings, the court should be particularly mindful to restrict their testimonies solely to the facts that relate to allegations of domestic violence.

Alongside the oral statements by parties – the alleged victim (abducting mother), alleged perpetrator (left-behind parent), the child, and other witnesses – the court might also need to hear the professional witnesses and experts, especially if their written findings have been challenged by any of the parties. Based on the results of the material and oral evidence, the court will assess the allegations of the risk of harm, and take this assessment into account when deciding on the return request, and on the protection measure order.

Oral hearings are particularly directed towards the testimony of the alleged victim of the violence. However, the fair trial guarantee dictates that the applicant in the return proceedings, the alleged perpetrator, should be heard as well. Personal appearance of the applicant raises some concerns, as it may cause undue delay in the consideration of the case, if the applicant lives in another Member State. The mechanism of cooperation and taking of evidence abroad should be employed here. Nevertheless, the court must give an opportunity to the left-behind father to address the allegations of domestic violence raised by the mother. Failing to do so amounts to a breach of fundamental rights, as established by *Karrer v. Romania*.[63]

Hearing a child in any proceedings relating to its protection and interest presents a general obligation, imposed by the UN Convention on the Rights of the Child (CRC). There are deeply entrenched differences between jurisdictions about hearing children in abduction cases, as well as on the weight to be attached to their views.[64] It is well established that

---

62 POAM Best Practice Guide, s. 5.1.3.1.

63 *Karrer v. Romania*, no. 16965/10, 21 February 2012.

64 M. Freeman and N. Taylor, 'Domestic Violence and Child Participation: Contemporary Challenge for the 1980 Hague Child Abduction Convention' (2020) 42 *Journal of Social Welfare and Family Law* 154–75; W. Schrama, M. Freeman, N. Taylor and M.R. Bruning (eds), *International Handbook on Child Participation in Family Law*, Intersentia, Cambridge 2021; M. Freeman, N. Taylor and R. Schuz, *The Voice Of The Child in International Child Abduction Proceedings Under the 1980 Hague Convention*, University of Westminster, London 2019, at <https://westminsterresearch.westminster.ac.uk/item/qx8q8/the-voice-of-the-child-in-international-child-abduction-proceedings-under-the-1980-hague-convention> accessed 27.01.2022.

hearing a child has to be performed bearing in mind his or her age and maturity. The court may nominate a guardian, depending on the national legal system. However, in the context of child abduction, the hearing should be narrowed down only to the issues relevant to establishing whether there is a grave risk of harm.

3.3. BURDEN AND STANDARD OF PROOF

The burden of proof under Article 13(1)(b) rests with the person opposing the child's return. It is, therefore, for the abducting mother to produce evidence to corroborate the defence raised. The court should be required to evaluate the evidence against the civil standard of proof, i.e. the ordinary balance of probabilities.

It is notable that, in respect of measures of protection in abduction proceedings, Regulation 2019/1111 imposes rules on the burden of proof regarding protection measures. These rules supersede national rules on burden of proof for protection measures. The burden of proof about the existence of adequate measures is, at first instance, placed on the left-behind parent. Article 27(3) of the Regulation explicitly states that the party seeking a return should present evidence to satisfy the court. However, the Regulation leaves the option open for the application of national standards of burdens of proof, as the court may collect evidence on its own, to determine the merits of the violence allegations. When it comes to the measure of protection the court may issue on its own, Article 27(5) indirectly places the burden of proof on the court.

Article 13(1)(b) requires that the real risk to the child must have reached such a level of gravity that it can be classified as 'grave'. The level of harm must be one that a child should not be expected to tolerate.[65] This includes not only physical or psychological abuse, or neglect of the child itself, but also the child's exposure to the harmful effects of witnessing physical or psychological abuse of their own parent and/or the consequences of such abuse, such as a reduction in the parenting capacities of that parent, or the ensuing separation from the abducting parent, should she not be able to return with the child. It follows that, in child abductions motivated by domestic violence, the risk of harm to the mother, and to the child, may be intertwined to the extent that, even if the domestic violence had been directed solely towards the mother, return may constitute a grave risk of harm to the child under Article 13(1)(b) of the Convention.

---

65 HCCH Revised Guide, p. 26.

Accordingly, protective measures for the abducting mother should also be considered as protective measures for the child.

Risk assessment is a 'decision-making process through which we determine the best course of action by estimating, identifying, qualifying or quantifying risk'.[66] Evaluating the level of risk of harm a victim may be facing, including the likelihood of repeated violence, is carried out with the aim of reducing harm to victims of violence by the proxy: women and children. Risk factors for domestic violence are related to the victim, the perpetrator, their relationship and the specific circumstances in the community where the risk takes place.[67] In the specific context of abduction proceedings, these factors may include that the victim is a vulnerable woman living in a community where she is insufficiently integrated, lacks language skills, is often financially dependent on her husband in the State of habitual residence, and perceives that authorities there would not provide protection, as it is her husband's homeland. Risk factors on the perpetrator's side include a history of violent behaviours, and previous breaches of protection orders. Risk factors inherent to their relationship include separation upon escalation of violence, and the victim having fled from home. Risk assessment and risk management for intimate partner violence varies significantly between EU Member States.[68]

The court should also consider the level and type of harm. In domestic violence cases, the level of harm may be categorised into three groups: (1) cases where the abuse is relatively minor; (2) cases that 'fall somewhere in the middle'; and (3) cases where 'the risk of harm is clearly grave'.[69] The third category refers to cases where protective measures would not ameliorate the risk, i.e. there has been grave physical, sexual or psychological abuse, and/or significant, severe and repeated violence, with a disregard for the law, including breaches of previous protection orders. The second category is perhaps the most common, i.e. cases where the abuse is substantially more

---

66 T.L. Nicholls, S.L. Desmarais, K.L. Douglas and P.R. Kropp, 'Violence Risk Assessments with Perpetrators of Intimate Partner Abuse' in J. Hamel and T. Nicholls (eds), *Family Interventions in Domestic Violence: A Handbook of Gender-Inclusive Theory and Treatment*, Springer, New York 2006, pp. 275–301.

67 European Institute for Gender Equality, *Risk assessment and management of intimate partner violence in the EU*, EIGE, Luxembourg 2019, pp. 24–27.

68 European Institute for Gender Equality, *Risk assessment and management of intimate partner violence in the EU*, EIGE, Luxembourg 2019, Annex 2, p. 48 et seq.

69 *Simcox v. Simcox*, 511 F.3d 594 (6th Cir. 2007); A.A. Zashin, 'Domestic Violence by Proxy: A Framework for Considering a Child's Return Under the 1980 Hague Convention on the Civil Aspects of International Child Abduction's Article 13(b) Grave Risk of Harm Cases Post *Monasky*' (2021) 33 *Journal of the American Academy of Matrimonial Lawyers* 571, 576.

than minor, but is less obviously intolerable.[70] The nature, frequency and intensity of the abuse, and the circumstances in which it was committed, will all be relevant considerations.[71] In considering the level of harm, courts should be taking into account all the circumstances of a case. If there is a history of physical abuse and menacing behaviour towards the applicant by the perpetrator, the applicant's heightened vulnerability places a duty on the domestic authorities to exercise an even greater degree of vigilance.[72]

The types of harm to be taken into account derive from the wording of Article 13(1)(b). The harm to the child may take the form of 'physical harm', 'psychological harm', or the child otherwise being placed in an 'intolerable situation'. The words 'physical or psychological harm' are not qualified, however they 'gain colour' from the third limb of the defence (i.e. 'or otherwise … placed in an intolerable situation').[73] 'Intolerable' is a strong word, but when applied in the context of Article 13(1)(b), it refers to 'a situation which this particular child in these particular circumstances should not be expected to tolerate'.[74] The Best Practice Guide recognises the significance of, and impact on, the victims of domestic violence at all levels, and acknowledges that different jurisdictions use different definitions of domestic violence and domestic abuse, with 'domestic violence' often denoting physical violence, and 'domestic abuse' usually referring to acts of psychological and emotional abuse. Courts should also consider the impact of domestic violence on the abducting mother's mental health, in terms of her subjective perception. Research has demonstrated that female victims of violence by a proxy are able to predict their risk of revictimisation with moderate accuracy.[75]

If the general risk of harm is severe, the mother's mental condition could impact on her parenting. It would bring the child to an intolerable situation, fulfilling the grave risk of harm defence under Article 13(1)(b).[76] By analogy, this also applies to a situation where the child (rather than the abducting mother) holds intense anxieties about a return that are not based on objective reality, but which would amount to the child's situation, on return, being intolerable.[77]

---

70 Ibid.

71 Revised Guide, p. 38.

72 *Hajduová v. Slovakia*, no. 2660/03, 30 November 2010, paras. 45–52.

73 *Re E (Children)* [2011] UKSC 27, para. 34, at POAM Best Practice Guide, s. 5.1.3.2.

74 *Re D (A Child) (Abduction: Rights of Custody)* [2006] UKHL 51, para. 52.

75 European Institute for Gender Equality Risk assessment and management of intimate partner violence in the EU, EIGE, Luxembourg 2019, p. 25.

76 POAM Best Practice Guide, s. 5.1.3.2.

77 *B v. P* [2017] EWHC 3577 (Fam), para. 66.

3.4. COLLECTING EVIDENCE ABROAD

It is notable that, in the context of return proceedings, all or some of the evidence will have to be obtained in another Member State. Collecting evidence abroad is another challenge, in the context of the area covered by this study. Obtaining such documentary evidence in a cross-border setting, even with the support of Central Authorities, may prove challenging, and may at times be unsuccessful within the strict timescales applicable to 1980 Hague Convention cases. The European Court of Human Rights' reasoning in *X v. Latvia* presupposes that, where available, the court will seek to obtain relevant documentary evidence from the State of habitual residence.[78]

Regular cross-border modes of collection of evidence by an Evidence Regulation or Evidence Convention may not be best suited to meeting the strict time framework of abduction proceedings.[79] Hence, its collection should be performed through Central Authorities, as envisaged by both the 1980 Hague Convention and Regulation 2019/1111.[80] Direct judicial cooperation is explicitly prescribed by Regulation 2019/1111,[81] while the activity of liaison judges – The International Hague Judicial Network – should be employed to this end.[82] Within the EU, courts should take advantage of Regulation 2020/1783 on the taking of evidence,[83] although this does not provide an urgent path for the collection of evidence.

4. DOMESTIC PROCEDURAL LAW ON ISSUING EU PROTECTION MEASURES

4.1. INVESTIGATION ON AVAILABILITY OF PROTECTIVE MEASURES

If the abduction court has performed sufficient gathering and evaluation of evidence for it to be satisfied that domestic violence constitutes a

---

78 *X v. Latvia*, no. 27853/09 Grand Chamber [2013], para. 107.

79 K. Siehr and M. Seibl, 'Evidence, procurement of' in J. Basedow et al. (eds), *Encyclopedia of Private International Law*, Elgar Online, 2017, pp. 710–19.

80 Reg. 2019/1111, Arts. 76–84; M. Župan, C. Hoehn and U. Kluth, 'Central Authority Cooperation under the Brussels II ter Regulation' in *Yearbook of Private International Law*, vol. 22, Verlag Dr. Otto Schmidt, Köln 2020/2021, pp. 217–31.

81 Ch. VI of Reg. 2019/1111.

82 <https://www.hcch.net/en/instruments/conventions/specialised-sections/child-abduction/ihnj> accessed 25.02.2022.

83 Regulation (EU) 2020/1783 of the European Parliament and of the Council of 25 November 2020 on cooperation between the courts of the Member States in

grave risk upon a child's return, it shall consider the availability and appropriateness of protective measures. The next steps in return proceedings have different pathways, depending on whether the return State is an EU Member State participating in civil cooperation, or is a non-EU State. In respect of the latter, the court must use all means of cooperation available to exchange information, and establish whether safe return can take place.

The abduction court, thus, has far more means available if a safe return is ordered in another EU Member State than in a non-EU state. Namely, the EU response to combating domestic violence based on the EU package of protection measures rules, though there is no convention in force with equivalent scope. However, employing the EU legal mechanism in the functioning of child abduction proceedings is far from an easy task. It largely depends on the mode of implementation of the EU protection measures package in the Member State domestic order, and is again dependant on national procedural law. The topic of issuing European protection orders instantly raises the issue of characterisation of a 'protection measure'. The dilemma of whether the protection measure belongs to civil or criminal law is far from being merely theoretical. This dichotomy in 'protection measures', from a national perspective, affects the procedure to be employed in issuing the measure, as well as matters of proof and evidence.[84] The Regulation and Directive were drafted on the assumption that protection orders can be procured mainly through both civil and criminal law. Even though most Member States provide for both civil and criminal protection orders, not all systems fit neatly into the 'civil vs criminal protection orders' dichotomy envisaged by the EU legislator.[85]

---

the taking of evidence in civil or commercial matters (taking of evidence) [2020] OJ L405/1.

84 R.B. Blázquez, 'European Judicial Cooperation and Protection of Gender-Based Violence Victims, Fact or Fiction?' (2020) 8 *Ceza Hukuku ve Kriminoloji Dergisi-Journal of Penal Law and Criminology* 95–115; T. Freixes and L. Román (eds), *Protection of the Gender-based Violence Victims in the European Union: Preliminary Study of the Directive 2011/99/EU on the European Protection Order*, Publications Universitat Rovira I Virgili/Publicacions Universitat Autònoma de Barcelona, Tarragona and Barcelona 2014, pp. 15–16.

85 S van der Aa, et al., 'Mapping the Legislation and Assessing the Impact of Protection Orders in the European Member States' (hereafter 'POEMs Project Final Report'), pp. 231 and 240, available at <http://poems-project.com/wp-content/uploads/2015/04/Intervict-Poems-digi-1.pdf> accessed 28.01.2022; see also EPOGENDER, 'Gender Violence: Protocols for the protection of victims and effectiveness of protection orders. Towards an efficient implementation of Directive 2011/99/EU', available at <https://ec.europa.eu/justice/grants/results/daphne-toolkit/content/epogender-gender-violence-protocols-protection-victims-and-effectiveness-protection-orders_en> accessed 28.01.2022.

In particular, civil protection orders are not available in some EU Member States, for example Portugal, Poland[86] and Croatia.[87]

This directly affects the evidencing of alleged violence in abduction proceedings, and opens up the topic of the inequality of arms. Criminal protection orders, as such, are not available in Finland, Denmark and Sweden. Instead, a distinct, 'quasi-criminal' route is used, whereby no link with substantive criminal proceedings is required. Taken in conjunction with the fact that protection orders are imposed by the public prosecutor, chief of police, or a district court,[88] this may affect the evidentiary threshold, and hinder utilisation of the Regulation 606/2013 protection measure in child abduction proceedings.

4.2. PROCEDURAL VARIANCES IN NATIONAL LEGAL SYSTEMS

Three general prohibitions include a ban on contacting the protected person, a ban on entering certain areas, and a ban on approaching the protected person. The way in which these three unified prohibitions[89] may be issued in connection with child abduction proceedings will largely depend on the national implementation and domestic procedural rules on the required evidence threshold. A civil protection order can normally be applied for by a claimant in civil summary proceedings. Normally, a court may impose a civil protection order *ex parte*, without hearing the left-behind father. Procedural fairness is guaranteed as long as he has been

---

86 K.E. Estankona, 'Regulation (EU) 606/2013 on mutual recognition of protection measures in civil matters. Spain as a certificate-issuing state?' in E.M. Garcia, *The Construction of Europe through Judicial Cooperation in Matters of Protection of Victims of Domestic Violence*, Tirant lo Blanch, Madrid 2019, p. 111.

87 In the Croatian legal system's generic legislation, protection orders, in event of domestic violence, can be obtained in either criminal or misdemeanour proceedings. But the 1980 Hague Convention Implementation Act provides that the civil court hearing the abduction proceedings may, at the proposal of the parties, the social welfare centre, or *ex officio*, impose the necessary measures to protect the best interests and well-being of the child, to secure the return of the child, and for the exercise of the right of contact. Still, due to the very clear standing of the generic law on domestic violence, the child abduction (civil) courts do not employ the above provision of the Implementing Act to issue protection measures, let alone the EPO-civil measure: POAM Project Report – Croatia, available at <https://research.abdn.ac.uk/wp-content/uploads/sites/15/2020/05/National-report_Croatia.pdf>.

88 POEMs Project Final Report, pp. 59, 231 and 240.

89 The bans on contacting the protected person, on entering certain areas, and on approaching the protected person.

summoned, and is allowed to appeal the decision.[90] Although evidentiary requirements for civil protection orders differ, to some extent, among the Member States, the evidentiary threshold is usually not very high. The victim merely has to demonstrate that she is in need of protection.[91]

In contrast, a criminal protection order is normally imposed by a criminal or misdemeanour court, on request by the police or the public prosecutor. A criminal protection order is always inseparably linked to criminal proceedings (i.e. there must be a suspicion of a crime),[92] and may be imposed for different types of crimes, some of which are more general (for example, assault, stalking and rape), and some more specific (for example, intimate partner violence or domestic abuse).[93] Because criminal protection orders are connected to criminal proceedings, the behaviour that will justify an arrest has to be behaviour that has been criminalised. It is usually required that offender be heard before an order is imposed. *Ex parte* criminal protection orders are possible in only a few Member States, and only in exceptional circumstances (for example, where the suspect cannot be located in spite of serious attempts, or the case requires urgent intervention), and only to the extent that the defendant can challenge the decision in subsequent hearings.[94] Unlike civil protection orders, most criminal protection orders have been developed as substitutes for detention or prison and, as such, require there to have been a level of violence that justifies an arrest.[95]

5. NATIONAL PROCEDURAL PATHWAYS: EVIDENCE IN CHILD ABDUCTION/PROTECTION MEASURES PROCEDURES

The application of the EU protection measures package is still rather infrequent all over Europe. It mirrors the situation of handling domestic

90 POEMs Project Final Report, p. 234. See also POAM Project Reports, available at <https://research.abdn.ac.uk/poam/resources/reports/>. E.g. in Italy, when the measure is granted *ex parte*, the defendant is heard within a few days, for the purposes of a confirmation of the measure: POAM Project Report – Italy.

91 POEMs Project Final Report, p. 242.

92 Ibid., p. 70.

93 For more details, see POAM Project Reports, available at <https://research.abdn.ac.uk/poam/resources/reports/> accessed 25.02.2022.

94 POEMs Project Final Report, p. 71.

95 Ibid., p. 242.

violence cases in general, where a monetary penalty is usually ordered.[96] In child abduction cases, protection measures are, in principle, not invoked. However, both international and European law impose obligations on an abduction court to issue a protection measure if a grave risk of harm is evidenced. Failure of authorities to properly implement such protection measures in domestic violence cases amounts to a human rights violation. In *Kontrová v. Slovakia*,[97] the European Court of Human Rights (ECtHR) reiterated the scope of the positive obligation, under Article 2 of the European Convention on Human Rights (ECHR), of the authorities to take preventive operational measures to protect an individual whose life is at risk from the acts of another individual. For a positive obligation to arise, it must be established that the authorities 'knew or ought to have known', at the time, of the existence of a 'real and immediate risk' to the life of an identified individual from the criminal acts of a third party, and that they failed to take measures within the scope of their powers which, judged reasonably, might have been expected to avoid that risk. It is not only criminal offences and misdemeanours that come under the scope of the ECtHR. In *Bevacqua and S v. Bulgaria*,[98] a positive obligation to assure protective measures in the private law sphere was also imposed. Holding a dispute to be a 'private matter' is incompatible with the authorities' obligations to protect the applicants' family life. In the context of our research, it is notable that Article 27(5) of Regulation 2019/1111 clearly imposes an obligation to assure safe return by issuing a protection measure.

It remains incumbent on national authorities to assure collection of evidence and impose measures of protection with cross-border effects. This task is made even more complex by the various national approaches to adjudication of child abduction proceedings, and differences in the implementation of the protective measures package.

The court that has jurisdiction over child abduction proceedings is not necessarily the same court that has jurisdiction to issue a protection measure.[99] The Member States are obliged to nominate the relevant courts, and in most States there will be an overlap, i.e. the civil court will deal with both matters. However, it will most likely not be the same court in

96 See POAM Project Report – Italy, p. 5; POAM Project Report – Croatia, p. 31, available at <https://research.abdn.ac.uk/poam/resources/reports/> accessed 25.02.2022.

97 *Kontrová v. Slovakia*, no. 7510/04, 31 May 2007.

98 *Bevacqua and S. v. Bulgaria*, no. 71127/01, 12 June 2008, paras. 83–84.

99 See the contribution by C. Honorati in this volume.

those Member States that have declared that they do not have the authority to issue a European protection order under Regulation 606/2013. In this scenario, where procedures run before different courts, a new question arises: can the evidence collected in the abduction proceedings be used before the court issuing the protection measure, or will the collection of evidence have to be duplicated? If the same court cannot issue both of the measures, and no coordination between the courts is in place, the answer is the latter.[100] If there is cooperation between the two national courts (court of abduction and court issuing the protection measure), it remains as an open issue whether the level of evidentiary burden set by national law and practice in establishing the grave risk of harm under Article 13(1)(b) would be sufficient for the purpose of issuing the protection order. One must bear in mind that, in child abduction proceedings, the States adapt national procedural law, use the guides for interpretation, and ultimately apply a rather consistent approach to the evidentiary burden of proof, as explained previously. However, the protective measures package has, so far, not been much used, and its burden of proof and evidence threshold aspects are mainly subject to national perceptions. If the same court deals with both aspects, as suggested by Article 27(5), it is self-evident that the measure will be issued within the child abduction procedure, and that one evidentiary standard will be applied.

Another problem that occurs in a scenario where different courts deal with abduction and protection measures, respectively, is that, within child abduction procedures, the evidence on domestic violence relates merely to a child who is in danger upon return. For example, if both child and mother have been victims of direct violence, the abduction court will probably concentrate on establishing the grave risk towards the child, and leave the specific aspects of violence relating to the mother outside of its focus. In that event, the court issuing the protection measure would have to start collecting evidence *ab novo*. In this situation, the court would most likely not meet the strict time-frame imposed by the abduction proceedings. In a case where the source of risk was related to the violence towards the mother, the abduction court should have collected relevant evidence on the violence specific to her, but that evidence may not be sufficient for the court deciding on the protective measure to issue such a measure.

The situation is complicated further by the fact that the evidence of violence is often outside the jurisdiction that is being asked to issue a

100 POAM Project Report – Italy, p. 12, available at <https://research.abdn.ac.uk/poam/resources/reports/> accessed 25.02.2022.

protection measure. The abduction court may use the cooperation tools to gather evidence, but there is no such communication tool to back up the evidence-collecting for the EU protection measure purposes. Another aspect of the problem is the veracity of evidence: under the 1980 Hague Convention, the court is required to take any evidence received from the Central Authority as reliable, which is not the case in national procedures relating to issuing protection measures, where the evidence is collected by means of evidence regulation.

Improper application of Regulation 606/2013 leads to a scenario where the only protection measure that can, ultimately, be issued, is a European protection order under the Directive. Regulation 606/2013 belongs to the 'European civil cooperation' package, and applies directly in all Member States. In several Member States, however, it has still not been given full effect. This non-compliance with the Regulation results either from a failure to notify a body responsible for issuing a certificate, or enforcing a protection order, or from a negative declaration to the effect that there are 'no authorities competent for ordering protection measures in civil matters and issuing of certificates', in the case of Croatia, Sweden and Portugal.[101] Croatia has indicated, in the *Judicial Atlas*,[102] that in civil matters it is not possible to issue a certificate pursuant to Regulation 606/2013 because there is no 'issuing body' in terms of Article 4(4). Despite the fact that neither the Directive nor the Regulation defines what gives a protection measure a criminal or civil law character, it does not mean that the matter is left to national law.[103] The Regulation clearly prescribes that the obligation of autonomous interpretation falls on the 'issuing bodies', and that the national system may be either civil, criminal or administrative in nature.[104] The CJEU has already given its opinion, indicating clearly that autonomously interpreted notions of civil matters do not have to coincide with the view of the Member State concerned.[105] A conclusion on mandatory direct application of the Regulation, in respect of the countries

101 Data in the *Judicial Atlas* do not correspond fully to reality, in respect of Spain and Portugal: see, further, POAM Best Practice Guide, s. 4.1.3.

102 <https://e-justice.europa.eu/352/EN/mutual_recognition_of_protection_measures_in_civil_matters> accessed 25.02.2022.

103 M. Bogdan, 'Some Reflections on the Scope of Application of the EU Regulation No. 606/2013 on Mutual Recognition of Protection Measures in Civil Matters' in *Yearbook of Private International Law*, vol. 16, Verlag Dr. Otto Schmidt, Köln 2014/2015, p. 408.

104 Recital 10 of Reg. 606/2013.

105 Case C-435/06, *C.* (Grand Chamber) of 27 November 2007, ECLI:EU:C:2007:714, paras. 40–52; Case C-523/07, *A.* of 2 April 2009, ECLI:EU:C:2009:225, paras. 21–28.

that have not nominated authorities to order protection measures and issue certificates, can be reached. The CJEU has recently rendered a decision in relation to a failure by a Member State to notify the European Commission of notaries who were acting as non-judicial authorities, exercising judicial functions like courts.[106] The CJEU held that a failure of a Member State to notify the Commission of a body responsible for issuing a measure was of merely indicative value.[107] Failure to nominate cannot deprive a protected person of the right prescribed by the Regulation. Regulation 606/2013 clearly indicates that it does not override a national system of judicial functions, but, on the contrary, relies upon such systems. A formal failure of notification should not affect the substantive situation that certain authorities are, within their respective national systems, able to issue protection measures. Consequently, irrespective of the failure to nominate, either the national court issuing protection measures in internal cases, or a child abduction court, should be able to issue the Regulation 606/2013 European protection order certificate. With the new Regulation 2019/1111 in mind, the abduction court is given competence to render the protection measure within the abduction proceedings.

However, as the POAM project's examination of the court practice indicates, the court is able to issue protection measures despite failing to nominate a responsible body. Such an improper implementation and interpretation of Regulation 606/2013 regarding the European protection order may result in procedural unfairness, and raise the objection of inequality of arms. This is the case with jurisdictions where the regulation is implemented only in such a way that incoming cases are dealt with, and the only possible way to issue a protection measure is by Directive. In terms of evidence, it means that, in principle, a higher level of evidence has to be presented, but also that the behaviour in question must have been criminalised. Criminal protection orders are not 'autonomous' measures that can be imposed outside the context of criminal proceedings; rather, they are inseparably linked to criminal proceedings. Such proceedings would have to be initiated in the Member State of refuge, as a consequence of a criminal act committed by the left-behind father. As the left-behind father usually remains in the State of habitual residence, this scenario is not very likely. In an attempt to localise the threat, the court would have to establish that there was violent behaviour in the State of habitual residence

[106] Case C-658/17, *WB*, of 23 May 2019, ECLI:EU:C:2019:444.

[107] 'Accordingly, the Republic of Poland's failure to notify the Commission of notaries who exercise judicial functions, as provided for in the second subparagraph of Article 3(2) of Regulation No. 650/2012, is of merely indicative value': Ibid., para. 48.

before abduction. The court might not be able to establish proof of a threat in the State of abduction, but may conclude that the mother may not be safe since the perpetrator knows where she is: he has initiated the return procedure! There might even be proof in the State of abduction, if the father has continued threats by way of messages and calls.[108] The left-behind father may even travel to the State of refuge and assault, stalk or threaten the abducting mother there. For criminal proceedings to be initiated in the Member State of refuge, the behaviour must be criminal, and of sufficient severity to justify an arrest, meaning that the evidential threshold is high. Consequently, if the behaviour (for example, threatening behaviour, stalking or domestic abuse) is not criminal, or the crime/requisite level of violence cannot be proven, or the victim does not wish to press criminal charges, no protection will be available to the victim.[109]

The benefits of civil protection orders in relation to evidence lie with the fact that the evidentiary threshold is usually not very high, with the victim merely having to demonstrate that she needs protection.[110] However, the weakness is the fact that they cannot be ordered *ex officio*, but only on the application of the party. If the protection measure would be used to only *mitigate* the risk, which subsequently may go against the mother's interests, she may be reluctant to apply for a measure, or to present the evidence needed for that measure to be issued. Regulation 2019/1111 indicates that the court should impose a measure, but does not take into account such reluctance. But domestic rules obliging the authorities to act only upon a complaint by the victim may also come under the scrutiny of the fundamental rights regime. In *Opuz v. Turkey*,[111] a victim of serious acts of violence that had been criminally prosecuted had, at a certain point, withdrawn her complains, under threats from her husband. Prosecution did not instantly proceed in the public interest, and the victim remained unprotected for months. The ECtHR found there had been a violation of the positive obligation under Article 2 of the ECHR, as the authorities could have ordered protective measures under the relevant legislation, such as, in particular, an injunction restraining the husband from contacting, communicating with or approaching the applicant's mother or entering defined areas. Although the woman had withdrawn her claims, once the

108 POAM Project Report – Germany, p. 14, available at <https://research.abdn.ac.uk/poam/resources/reports/> accessed 25.02.2022.

109 POEMs Project Final Report, p. 242.

110 Ibid.

111 *Opuz v. Turkey*, no. 33401/02, ECHR 2009.

situation had been brought to the authorities' attention, they could not rely on the victims' attitude in order to excuse their failure to take adequate measures to prevent threats to physical integrity being carried out.[112] It has been confirmed in national case law that the standard burden of proof in domestic civil procedure may not always be appropriate to meet the requirements of child abduction adjudication. The Czech Constitutional Court thereby criticised the approach of the abduction court that had dismissed the allegation of domestic violence by claiming that the expert evidence collected on the motion of the party was not objective proof. The Constitutional Court found violations of the right to a fair trial and the best interest of a child, with the lower courts having failed to examine the potential risk thoroughly, and assess the allegations *ex officio*.[113]

6. CONCLUSION

It is well known that unified laws on child abduction and protective measures, respectively, rely on national procedural law. Variations in these national laws (and the fact that they are confined to dealing with internal situations) may hinder uniform interpretation. When dealing with evidence in child abduction proceedings involving allegations of domestic violence, authorities should strive to simultaneously satisfy the *ratios* of numerous intertwined international and European instruments. General EU child-centred policy, as well as the EU's strategy to combat gender-based violence, must not be sacrificed for rushed procedures, just to meet the strict time-frames for return of children. A judge should rely on the documentary evidence first, but should also have the benefit of oral hearings. A judge should make a decision without a detailed examination of the facts, to avoid falling into welfare determinations. However, the proceedings must not be too cursory, either, as these may end with incomplete or arbitrary determination.

Evidencing the alleged domestic violence, in the context of international parental abduction, has a twofold purpose. On the one hand, it serves to determine that there is a grave risk, which may be a reason

---

112 Ibid., paras. 138–149.

113 Decision of the Constitutional Court No II. ÚS 378/17 dated 9 May 2017 – Art. 13(b), National report on the practical operation of the 1980 Hague convention <https://assets.hcch.net/docs/85c2ce9b-2e0e-4e67-aad6-1c0c8c441a00.pdf> accessed 28.01.2022.

for refusing return. On the other hand, proven domestic violence is the basis for issuing undertakings. The latter may include the imposition of a protection measure. If that measure has transboundary effects, the safe and controlled return of the child and the mother may be ordered, despite the existence of a serious risk.

Although the uniform interpretation of the burden of proof and evidentiary standards, in the adjudication of child abduction proceedings, is a long-term mandate of the Hague Conference on Private International Law, national approaches vary. EU child abductions are subject to Regulation 2019/1111, which imposes specific requirements regarding the burden of proof. It specifically refers to the obligation of the applicant for return, regarding safeguarding measures, but also to the court, both in respect of the safeguard measures in the State of habitual residence, and in the refugee State (Article 27(3) and (5)).

The differences in the implementation of the protective measures package may lead to different procedural outcomes, depending on the jurisdiction seised. National instead of Euro-autonomous characterisation of the 'protection measure' may lead, in particular, to an inability to apply the European protection order of Regulation 606/2013, which, in abduction cases, is more beneficial that the order under the Directive. Hence, this scenario can end with inequality of arms, depending on the jurisdiction seised.

National procedural standards of applying for protection, evidentiary standards, and burdens of proof in cases of alleged domestic based violence, are varied. However, they are subject to the relevant European and international instruments and practices in force. National procedural rules should also be interpreted in light of the above-listed obligations that Member States have undertaken, under the Conventions and EU law. Guided by a balanced appreciation of contemporary policies and doctrines relating to child protection and combating domestic violence, authorities should approach the matter of evidence open-mindedly. Conventions enacted decades ago are living instruments requiring evolutive interpretation. Adaptation of the domestic legislation is advantageous. Domestic procedural law should be arranged in a way that enables a judge to be able to meet the complex tasks and requirements that lie within a mosaic of rules aimed at protecting the child, protecting the mother, and assuring that the rights of the left-behind parent are observed, but, at the same time, to be able to align with the strict time-frame of the return mechanism.

JURISDICTION TO TAKE PROTECTIVE MEASURES IN THE STATE OF REFUGE IN CHILD ABDUCTION CASES

Costanza HONORATI

1. SEEKING PROTECTION MEASURES AGAINST DOMESTIC VIOLENCE IN HAGUE RETURN PROCEEDINGS

This contribution focuses on where to apply for measures for the protection of a mother who, with the intent of escaping domestic violence, has removed her child from his/her habitual residence, and taken him/her to a different State, thus committing international abduction. The underlying situation is one where the left-behind father starts return proceedings in the State of refuge and the court will seek to order the return of the child pursuant to the 1980 Hague Convention. This contribution will, therefore, concentrate on jurisdictional issues enabling the granting of measures for the protection of the mother in the State of refuge, pending the Hague return proceedings. The interconnected issue of whether domestic violence, in practice, amounts to a grave risk of harm for the child and is, thus, a cause for refusing the return of the child is dealt with in a separate contribution.[1]

While the scope of this contribution – and, indeed, the aim of the whole POAM research project – focuses on the issuance and circulation of protection measures, this should not be seen as implying that the present author minimises or overlooks the effects of domestic violence in abduction cases. Indeed, domestic violence is a serious plague, far from being extinguished, and with rising figures. Courts should never handle a case superficially or mechanically where domestic violence is alleged, and such violence should always be weighed in and considered with extreme caution. In fact, when proved at a reasonable level, domestic violence may well be considered a ground for refusing return, as it will expose the child to a real and actual risk of grave harm. For an overall analysis of this kind of consideration, the reader is referred to other legal analyses, whose content and conclusions are fully endorsed here.[2]

It is precisely because an exception based on domestic violence should always be taken seriously, even when it does not reach the standard of proof for refusing return, that focusing on protection measures is of relevance. Besides some (rare) cases where domestic violence reaches the required standard of proof, and some other cases (unfortunately not so rare), where domestic violence allegations are ill-used and used in the first pleading by unprofessional legal advisers only to catch the court's empathy, in the majority of cases there may be hints of proof of some form of violence – not necessarily physical, as domestic violence may also take the form of psychological abuse – giving the court a clear picture of an unfriendly,

---

1 The subject is dealt with by M. Freeman and N. Taylor, in this volume.

2 O. Momoh, 'The interpretation and application of Article 13(1) b) of the Hague Child Abduction Convention in cases involving domestic violence: Revisiting *X v. Latvia* and the principle of "effective examination"' (2019) 15 *Journal of Private International Law* 626 et seq.; C. Bruch, 'The Unmet Needs of Domestic Violence Victims and their Children in Hague Child Abduction Convention Cases' (2004) *Family Law Quarterly* 529; M. Weiner, 'International Child Abduction and the Escape from Domestic Violence' (2000) *Fordham Law Review* 593 et seq.; M. Kaye, 'The Hague Convention and the Flight from Domestic Violence: How Women and Children are being Returned by Coach and Four' (1999) 13 *International Journal of Law, Policy and the Family* 191, 192 et seq.; and, in more general terms, but with specific attention to the problem of domestic violence, reference may also be made to: C. Honorati, 'Il ritorno del minore sottratto e il rischio grave di pregiudizio ai sensi dell'art. 13 par. 1 lett. b della convenzione dell'Aja del 1980' (2020) *Rivista di diritto internazionale privato e processuale* 796 et seq.; M. Distefano, *Interesse superiore del minore e sottrazione internazionale dei minori*, Cedam, Padova 2012, pp. 131 et seq.

stressful and traumatic or fearful environment. While this may not amount to a justification for non-return, the court may feel uncomfortable (and should, indeed, avoid) returning the child (and the mother with him/her) with no protection, as if the challenge of domestic violence had not been raised. It is for this middle-ground, i.e. cases where domestic violence is not clearly and manifestly unfounded and is clearly also not so grave as to justify the refusal of returning the abducted child, that the court may need to issue a protection measure for the child and/or the mother. The background to this contribution is, therefore, those cases where there is *some proof* of domestic violence, although this may not be of such gravity as to convince the court to refuse return. The crucial and delicate question of how to meet the evidential threshold in domestic violence cases is handled elsewhere.[3]

2. THE LACK OF RULES ON JURISDICTION IN REGULATION 606/2013 AND ITS DIFFICULT COORDINATION WITH BRUSSELS IIA

The issue of jurisdiction deserves particular attention because, surprisingly, Regulation 606/2013[4] lacks any guidance on this basic requirement. As has been noted previously, the Regulation sets only uniform rules that provide for the circulation and enforcement of protection measures in civil matters, but not rules on international competence for issuing protective measures.[5] Interestingly, the Commission's original proposal did contain a jurisdictional rule;[6] but this was removed from the final version of the instrument with no apparent explanation.

The failure to include a jurisdictional rule in the final version of the Regulation appears questionable.[7] Various different reasons may be given

3 The subject is dealt with by M. Zupan and M. Mrčela, in this volume.

4 Regulation (EU) No 606/2013 of the European Parliament and of the Council of 12 June 2013 on mutual recognition of protection measures in civil matters [2013] OJ L181/4.

5 On the structure, scope and content of Reg. 606/2013, see the contribution by A. Dutta in this volume.

6 Proposal of the Commission for a Regulation of the European Parliament and of the Council on mutual recognition of protection measures in civil matters, COM(2011) 276 final. The proposed Article 3 was as follows: 'The authorities of the Member State where the person's physical and/or psychological integrity or liberty is at risk shall have jurisdiction.'

7 See, e.g. the criticism expressed by A. Dutta, 'Cross-border protection measures in the European Union' (2016) 12 *Journal of Private International Law* 169, 171 et seq.

to explain such decision, all of which lead, nonetheless, to an unsatisfying legal gap.

Firstly, one may suppose that the instrument was drafted having in mind cases that are fully internal to a particular State at the time the measure is issued, and where the need for recognition abroad of such measure arises only subsequently. In other words, if the case is a purely internal one, a ground for jurisdiction is not needed at the stage when the measure is taken. Regulation 606/2013 will, instead, come into play only later, when the protected person needs to move to a different Member State, and requires the extension of the protection order's effects to that Member State. This may appear consistent with the assumption, made by Article 2(2), that the Regulation applies to cross-border cases, such as 'where the recognition of a protection measure ordered in one Member State is sought in another Member State'.

While this construction may explain some cases, it seems that it does not fit all possibilities. The same wording of the Regulation, in fact, seems to encompass the case where the person causing the risk is resident in a Member State different from the one in which the protection order is issued. In particular, Articles 8 and 11 of Regulation 606/2013, which deal with the obligation to notify the person causing the risk of the issuing of the certificate, and of the adjustment of the protection measure, both refer to a situation: 'where the person causing the risk resides in a Member State *other than the Member State of origin* or in a third country'.[8]

In other words, while the person to be protected will likely find him- or herself in the forum, the (assumed) abusive and violent other party may already be in a different country when the measure is adopted (and not only at a later stage, causing an issue of recognition to arise). In such a situation, the court will have to face the question of jurisdiction and search for a legal basis that permits the adoption of a restrictive measure against such person. This may be the case with measures addressed to the father, who is in a Member State other than the forum, that forbid him from approaching the residence of the mother in the forum, and which, consequently, limit access rights to the child residing with the mother. In essence, while there may be cases where the international element arises only at a later stage, surely the EU legislator will also have considered the possibility that the situation will also be a cross-border one at the stage where the measure is issued. To limit the application of Regulation 606/2013 to measures that

8 Articles 8(2) and 11(4) Reg. 606/2013. Emphasis added.

are taken in internal cases, and where the need for cross-border circulation arises only later, would mean greatly reducing the potential use of this instrument. Therefore, a rule on jurisdiction must be searched for.

Jurisdiction could, then, be governed either by *other* EU instruments on jurisdiction, or by national law. National law will rarely be an appropriate ground. Although Regulation 606/2013 is founded on mutual trust, this does not mean that whatever decision is adopted under any national forum (included so-called 'exorbitant fora') should be recognised across the EU. Indeed, as a general principle, EU instruments that provide for automatic recognition and abolish the exequatur procedure, such as Regulation 606/2013, rely on the fact that a decision is being adopted under uniform rules of jurisdiction. It is, therefore, consistent with the general EU legal framework to consider that the EU legislator has relied on the idea that, in cross-border cases, the decision would be granted under one of the already available EU instruments governing international competence. In particular, reference should be made to the Brussels Ia Regulation on civil and commercial matters,[9] and, parallel to this, the Brussels IIa[10] (and IIb[11]) Regulations on matrimonial matters, parental responsibility and international abduction.

The application of the Brussels Ia Regulation in order to ground jurisdiction over protection measures in civil matters is undisputed. Firstly, such protection measures are not excluded from the scope of the Brussels Ia Regulation (see Article 1 thereof); secondly, Article 67 of the Brussels Ia Regulation gives priority to other EU provisions governing jurisdiction, recognition and enforcement in 'specific matters'. Hence, there will be no problem with cases where jurisdiction is based on the Brussels Ia Regulation, and recognition and enforcement is grounded in Regulation 606/2013.

Whether such a patchwork of rules is meaningful and useful is, however, open to discussion, especially since Regulation 606/2013 has applied from

9 Regulation (EU) No 1215/2012 of the European Parliament and of the Council of 12 December 2012 on jurisdiction and the recognition and enforcement of judgments in civil and commercial matters [2012] OJ L351/1.

10 Council Regulation (EC) No 2201/2003 of 27 November 2003 concerning jurisdiction and the recognition and enforcement of judgments in matrimonial matters and the matters of parental responsibility, repealing Regulation (EC) No 1347/2000 [2003] OJ L338/1.

11 Council Regulation (EU) 2019/1111 of 25 June 2019 on jurisdiction, the recognition and enforcement of decisions in matrimonial matters and the matters of parental responsibility, and on international child abduction (recast) [2019] OJ L178/1.

the same date as the Brussels Ia Regulation, i.e. since January 2015.[12] Both instruments depart from the regime set by the previous Brussels I Regulation (Regulation 44/2000), and provide for a fast and effective enforcement of decisions, grounded on the abolition of exequatur and the issuance of a certificate. This issue will be investigated further below.[13]

More complex is the relationship between Regulation 606/2013 and the Brussels IIa Regulation. The framework here is complicated by an express rule, Article 2(3) of Regulation 606/2013, according to which: 'the Regulation shall not apply to protection measures falling within the scope of Regulation (EC) No 2201/2013'. This provision is unsatisfactory overall, and has an unclear rationale.[14]

It has been suggested[15] that the exclusion was drafted in view of orders, prohibiting contacts between spouses, that are imposed in connection with proceedings relating to divorce, legal separation or marriage annulment. It is, however, unclear and disputable that such orders would fall under Brussels IIa Regulation, given that ancillary measures to divorce and separation are not covered by the Regulation.[16]

Recital 11 gives a tentative explanation for such an approach, stating that:

> This Regulation *should not interfere* with the functioning of Council Regulation (EC) No 2201/2013 of 27 November 2013 concerning jurisdiction and the recognition and enforcement of judgments in matrimonial matters and the matters of parental responsibility ('Brussels IIa Regulation'). Decisions taken under the Brussels IIa Regulation should continue to be recognised and enforced under that Regulation.[17]

---

12 More precisely, from 15 January 2015 (Brussels Ia Regulation), and 11 January 2015 (Reg. 606/2013). See also C. Moioli, *Le nuove misure 'europee' di protezione delle vittime di reato in materia penale e civile*, 2015, s. 4 <http://rivista.eurojus.it/le-nuove-misure-europee-di-protezione-delle-vittime-di-reato-in-materia-penale-e-civile/> accessed 06.09.2021, emphasising how Reg. Brussels I*bis* overlaps with Reg. 606/2013, therefore reducing the impact of the latter.

13 See section 3 in this contribution.

14 For a similar criticism, A. Dutta, 'Cross-border protection measures in the European Union' (2016) 12 *Journal of Private International Law* 169, 180 et seq.

15 By M. Bogdan, 'Some Reflections on the Scope of Application of the EU Regulation No. 606/2013 on Mutual Recognition of Protection Measures in Civil Matters' (2015) 16 *Yearbook of Private International Law* 405.

16 Recital 8 of the Brussels IIa Regulation states that the Regulation applies only to the dissolution of matrimonial ties, and should not deal with 'any other ancillary measures'. See further, below, at section 3.

17 Emphasis added.

It seems that the legislator conceived the Brussels IIa Regulation as a 'closed package': a complete and self-standing system, having its own rules on jurisdiction and on circulation of decisions, with which no other instrument should 'interfere'. This approach is questionable, given the multiple instruments in civil justice that the EU legislator has adopted over the years, and which are meant to coordinate with one another in the same area of Freedom, Security and Justice. Such approach would have had at least a technical justification, if, as originally planned by the Commission, Regulation 606/2013 was also a complete and self-standing instrument. Instead, this is not the case. Regulation 606/2013 provides no solution, and one is left with great uncertainty, and is forced to search jurisdictional rules within other EU instruments on jurisdiction.

In all cases, on a textual construction, Article 2(3) of the Regulation 606/2013 will exclude most protective measures that are adopted in view of alleged domestic violence, as these are usually connected to family law proceedings. This is regrettable. Although the Regulation has a general scope of application, and applies to all kinds of protection measures when a person's 'physical or psychological integrity may be at risk' (see Article 3(1)), there is no doubt that the Regulation could be of greatest relevance mainly in the field of domestic violence[18] (stalking may be another possible case). It is also well known that violence escalates during matrimonial crises, or when a separation or divorce is sought. Excluding all cases where there is a matrimonial or parental responsibility issue from the scope of Regulation 606/2013 (as these fall under Brussels IIa) would deprive Regulation 606/2013 of its greatest, and most relevant, purpose.

Keeping in mind the above-mentioned considerations and limitations to the Brussels Ia and IIa Regulations, this contribution now turns to examination of the available grounds of jurisdiction for protection measures to be issued in the State of refuge, in the context of international abduction. It should be noted that the situation where measures are requested and issued in the State of habitual residence of the child, once the child and the mother have returned there, is not dealt with here.

---

18 M. Bogdan, 'Some Reflections on the Scope of Application of the EU Regulation No. 606/2013 on Mutual Recognition of Protection Measures in Civil Matters' (2015) 16 *Yearbook of Private International Law* 405.

3. A STRAIGHTFORWARD (BUT INEFFECTIVE) PATH: PROTECTION MEASURES AS SELF-STANDING MEASURES UNDER BRUSSELS IA

Where the abducting mother feels compelled to relocate abroad with her child because of domestic violence, she may find it appropriate, at a given stage, to seek protection measures that are effective both in the State of refuge and in the State of the child's habitual residence, to which she might find herself returning, depending on the outcome of the Hague proceedings.

The first option she has is to seek such measures in a venue unrelated to the Hague return proceedings. In this scenario, the measure is completely disconnected from the abduction proceedings, and the seised court will only assess the relationship between the man and the woman.

In this case, the alleged violence against the woman amounts to a (civil) tort. As is well known, Article 7(2) of the Brussels Ia Regulation gives jurisdiction over torts to the courts of the place 'where the harmful event may occur', which, in this case, could be the State of refuge.[19] Such a ground will be met, in the first place, where the man has followed the woman, and is now present in the State of refuge, therefore constituting an actual risk of harm. However, jurisdiction may also be grounded in a situation where the man has showed his intention to harm the woman by making threats to her, for example, via phone or email. The physical presence of the man in the State of refuge is, therefore, not necessary, as long as the woman has received the threats there. Indeed, Article 7(2) of the Brussels Ia Regulation also covers the risk of a prospective tortious event, and the likelihood of damage occurring in a particular Member State will also ground jurisdiction there.[20]

Once a protective order has been issued, the question arises of its circulation and enforceability in a different Member State. Regulation 606/2013

---

[19] Art. 7(2) states: 'A person domiciled in a Member State may be sued in another Member State … in matters relating to tort, delict or quasi-delict, in the courts for the place where the harmful event occurred or may occur.'

[20] In Case C-167/00, *Henkel*, ECLI:EU:C:2002:555, paras. 47–48, the Court of Justice had already given an extensive interpretation of Art. 5(3) of the 1968 Brussels Convention (which, at that time, only referred to the place where 'the harmful event occurred'), stating that such rule also covered actions 'whose aim is to prevent the imminent commission of a tort'. Following the entry into force of the Brussels I and Ia Regulations, the Court of Justice has repeatedly stated that the likelihood of damage occurring in a particular Member State shall also ground jurisdiction based on Article 7(2), subject to

and the Brussels Ia Regulation appear to be concurrent, and may be applied as alternatives to one another, as nothing in the wording of either seems to exclude the other.[21] One may suggest that a protection order would be better circulated under Regulation 606/2013 rather than under the Brussels Ia Regulation, as the former is a dedicated instrument that should be more effective and bring added value over the more general instrument.

However, that this really is the case, and that there really is added value in Regulation 606/2013, should be verified in each individual case, the difference between the two procedures being very subtle.

Both regimes are, in fact, grounded on the abolition of the exequatur procedure in the Member State of enforcement, and the concurrent issuance of a certificate in the Member State of origin when the conditions for the enforcement of the decision are fulfilled. As is well known, this model, which was first tested by the Brussels IIa Regulation in 2005 with reference to some very peculiar decisions in parental responsibility cases, is now the common cornerstone of all EU instruments in civil justice. The requirements for the issuance of the certificate are, thus, very similar under both instruments, although the regime under Regulation 606/2013 may seem less detailed (and probably less cumbersome). The same may be said, in principle, for the grounds of opposition to enforcement, based mainly on public policy, and on irreconcilability with a decision given or recognised in the requested Member State.[22]

There are, however, some minor differences that could be relevant in specific cases. For example, the instruments take different approaches to decisions adopted *inaudita altera parte*, i.e. under procedures that do not provide for prior notice to be given to the person causing the risk, something that is often the case for civil protection measures, as it allows

the requirement that the right in respect of which infringement is alleged is protected in that Member State (see Case C-523/10, *Wintersteiger*, ECLI:EU:C:2012:220, para. 25; Case C-170/12, *Pinckney*, ECLI:EU:C:2013:635, para. 33; Case C-441/13, *Hejduk*, ECLI:EU:C:2015:28, para. 29). While such a clarification may result in a limitation with regard to infringement of intellectual property rights or personality rights, it certainly does not apply with regard to physical or psychological harassment or abuse. For a more general overview, see also G. van Calster, *European Private International Law Commercial Litigation in the EU*, Hart Publishing, Oxford 2016, pp. 176 et seq.

21 See above, at section 2. See also Recital 16 to Reg. 606/2013, stating that the provisions of the Regulation 'should be without prejudice to the right of the protected person to invoke that protection measure under any other available legal act of the Union providing for recognition'.

22 Compare Art. 13 of Reg. 606/2013 with Arts. 45 and 46 of the Brussels Ia Regulation.

for a 'surprise effect', granting better protection to the alleged victim. Interestingly, however, the Brussels Ia Regulation may result in better protection, at least in some cases. For the certificate to be issued under Regulation 606/2013, it is in fact necessary not only for the final decision on the protection measure to have been notified to the person causing the risk, but also that, when the decision was adopted *inaudita altera parte*, such person had the right to challenge the protection measure under the law of the Member State of origin (see Articles 6(1) and 6(3) of Regulation 606/2013). A decision will, therefore, not be allowed to circulate until the person causing the risk has been made aware of the protection measure, and has been heard by the court of the Member State of origin. Under the Brussels Ia Regulation, instead, where the measure has been ordered without the defendant being summoned to appear, the necessary certificate may be issued on proof of service of the judgment (compare Article 42(c) of the Brussels Ia Regulation). It is true that a judgment given in default of appearance is subject to refusal of recognition and refusal of enforcement (pursuant to Articles 45 and 46 of the Brussels Ia Regulation, respectively), but this will require *subsequent*[23] action to be taken in the State of enforcement on the part of the person causing risk, in the meantime allowing the measure to fully produce its protective effects.

Furthermore, irrespective of the duration of the protection measure granted, the effects of recognition, and of the certificate issued, will, under Regulation 606/2013, be limited to a period of 12 months, starting from the date of issuance of the certificate (see Article 4(4), Regulation 606/2013). For longer-lasting effects, enforcement under the Brussels Ia Regulation will, therefore, be more suitable.

On the other hand, Regulation 606/2013 contains more limited grounds for refusing the enforcement, as it does not include grounds for refusal or suspension under the law of the requested Member State, as long as they are not incompatible with the Regulation, as allowed by Article 41 of the Brussels Ia Regulation. Depending on the State in which enforcement is required, this could be a ground for refusal that one should look into.

In light of the above, a careful assessment of the situation, and a comparison of the pros and cons of each instrument – something that is possible only for an experienced private international lawyer – should be carried out before deciding how to deal with a foreign measure.

A different situation may also raise a different opportunity to apply for protection measures, independently from the Hague return proceedings.

---

23 Emphasis added.

The runaway wife and abducting mother may seek divorce or separation from the violent spouse, and in the course of such proceedings may also wish to apply for protection measures from her former spouse, such as a no contact or no access order. From the wife's point of view, this appears reasonable, as evidence of domestic violence would, among other considerations, justify applying for damages under a fault-based divorce, where this is provided by the *lex fori*. As seen above, this may be the kind of situation where the legislator feared 'interferences' between the two Regulations and, hence, ordered the Brussels IIa Regulation to prevail over Regulation 606/2013. Prima facie, in fact, one could argue that the court having jurisdiction over the principal question (the couple's separation/ divorce) would also have jurisdiction over the ancillary request for protection measures, asked in such proceedings.

The application of the Brussels IIa Regulation is, however, less obvious than one would think. In a very early decision, the *De Cavel I* case, the CJEU clarified that protective measures (in that case, provisional measures relating to property, but the reasoning may be applied in more general terms) 'can serve to safeguard a variety of rights' and that, consequently, 'their inclusion in the scope of the Convention [at the time, the 1968 Brussels Convention] was determined not by their own nature but *by the nature of the rights which they serve to protect*'.[24] Furthermore, Brussels IIa applies only to the dissolution of matrimonial ties and, pursuant to its Recital 8, 'should not deal with issues such as the grounds for divorce, property consequences of the marriage or *any other ancillary measures*'.[25] This leads to the conclusion that the tortious behaviour of the violent husband will not fall under the scope of the application of the Brussels IIa Regulation, even if committed in the context of a matrimonial relationship. As in the previous scenario, the wife in need of protection will have to apply to the court having jurisdiction on tort, under the Brussels Ia Regulation, which may be different from the court seised of the separation/divorce proceedings thus requiring her to institute separate proceedings elsewhere.

---

24 Case C-143/78, *Jacques de Cavel v. Louise de Cavel*, ECLI:EU:C:1979:83, para. 8 (emphasis added). In this case, the Court considered that judicial decisions authorising provisional protective measures, such as the placing under seal or freezing of the assets of the spouses, in the course of proceedings for divorce, did not fall within the scope of the Convention if those measures concerned, or were closely connected with, either questions of the status of the persons involved in the divorce proceedings, or proprietary legal relations resulting directly from the matrimonial relationship or the dissolution thereof.

25 Emphasis added.

There is only one way in which the Brussels IIa Regulation could be applied to protection measures being sought outside of, and independently from, abduction proceedings. This would be to ground jurisdiction on Article 20 of the Regulation. According to the rule therein, a court may, in urgent cases, take provisional measures that are available under the *lex fori* in respect of persons who are present in that State, even if that court has no jurisdiction as to the substance of the matter under the Regulation. This rule would allow the court of the State of refuge to take protective measures under national law in respect of the abducting mother who is present in such Member State. Any such measure, however, being established on a national ground for jurisdiction, will not be eligible for circulation under the Brussels IIa Regulation and will have limited territorial effects, hence will be of little help for the escaping mother. This situation will be dealt with below,[26] as similar problems arise when the measure is taken in view of the protection of the abducted child.

As seen above, notwithstanding some difficulties and uncertainties, Article 7 of the Brussels Ia Regulation, and possibly Article 20 of the Brussels IIa Regulation, may indeed confer jurisdiction on the State of refuge to adopt protection measures that, depending on which of these regimes is used, may be capable of being recognised and enforced in the State of the child's habitual residence. The major problem with this pathway, however, is that it seems too theoretical, and very unlikely to happen in practice.

The procedure presupposes an application by the mother/spouse, seeking measures for her own protection (and, indirectly, for the protection of the child). The underlying assumption is that the mother will seek such protection *upon her return* to the State of the child's habitual residence. This assumption is, however, ill-founded and unverified. In most cases, the mother, either through ignorance of the law, or because she is driven by desperation, assumes that she will protect herself and her child against domestic violence by *escaping to a different country*. It is not in her plans, and not in her interests, to return to the State that she has just escaped from. It is even less likely that such a mother will seek to have protection measures enforced in such State. Indeed, asking for, and obtaining, a measure that is capable of guaranteeing protection upon her return may even be counterproductive to the mother's plans.

Things may be different if the Hague return proceedings have already been instituted. In this case, and if the mother senses that a return order is the most likely outcome, then she may value measures to protect herself.

26 See below, at section 4.

But, even in this case, the pathway described here, which requires the filing of new and separate proceedings for a protection measure, will rarely be viable, especially if the Hague return proceedings are expected to keep to the six-week time-frame.

For all the above-mentioned reasons, this first path, although clear and straightforward from the technical (legal) point of view, will not, in practice, lead to real and effective protection against domestic violence in cases where a child has been wrongly removed or retained.

4. A 'CREATIVE' PATH: PROTECTION MEASURES ISSUED IN THE HAGUE RETURN PROCEEDINGS: PROTECTING THE CHILD BY PROTECTING THE MOTHER

Preventing and combating domestic violence is increasingly a front-line issue nowadays, both at a national and a supranational level. It also is one of the policies of the EU legislator, who has adopted several measures in this field.

What is even more important, with regard to the present contribution, is the growing awareness and evidence that domestic violence directed towards a mother has a severe impact on her children, including in situations where they do not directly witness the abuse. Being aware of violent behaviour against one's own mother is a psychological and emotional stressor that affects the child's life in many respects. Furthermore, in the longer term, such behaviour may be internalised by the child and accepted as a model, leading the adult-to-be to consider violence as the ordinary way to solve conflicts or address difficult situations.[27]

---

27 See Best Practice Guide – Protection of Abducting Mothers in Return Proceedings (hereafter 'POAM Best Practice Guide'), reprinted in this volume, s. 2.1.3. In particular, see also the views of B. Hale, 'Taking Flight – Domestic Violence and Child Abduction' (2017) 70 *Current Legal Problems* 7, finding that 'domestic violence directed towards a parent can be seriously harmful to the children who witness it or who depend upon the psychological health and strength of their primary carer for their well-being'; also J.L. Edleson, 'Should childhood exposure to adult domestic violence be defined as child maltreatment under the law?', available at <http://www.mincava.umn.edu/link/documents/shouldch/shouldch.shtml> accessed 06.09.2021. In general terms, see also Robert Koch-Institut (eds), 'Gesundheitliche Folgen von Gewalt unter besonderer Berücksichtigung von häuslicher Gewalt gegen Frauen', Heft 42, Berlin 2008, available at <https://pub.uni-bielefeld.de/download/1857826/2656432/Gesundheitliche_Folgen_von_Gewalt.pdf> accessed 06.09.2021, for further legal references.

As early as 2006, the European Economic and Social Committee (EESC) circulated the *Opinion on Children as indirect victims of domestic violence*, calling for further action.[28] The document clearly acknowledged how domestic violence not only constituted a threat to the lives and well-being of women, but also affected and endangered the welfare of children. Based on academic evidence, it recognised that:

> Violence against the mother is a form of violence against the child. Children who witness domestic violence and have to experience and watch their father, stepfather or mother's partner hitting and abusing her are always victims of psychological violence. Although domestic violence does not constitute direct violence against children, *violence against the mother is always harmful to children.*[29]

The *Opinion* expands on the effects of domestic violence on children,[30] concluding that children who grow up in a context of domestic violence are

---

28 Opinion of the European Economic and Social Committee on Children as indirect victims of domestic violence, [2006] OJ C 325, pp. 60–64.

29 Ibid., para. 2.24 (emphasis added). It then continues as follows: 'Furthermore … domestic violence against women and child abuse often occur in the same families. Men who abuse their partners often also perpetrate violence against children. Because they live in a climate where it is routine, women who suffer violence may sometimes also be violent in turn towards their children' (para. 2.25).

30 See ibid., para. 2.3, where it reads: 'Growing up in a climate of physical and psychological violence can have serious consequences for children. Children – even young children – feel very helpless and vulnerable in the face of the father's, stepfather's or mother's partner's violence and her powerlessness. They also sometimes feel responsible for what is happening. They often believe that the violence is their fault, or they try to intervene and protect the mother, and are then themselves abused. Although the effects on each individual child are different and not all children develop behavioural problems as a result of violence, and although there are no empirically established criteria for determining how great the risk is (if any) in each individual case, there do seem to be clear links. The main stress factors that need mentioning are: living in a threatening atmosphere; not knowing when an attack will happen next; fear for the mother's survival; the feeling of helplessness in the situations in question; the feeling of isolation, because such children are often warned not to tell outsiders; conflicts of loyalties towards the parents; and impairment of the parent–child relationship. This can cause children to develop massive problems and behavioural disorders, including psychosomatic symptoms and psychological problems such as low self-esteem, restlessness, sleep disorders, difficulties at school, anxiety, aggression, and even suicidal thoughts. … Growing up in a context of domestic violence can also have an impact on the children's attitude to violence and to their own violent behaviour. By observing their parents' behaviour or experiencing violence themselves, children can take on the adults' problematic behaviour patterns. The cycle of violence can lead boys to learn the role of perpetrator and girls to learn that of victim, and can mean that they themselves become perpetrators or victims of domestic violence when they are adults. The effects on children who experience or witness their mother being killed by her partner seem to be particularly severe.'

exposed to numerous stress factors that can have significant and long-term effects on their well-being and behaviour. Most interestingly, one of the policy recommendations of the EESC points to '[i]mproving cooperation between women's protection and child protection',[31] disclosing how empirical results point unambiguously to the need for better coordination between these two protection aims.

Proceeding from this starting point, the POAM research team investigated how cases of domestic violence resulting in the international abduction of a child should make room for the adoption of protection measures for the mother, within the framework of the Hague return proceedings. The underlying assumption is that, in the very particular scenario of abduction against a background of domestic violence, the dichotomy between mother and child is an artificial one, given that what happens to one will clearly affect the other. Protecting the mother will *always* mean also protecting the child (albeit indirectly). Moreover, a child cannot be fully and properly protected if its own mother is at risk of physical or psychological harm. This is now recognised by the newly adopted Hague *Guide to Good Practice on Article 13(1)(b)*, which makes it clear that '[t]he Article 13(1)(b) exception does not require … that the child be the *direct* or *primary* victim of physical harm'.[32] While protection measures for the mother can, and should, also be requested in the State

---

31 Ibid., para. 2.3.8.

32 Hague Conference on Private International Law, *Guide to Good Practice under the HCCH Convention of 25 October 1980 on the Civil Child Abduction – Part VI, Article 13(1)(b)*, The Hague 2020 (hereafter 'HCCH Guide'), para. 33 (emphasis added) <https://www.hcch.net/en/publications-and-studies/details4/?pid=6740&dtid=3> accessed 06.09.2021. The different approach is more evident if compared to the previous, and more 'traditional', wording offered by the Permanent Bureau of the Hague Conference, *Draft Guide to Good Practice on Article 13(1)(b) of the Hague Convention of 25 October 1980 on the Civil Aspects of International Child Abduction*, The Hague 2017 <https://assets.hcch.net/docs/0a0532b7-d580-4e53-8c25-7edab2a94284.pdf> accessed 06.09.2021, whose paras. 52–53 read as follows: 'The wording of Article 13(1)(b) [that his or her return would expose the child] clarifies that the issue is whether the return of the child would subject the *child* to a grave risk, and not whether the return would place another party's safety at grave risk. Thus, it is the situation of the child which should be the prime focus of the inquiry. However, Article 13(1)(b) does concern itself with the predicament of, for example, a taking parent, to the extent that the situation of the taking parent has an impact on the child. In a situation where there is evidence of a serious risk of harm to the taking parent upon his/her return with the child to the State of habitual residence, which cannot be adequately addressed by protective measures in that State, and which, if it occurred, would *expose the child* to a grave risk in accordance with Article 13(1)(b), the grave risk exception may be established.'

of prior habitual residence, the Hague return court should not rely solely on the theoretical obligation of such State to protect *the mother*, given the possible effects of such a situation on the child.

Of course, the Hague return proceedings cannot deal with domestic violence, as such, as is the case with any other matter related to the mother. The Hague return proceedings have a very precise and limited object, and should focus only on the return of the child. However, it is a primary responsibility of the court of the State of refuge to *protect* the child, upon ordering his or her return. This implies that, when the risk of harm is grave and there is no way to mitigate such harm, the court is left with no option but to refuse return. Adopting effective protective measures is the only way to ensure a safe return and, thus, the only way to order return. Adopting effective protection measures is even more crucial in the EU context, given that the Brussels IIa framework implements an even stronger child return policy. The point is well known and well explored, and needs no further investigation.[33]

Based on the Brussels IIa Regulation, two alternative grounds for achieving the necessary protection can be explored, although neither of these seems to be a perfect fit.

The first option would be to base the jurisdiction to take a protection measure on the provision dealing with this kind of order, i.e. Article 20 of the Regulation. As explored above (at section 3), this provision allows a court (in our case, a court in the State of refuge), in an urgent case, to take any 'provisional or protective measure' with regard to a 'person present on its territory'. The territorial requirement may be referred to either the mother or the child who finds themselves in the State of refuge, depending on whether the protective aim relates to mother or child. For the reasons explained above, however, it is maintained that, where evidence of (past) domestic violence reaches a reasonable standard, such a dichotomy is ill-founded, and any measure prohibiting (or regulating) the contacting

[33] C. Honorati, and A. Limante, 'Jurisdiction in Child Abduction Proceedings' in C. Honorati (ed), *Jurisdiction in Matrimonial Matters in Parental Responsibility and International Abduction: A Handbook on the Application of Brussels IIa Regulation in National Courts*, Giappicchelli and Peter Lang, Torino and Frankfurt 2018, pp. 128–31; P. McEleavy, 'The New Child Abduction Regime in the European Union: Symbiotic Relationship or Forced Partnership?' (2005) *Journal of Private International Law* 5 et seq.; A Schulz, 'The New Brussels II Regulation and the Hague Conventions of 1980 and 1996' (2004) *International Family Law* 22 et seq.; M. Ballesteros, 'International Child Abduction in the European Union: the Solution Incorporated by the Council Regulation' (2004) *Revue générale de droit* 343 et seq.

or approaching of the mother will, in fact, also protect the emotional well-being of the child. Furthermore, such measure will reassure both the mother and child who are bound to return. In concrete terms, a provisional measure should probably concern both child and mother, and always consider both sides of the matter.

While jurisdiction would easily be assumed on the basis of Article 20, the problem arises at the stage of recognition and enforcement of such measures. As is well known, measures based on Article 20 have only territorial effects, and are not enforceable outside the territory of the Member State where they were taken.[34] In this situation, the point is made that such a protection measure should be recognised and enforced under Regulation 606/2013.

Circulating under Regulation 606/2013 a protection measure based on Article 20 of the Brussels IIa Regulation may seem at odds with the structure of the latter Regulation, given that measures based on Article 20 are clearly not imbued with extraterritorial effects. The result is, however, acceptable and consistent, in light of the structure and scope of Regulation 606/2013. This instrument has a special scope of application, and envisages only certain types of protection measures, defined by Article 3 as those 'imposing *one or more of the following obligations* [i.e. a prohibition or regulation on entering a place, having contact or approaching the protected person] on the person causing the risk *with a view to protecting* another person, when the latter person's physical or psychological integrity may be at risk'.[35] In brief, Regulation 606/2013 only applies to a certain type of measure having a well-defined content, issued for the protection of a person's integrity. The special aim and scope of Regulation 606/2013 justifies that, while a 'normal' provisional or protection measure grounded in Article 20 will not be recognised and enforced in other Member States, such recognition and enforcement may occur when the measure is taken in view of a special

34 I. Kunda and D. Vrbljanac, 'Provisional and Protective Measures' in C. Honorati (ed), *Jurisdiction in Matrimonial Matters in Parental Responsibility and International Abduction: A Handbook on the Application of Brussels IIa Regulation in National Courts*, Giappicchelli and Peter Lang, Torino and Frankfurt 2018, pp. 249 et seq. The point of the limited territorial effect of provisional measures based on Article 20 was clarified by the CJEU in Case C-256/09, *Purrucker v. Vallés Pérez*, ECLI:EU:C:2010:437. On this decision, see also O. Feraci, 'Riconoscimento ed esecuzione all'estero dei provvedimenti provvisori in materia familiare: alcune riflessioni sulla sentenza Parrucker' (2011) *Rivista di diritto internazionale privato e processuale* 107 et seq.; C. Honorati, 'Parrucker I e II ed il regime speciale dei provvedimenti provvisori e cautelari a tutela dei minori' (2011) *Int'l Lis* 66 et seq.

35 All emphasis added.

(protective) aim that the EU legislator considers so relevant as to adopt a specific instrument in order to guarantee the production of extraterritorial effects.

It could also be argued that Regulation 606/2013 is not only *lex specialis*, but also *lex posterior*, with regard to the Brussels IIa Regulation, and that the *ratio legis* embodied in the later instrument should be upheld. Indeed, when multiple options are given, the interpreter is called to choose a construction giving an *effet utile* to all instruments concerned, and not one that frustrates and deprives all utility of one of the instruments (especially the more recent one).

Furthermore, as Regulation 606/2013 refers elsewhere for rules on jurisdiction, it cannot be excluded that jurisdiction is grounded in national rules.[36] Indeed, as seen above, one possible construction is that protection measures falling under Regulation 606/2013 may be granted on the basis of national fora. This is, however, also the case when triggering Article 20 of the Brussels IIa Regulation, which makes implicit reference to measures available under the *lex fori*. It would be odd to allow a provisional measure to circulate under Regulation 606/2013 when it is grounded *only* in national fora, and then refuse to circulate it under the same instrument when the same national fora is triggered by a uniform rule, as Article 20 of the Brussels IIa Regulation is.

Finally, this construction is also consistent with the limitation set by Article 2(3) of Regulation 606/2013. Circulating provisional measures taken on the grounds of Article 20 of the Brussels IIa Regulation under the special regime set by Regulation 606/2013 would not amount to an 'interference' with Brussels IIa, as circulation of this kind of measure is not envisaged by the latter Regulation.

A second possibility may be explored, in relation to applying for protection measures in the context of abduction proceedings. This approach builds on the special rules provided by the Brussels IIa Regulation, in order to enhance the Hague return proceedings in intra-EU cases. In particular, Article 11(4) of the Brussels IIa Regulation is meant to support and foster the very strict return policy envisaged by the Brussels IIa Regulation, by forbidding the court of the State of refuge to refuse the return of the child if 'adequate arrangements' have been taken to secure the protection of the child after his or her return. The underlying idea is that, even when return constitutes a grave risk for the child, a return order should, nevertheless, be issued if effective and adequate arrangements are to be taken to protect

36 See above, at section 2.

the child on his or her return.[37] Of course, the subject to be protected is the child and not the mother. However, as has already been seen, in cases where there is reasonable evidence of domestic violence affecting the mother, the court should be very cautious, and should be prepared to protect the child from any possible risk, including risk of indirect harm. One could, therefore, argue that 'adequate arrangements', for the purposes of Article 11(4), could also be made to protect the mother in return proceedings involving allegations of domestic violence.

The real problem with this provision is that it is doubtful that it may be used as an effective jurisdictional ground for international cases, especially because any provisional and urgent measure will have limited territorial effects. The rule requires 'arrangements' to be made, directly or through the channels of judicial or administrative cooperation, so that measures are taken in the State of habitual residence.[38] On its face, it does not require the court of the State of refuge to grant protective measures directly. In the current Brussels IIa framework, protection measures, the need for which arise in the course of abduction proceedings, be they focused on the mother or the child, are a matter for the court of the State of habitual residence. This is a weak point of the current Regulation, as is confirmed by the fact that the Brussels IIb Regulation, coming into application from August 2022, will provide for a different, better solution. Investigating this will be the object of the next and last section of this contribution.

5. THE WAY FORWARD: PROTECTION MEASURES IN ABDUCTION PROCEEDINGS UNDER THE NEW BRUSSELS IIB REGULATION

The analysis conducted above pointed to a gap in the current legal framework of mother/child protection when domestic violence is a

---

37 This approach is also inherent in the 1980 Hague Convention, and has, today, been made clear by the HCCH Guide, para. 44–48.

38 See, e.g. the European Commission, *Practice Guide for the Application of the Brussels IIa Regulation* (hereafter 'Practice Guide of the Brussels IIa Regulation'), Brussels 2014, para. 4.3.3, p. 55, stating that the mere possibility of protective measures is not enough to order return, since 'it must be established that the *authorities of the Member State of origin have taken concrete measures* to protect the child in question' (emphasis added). Similarly, see E. Pataut and E. Gallant, 'Article 11 para. 46' in U. Magnus and P. Mankowsky (eds), *Brussels IIbis Regulation Commentary*, Otto Schmidt, Cologne 2017; and R. Hausmann, *Internationales und Europäisches Ehescheidungsrecht. Kommentar*, CH Beck, Munich 2013, para. 124, p. 200.

background feature of an international abduction case. Although different pathways for achieving protection may be outlined, none of them are fully appropriate.

Seeking protection measures as self-standing measures, to be filed in proceedings independent from the Hague return proceedings, may be the right pathway from a theoretical and abstract point of view, but it is not an appealing one, and it may be counterproductive to the interests of the mother seeking protection (see section 3 above). The hope that protection measures will be taken in the framework of the Hague return proceedings, as established by the court on its own motion, in the interest of the child, or applied *ex parte*, appears more appropriate to the needs of the mother, but is less convincing from the point of view of the legal structure of the rule (see section 4 above).

Things may be changing in the near future, when the new Brussels IIb Regulation comes into effect. Pursuant to Article 100 thereof, the Regulation will apply to all legal proceedings instituted on or after 1 August 2022. Legal proceedings instituted before (and still pending at) that date, and recognition of decisions rendered in such proceedings, will continue under the current Brussels IIa Regulation.

Hague Proceedings instituted after that date will, thus, benefit from the new Article 27(5), which reads:

> Where the court orders the return of the child, the court may, where appropriate, take provisional, including protective, measures in accordance with Article 15 of this Regulation in order to protect the child from the grave risk referred to in point (b) of Article 13(1) of the 1980 Hague Convention, provided that the examining and taking of such measures would not unduly delay the return proceedings.

Article 15, to which the rule refers, is concerned with '[p]rovisional, including protective, measures in urgent cases'. Its paragraph 1 states that:

> In urgent cases, even if the court of another Member State has jurisdiction as to the substance of the matter, the courts of a Member State shall have jurisdiction to take provisional, including protective, measures which may be available under the law of that Member State in respect of:
>
> (a) a child who is present in that Member State; or
> (b) property belonging to a child which is located in that Member State.

What is more interesting, and which makes these measures special, is that, as a derogation to the general rule, a measure grounded in Article 27(5) will be recognised and enforced in all Member States. This result does not stem clearly from the rule, but is reached indirectly through a rather cumbersome referral to the definition of 'decision'. According to Article 2(1)(b), for the purposes of recognition and enforcement under the Brussels IIb Regulation, the notion of decision includes:

> provisional, including protective, measures ordered by a court which by virtue of this Regulation has jurisdiction as to the substance of the matter or measures ordered in accordance with Article 27(5) in conjunction with Article 15.

While the final outcome may not be immediately obvious to a lawyer less experienced in private international law, the result is, nonetheless, unequivocal. The court of the State of refuge, while not having jurisdiction over the substance of parental responsibility or custody, will have jurisdiction to take provisional and protective measures addressing the child, and such measures will have extraterritorial effects. The only difference between this and a decision on the substance is that the provisional measure is inherently limited in time, and will cease to apply when any further measure is taken by the court having jurisdiction over the substance (see Article 15(3)). The rule mirrors Article 11 of the 1996 Hague Convention, which also reflects the same extraterritorial, but temporary and limited, effects.

Article 27(5) is a very welcome step forward in the field of child protection. Indeed, it gives answers to a few of the issues that have been highlighted above. In particular, it sets a clear jurisdictional rule for protective measures to be taken by the State of refuge, in the context of abduction proceedings. Protecting the child will no longer be a question only for the State of habitual residence, but will become a clear responsibility of the State of refuge, which will be required to take an active role in achieving this result.

The rule also opens the door to extraterritorial effects of (some, very special) provisional measures that are taken by the court that does not have jurisdiction on the substance. This will exclude any need to revert to complicated legal constructions in order to achieve this result. It will also exclude the need to apply Regulation 606/2013.[39]

---

39 It may be noted that reference to Reg. 606/2013 will still be useful in cases where a woman seeks protection against domestic violence in a State different from the one of her own habitual residence, outside of a pattern of international abduction of children. Art. 27(5) of the Brussels IIb Regulation, in fact, only applies to cases of international abduction of children.

While these are all very important steps forward, one last step is still missing. The rule still makes reference only to the protection of *the child*, and gives no consideration whatsoever to the primary caregiver, who may also be in need of protection. It is a pity that the legislator did not include the parent who is a victim of domestic violence in the scope of the application of the rule.[40] A reference could, at least, have been made in the corresponding Recital. Instead, Recital 46, when giving examples of possible protection measures, does not refer, even implicitly, to situations that could involve the mother, as explored in the POAM project.[41] Once again, the mother is left alone to face a terrible dilemma: either return with the child and go back to the situation of violence she had escaped from, or stay safe and protected, but abandon her child. Pleading for protection measures will be her own responsibility, and will require her to file a separate proceeding, according to one of the pathways described under section 3.

Building further awareness of this situation, and the underlying gaps and needs, was one of the aims of the POAM research project and of this contribution in particular. Although the Brussels IIb Regulation represents an improvement, more is still to be done. It is up to the legal practitioner – be it the judge, the practising lawyer, or the academic – to make good use of all available means to achieve adequate protection for any woman suffering from domestic violence.

---

40 Such a proposal had already been suggested by K. Trimmings, *Child Abduction within the European Union*, Hart Publishing, Oxford 2013, p. 154, in light of a possible amendment to Article 11(4) of the Brussels IIa Regulation.

41 Recital 46 gives the following example: 'Such provisional, including protective, measures could include, for instance, that the child should continue to reside with the primary care giver or how contact with the child should take place after return until the court of the habitual residence of the child has taken measures it considers appropriate.'

THE CROSS-BORDER CIRCULATION OF CIVIL PROTECTIVE MEASURES ISSUED IN THE CONTEXT OF RETURN PROCEEDINGS

Katarina TRIMMINGS

1. INTRODUCTION

The implementation of measures of protection in return proceedings, through their recognition and, if needed, enforcement in the State of habitual residence of the child, is vital to ensure their effectiveness.

This contribution will explore how civil protection measures ordered in the State of refuge can be circulated in other Member States, including the State of habitual residence of the child, with reference to two instruments: Regulation 606/2013[1] and the 1996 Hague Child Protection Convention.[2] In theory, measures for the protection of the abducting mother can be taken in the State of refuge, either at the request of the abducting mother in proceedings that are separate from the return proceedings, or *ex officio* by the court dealing with the return application, in the return proceedings.

Two scenarios will, therefore, be explored. The first is a situation where the protection measures would be taken outside of the return proceedings, at the request of the abducting mother. As Regulation 606/2013 contains no rules on jurisdiction, jurisdiction in such a situation could, theoretically, be based on either Article 7(2) of the Brussels Ia Regulation,[3] or Article 20 of the Brussels IIa Regulation,[4] where matrimonial proceedings are pending between the abducting mother and the left-behind father in the State of refuge. It is envisaged that, in both cases, cross-border circulation of the protection measures would be facilitated by Regulation 606/2013.

The second is a situation where measures for the protection of the abducting mother would be taken by the court dealing with the return application, in the return proceedings. Jurisdiction would be based on the Brussels IIa Regulation: either Article 11(4) or Article 20 (matters related to parental responsibility). The underlying rationale is that measures to protect the mother will indirectly protect the child by ameliorating the grave risk of psychological harm or other intolerable situation to the child.[5] It is understood that there remain concerns amongst judges and

---

1 Regulation (EU) No 606/2013 of the European Parliament and of the Council of 12 June 2013 on mutual recognition of protection measures in civil matters [2013] OJ L 181.

2 Hague Convention of 19 October 1996 on Jurisdiction, Applicable Law, Recognition, Enforcement and Co-operation in Respect of Parental Responsibility and Measures for the Protection of Children.

3 Regulation (EU) No 1215/2012 of the European Parliament and of the Council of 12 December 2012 on jurisdiction and the recognition and enforcement of judgments in civil and commercial matters [2012] OJ L 351.

4 Council Regulation (EC) No 2201/2003 of 27 November 2003 concerning jurisdiction and the recognition and enforcement of judgments in matrimonial matters and the matters of parental responsibility, repealing Regulation (EC) No 1347/2000 [2003] OJ L 338.

5 It is regrettable that Council Regulation (EU) 2019/1111 of 25 June 2019 on jurisdiction, the recognition and enforcement of decisions in matrimonial matters and the matters of parental responsibility, and on international child abduction ('the Brussels IIb Regulation') missed the opportunity to clarify that the risk to the child and the risk to the mother are

other key players in some Hague return courts as to whether they have the jurisdiction to order protection for mothers in return proceedings.[6] To tackle this issue, the POAM project's *Best Practice Guide*[7] seeks to persuade such judges and jurisdictions by noting, firstly, that a child's exposure to domestic violence suffered by their parent can constitute a grave risk of harm.[8] Moreover, Article 19(1) of the UNCRC provides that 'State Parties shall take all appropriate legislative, administrative, social and educational measures to protect the child from all forms of physical or mental violence'. Subsequently, the UN Committee on the Rights of the Child clarified that mental violence referred to 'psychological maltreatment, mental abuse, verbal and emotional abuse or neglect', which included 'exposure to domestic violence'.[9] Therefore, where the domestic violence is perpetrated on the mother, and she is the main subject for whom protective measures are required within the return proceedings, courts should recognise that a child's exposure to violence may itself constitute a grave risk of harm, including harm due to the parent's inability to care properly for that child as a result of the violence.[10] The child's interests and security are inextricably linked to the mother's, especially where she is the primary carer.

Accordingly, an assessment in relation to an individual child, in cases of domestic violence, cannot ignore the impact on the child of the violence

often intertwined, and therefore, in such circumstances, in order to protect the child, the mother will also need to be protected. See Brussels IIb Regulation, Art. 15; K. Trimmings and O. Momoh, 'Intersection between Domestic Violence and International Parental Child Abduction: Protection of Abducting Mothers in Return Proceedings' (2021) 35 *International Journal of Law, Policy and the Family* 1, 17.

6 Findings from POAM National Reports <Project Reports – POAM Project (abdn.ac.uk)> accessed 22.12.2021. See also the contribution by C. Honorati in this volume.

7 The Best Practice Guide – Protection of Abducting Mothers in Return Proceedings ('POAM Best Practice Guide'), reprinted in this volume.

8 *Re E* [2011] UKSC 27, paras. 34 and 52.

9 UN Committee on the Rights of the Child, General Comment No. 13, 2011.

10 See Permanent Bureau, 'Guide to Good Practice under the HCCH Convention of 25 October 1980 on the Civil Aspects of International Child Abduction – Part VI – Article 13(1)(b)', para. 57 ('HCCH Guide'). As reflected on by Baroness Hale, 'one of the principal reasons' for the HCCH Guide was to protect 'victims of domestic violence and abuse from the hard choice of returning to a place where they do not feel safe and losing their children': B. Hale, 'Taking Flight – Domestic Violence and Child Abduction' (2017) 70 *Current Legal Problems* 3, 15. See also D. Bryant AO, QC, 'Response to Professors Rhona Schuz and Merle H Weiner ("the authors"), A Mistake Waiting to Happen: the Failure to Correct the Guide to Good Practice on Article 13(1)(b)' (2020) *International Family Law Journal* 207, emphasising that the HCCH Guide provides ample support for the notion that a child's exposure to domestic violence can constitute a grave risk of harm.

perpetrated on the primary carer.[11] Therefore, to break the impasse for judges and other key players who may feel that their domestic laws concerning return proceedings cater only for the protection of the child, as opposed to the abducting parent, the way forward is to engage the above analogy, and recognise that the duty to protect the child necessitates a duty to protect the abducting parent.

2. REGULATION 606/2013

Regulation 606/2013 is based on Article 81 of the Treaty on the Functioning of the European Union (TFEU),[12] and provides for the mutual recognition of civil protection measures across the EU by establishing 'rules for a simple and rapid mechanism for the recognition of protection measures ordered in a Member State in civil matters'.[13] The Member State that issued the protection order is referred to in the Regulation as 'the Member State of origin' and the other Member State is termed 'the Member State addressed'.[14] For a protection measure to fall within the scope of the Regulation, the issuing authority does not necessarily need to belong to the civil justice system;[15] however, a protection order issued by the police would not be eligible.[16]

The restrictions that can be placed on the person causing risk, with a view to safeguarding the protected person's physical or psychological integrity, include:

(1) a prohibition or regulation on entering the place where the protected person resides, works, or regularly visits or stays;

---

11 As early as 2001, the Hague Conference itself recognised that, in considering the protection of the child, 'regard should be given to the impact on a child of violence committed by one parent against the other': Permanent Bureau, 'Conclusions and Recommendations of the Fourth Meeting of the Special Commission', para. 42. More generally, see I. Pretelli, 'Three Patterns, One Law: Plea for a Reinterpretation of the Hague Child Abduction Convention to Protect Children from Exposure to Sexism, Misogyny and Violence Against Women' in M. Pfeiffer et al. (eds), *Liber Amicorum Monika Pauknerová*, Wolters Kluwer, Prague 2021, pp. 363–93.

12 Consolidated Version of the Treaty on the Functioning of the European Union [2012] OJ C 326/49.

13 Reg. 606/2013, Art. 1.

14 Ibid., Art. 3.

15 Ibid., Recital 10.

16 Ibid., Recital 13.

(2) a prohibition or regulation of contact, in any form, with the protected person, including by telephone, electronic or ordinary mail, fax or any other means; and
(3) a prohibition or regulation on approaching the protected person closer than a prescribed distance.[17]

The recognition of the protection measure is automatic, meaning that 'a protection measure ordered in a Member State shall be recognised in the other Member States without any special procedure being required and shall be enforceable without a declaration of enforceability being required'.[18]

A protected person who wishes to invoke their protection measure in another Member State is required to produce:[19]

(1) a copy of the protection measure;
(2) a certificate issued by the Member State of origin under Article 5 of the Regulation; and
(3) where necessary, a translation or transliteration of the certificate.

The protected person can bring enforcement proceedings in the Member State addressed if necessary, and the enforcement, including the sanctions and procedures relating to the breach of the protection order, are left to the law of that Member State.[20]

There are only limited grounds on which a court in the Member State addressed can refuse to recognise and, where applicable, enforce a protection measure issued in another Member State (upon application by the person causing the risk). These grounds include that the protection measure is 'manifestly contrary to public policy in the Member State addressed', or 'irreconcilable with a judgment given or recognised in the Member State addressed.'[21]

Regulation 606/2013 contains no rules on international jurisdiction; therefore, other international instruments, namely the Brussels Ia or Brussels IIa Regulations, must be resorted to for the purpose of establishing jurisdiction.[22] Having established jurisdiction, it is envisaged that the

---

17 Ibid., Art. 3(1).
18 Ibid., Art. 4(1).
19 Ibid., Art. 4.
20 Ibid., Art. 4(5).
21 Ibid., Art. 13(1).
22 A. Dutta, 'Cross-Border Protection Measures in the European Union' (2016) 12 *Journal of Private International Law* 169, 171. This contrasts with the Commission

measures for protection against domestic violence will not be circulated under Brussels Ia or Brussels IIa; instead, they will be recognised and (if needed) enforced as 'special' measures of protection under Regulation 606/2013.[23]

2.1. MEASURES FOR THE PROTECTION OF THE ABDUCTING MOTHER ISSUED AS SELF-STANDING MEASURES

This section addresses measures for the protection of the abducting mother issued in proceedings separate from the Hague Convention return proceedings, i.e. as self-standing measures.

2.1.1. Jurisdiction Based on Article 7(2) of the Brussels Ia Regulation

Article 7(2) of the Brussels Ia Regulation makes provision for the jurisdiction to make protective measures on the basis of a tort, 'where the harmful event may occur' (i.e. in the State of refuge). Article 7(2) states: 'A person domiciled in a Member State may be sued in another Member State … in matters relating to tort, delict or quasi-delict, in the courts for the place where the harmful event occurred or may occur'.

In order for Article 7(2) to be applicable, the left-behind parent would either need to be physically present in the State of refuge, or to have threatened the abducting parent via electronic means (telephone, email) of his intention to cause harm to, or assault, the mother in the State of refuge. It is envisaged here that the protection order would be circulated under Regulation 606/2013 rather than under Brussels Ia. The rationale is that the judgment is concerned with a specific type of protection measure, governed by a dedicated instrument: Regulation 606/2013. However, the question is open as to whether Regulation 606/2013 ousts Brussels Ia.

Proposal for the Regulation, which contained, in Article 3, a rule that conferred jurisdiction on '[t]he authorities of the Member State where the person's physical and/or psychological integrity or liberty is at risk': Proposal of the Commission for a Regulation of the European Parliament and of the Council on mutual recognition of protection measures in civil matters, COM (2011) 276 final.

23 It is believed that such an interpretation does not contradict Recital 11, which explains that Regulation 606/2013 'should not interfere with the functioning of the Brussels IIa Regulation' and, where possible, '[d]ecisions taken under the Brussels IIa Regulation should continue to be recognised and enforced under that Regulation'.

This was suggested by the European Commission in their Proposal,[24] but Regulation 606/2013, despite setting out its delineation with Brussels IIa, remains silent on this question. Therefore, both instruments could be applied as alternatives to one another. A cross-border enforcement under Brussels Ia could be possible, at least once the expiry date of the Article 5 certificate under Regulation 606/2013 has been reached.[25] Recital 16 to Regulation 606/2013 points in this direction, as it says that the provisions of the Regulation 'should be without prejudice to the right of the protected person to invoke that protection measure under any other available legal act of the Union providing for recognition'. It has, however, to be noted that, according to the CJEU,[26] provisional measures are only enforceable under the Brussels I regime if the respondent has been heard.[27] However, even in terms of such *ex parte* measures, these preconditions will be met after the expiry period of the certificate under Regulation 606/2013 has elapsed. An *ex parte* protection measure can only be enforced under Article 8 of Regulation 606/2013 if the certificate has been brought to the notice of the person causing the risk.

2.1.2. *Jurisdiction Based on Article 20 of the Brussels IIa Regulation (Pending Matrimonial Proceedings)*

Jurisdiction based on Article 20 of the Brussels IIa Regulation relates to circumstances where matrimonial proceedings are pending between the taking parent and the left-behind parent, in the State of refuge. Article 20(1) states:

> In urgent cases, the provisions of this Regulation shall not prevent the courts of a Member State from taking such provisional, including protective, measures in respect of persons or assets in that State as may be available under the law of that Member State, even if, under this Regulation, the court of another Member State has jurisdiction as to the substance of the matter.

In essence, where there are proceedings for divorce or judicial separation pending between the abducting mother and the left-behind father, in the

24 Proposal of the Commission for a Regulation of the European Parliament and of the Council on mutual recognition of protection measures in civil matters, COM (2011) 276 final, 6.

25 A. Dutta, 'Cross-Border Protection Measures in the European Union' (2016) 12 *Journal of Private International Law* 169, 182.

26 Case C-125/79, *Denilauler*, 21 May 1980, ECLI:EU:C:1980:130.

27 This has been put on a statutory basis by the Brussels Ia Regulation, Art. 2(a)(2). See also Brussels Ia Regulation, Art. 42(2)(c).

State of refuge, Article 20 of the Brussels IIa Regulation gives jurisdiction to the courts of the State of refuge to take provisional protective measures, based on the presence of the abducting mother in the territory of that Member State. The problem with Article 20 is that protective measures taken under this provision are not enforceable outside the territory of the Member State where they were taken. This is according to the CJEU decision in *Purrucker*,[28] although this will change after August 2022 when the Brussels IIb Regulation comes into effect. Nevertheless, a functional construction of Regulation 606/2013 envisages here that the protective measures would be circulated under Regulation 606/2013. This, however, may be problematic, as Article 2(3) of Regulation 606/2013 states that the Regulation should not apply to protection measures falling within the scope of the Brussels IIa Regulation. The Explanatory Memorandum to the EC Proposal for Regulation 606/2013 uses examples of protective measures concerning 'a couple which has not been married, same sex partners or neighbours' that would be covered by the proposed Regulation. Implicitly, therefore, Regulation 606/2013 would not cover protective measures taken in respect of a married couple in the context of matrimonial proceedings.

2.2. MEASURES FOR THE PROTECTION OF THE ABDUCTING MOTHER ISSUED AS INDIRECT PROTECTIVE MEASURES FOR THE CHILD

This section addresses measures for the protection of the abducting mother issued *ex officio* by the Hague Convention return court in return proceedings, i.e. as indirect protective measures for the child.

2.2.1. Jurisdiction Based on Article 20 of the Brussels IIa Regulation (Matters Related to Parental Responsibility)

Article 20 of the Brussels IIa Regulation gives jurisdiction to the courts of the State of refuge, based on the presence of the child in the territory of that Member State. With reference to the same provision under

28 Case C-256/09, *Purrucker v. Vallés Pérez*, 15 July 2010, ECLI:EU:C:2010:437. See also European Commission, 'Practice Guide for the Application of the Brussels IIa Regulation', 38 <https://op.europa.eu/en/publication-detail/-/publication/f7d39509-3f10-4ae2-b993-53ac6b9f93ed> accessed 27.12.2021.

Article 20(1), the difficulty with Article 20 is that, currently, the protective measures are not enforceable outside the Member State that issues such measures.[29]

2.2.2. Jurisdiction Based on Article 11(4) of the Brussels IIa Regulation

Article 11(4) of the Brussels IIa Regulation[30] can be seen as a ground of jurisdiction for 'adequate arrangements' that would guarantee a safe return of the child in cases involving the 'grave risk of harm' defence. Article 11(4) of Brussels IIa states:

> A court cannot refuse to return a child on the basis of Article 13b of the 1980 Hague Convention if it is established that adequate arrangements have been made to secure the protection of the child after his or her return.

Article 11(4) can also be used as a jurisdictional ground for measures to protect the mother, in return proceedings involving allegations of domestic violence. On a functional construction of Regulation 606/2013, the POAM project's *Best Practice Guide* envisages the possibility that such protective measures can then be circulated under Regulation 606/2013.

Therefore, in circumstances where jurisdiction to take measures of protection is based on either Article 11(4) or Article 20 (parental responsibility) of the Brussels IIa Regulation, cross-border circulation of such measures will be facilitated by Regulation 606/2013 (as measures for protection against domestic violence taken under either of these jurisdictional bases cannot be recognised and enforced under Brussels IIa). The problem, however, may be seen again in Article 2(3) of Regulation 606/2013, which, as explained previously, states that this Regulation should not apply to protection measures falling within the scope of the Brussels IIa Regulation. Nevertheless, there are two arguments on which the applicability of Regulation 606/2013 here can be justified. These two arguments are intertwined, and are linked with the concept of 'legislative intent'. First, it is proposed here that the purposive approach to statutory interpretation should be adopted when interpreting Article 2(3). According to this approach, the courts should construe statutory

29 See section 2.1.2 above.

30 Soon to be Art. 27(3) of the Brussels IIb Regulation, when this comes into effect in August 2022: Council Regulation (EU) 2019/1111 of 25 June 2019 on jurisdiction, the recognition and enforcement of decisions in matrimonial matters and the matters of parental responsibility, and on international child abduction.

language in accordance with the object and intent of the legislation.[31] It is a method of statutory interpretation that considers the purpose of the provision, and interprets the provision in accordance with this purpose.[32] The purposive approach is derived from the European 'teleological' approach, which focuses on the spirit and purpose of the legislation. The purposive approach to statutory interpretation is used in the European Court of Justice, and domestic judges are required to apply the purposive approach whenever applying a piece of EU law.[33] This modern approach to statutory interpretation requires that the words of a statute be read 'in their entire context and in their grammatical and ordinary sense harmoniously with the scheme of the Act, the object of the Act, and the intention of Parliament'.[34] A principal corollary to the teleological method is the doctrine of 'effectiveness', invariably called by its French name, *effet utile*.[35] The doctrine provides that, once the purpose of a provision has been clearly identified, its detailed terms will be interpreted so 'as to ensure that the provision retains its effectiveness'.[36] Accordingly, the legislation is interpreted to produce the desired effect.

On examining the legislative intent expressed in the Explanatory Memorandum to the EC Proposal for Regulation 606/2013, one of the obvious intentions of the legislator was for protective measures to be utilised effectively.[37] The Explanatory Memorandum gives examples of protective measures that would, or would not, fall within the scope of the Regulation. Notably, none of these examples concern parental

---

31 See, e.g. A. Edgar and K.M. Stack, 'The Authority and Interpretation of Regulations' (2019) 82 *Modern Law Review* 1009.

32 In contrast, the literal approach interprets the meaning of the statute based primarily on its wording. See, generally, on statutory interpretation, e.g. G. Wilson, *English Legal System*, Pearson Education, London 2013, pp. 51–73.

33 See, e.g. N. Fennelly, 'Legal Interpretation at the European Court of Justice' (1996) 20 *Fordham International Law Journal* 656, 672.

34 *Re Rizzo & Rizzo Shoes Ltd.* [1998] 1 SCR 27.

35 K. Gombos, 'EU Law viewed through the eyes of a national judge', 4 <https://ec.europa.eu/dgs/legal_service/seminars/20140703_gombos_speech_en.pdf> accessed 26.12.2021, citing K. Lenaerts, 'L'égalité de traitement en droit communautaire. Un principe unique aux apparences multiples en Cahiers de droit européen', 1991, pp. 3–41, particularly p. 38, <https://bib.kuleuven.be/rbib/collectie/archieven/cde/1991-1-2.pdf> accessed 04.03.2022.

36 Ibid.

37 See Proposal for a Regulation of the European Parliament and of the Council on mutual recognition of protection measures in civil matters, COM/2011/0276 final – COD 2011/0130, Explanatory Memorandum, 52011PC0276 <https://eur-lex.europa.eu/legal-content/EN/TXT/?uri=COM%3A2011%3A0276%3AFIN> accessed 20.12.2021.

responsibility; instead, all of them pertain to relationships between adults and are, therefore, relevant only to Article 20 cases where protective measures have been taken in the context of matrimonial proceedings.[38] This implies that the rule in Article 2(3) does not apply to protective measures issued in proceedings concerning parental responsibility. It follows that, on a functional construction, Regulation 606/2013 applies to protective measures taken in return proceedings. Indeed, if Article 2(3) was intended to impose a blanket ban on the application of Regulation 606/2013 in respect of all proceedings falling under the Brussels IIa Regulation, then Regulation 606/2013 could not be applied in respect of nearly all family law proceedings, as Brussels IIa covers a significant proportion of family law matters. As a result, this would make Regulation 606/2013 nearly redundant, and its usefulness would be cancelled out, especially in circumstances where it is most needed, i.e. matters pertaining to children and parental responsibility.

3. THE 1996 HAGUE CHILD PROTECTION CONVENTION

Article 11 of the 1996 Hague Child Protection Convention provides the State of refuge with jurisdiction to issue measures based on the presence of the child in the territory of the State of refuge. Article 11(1) provides:

> In all cases of urgency, the authorities of any Contracting State in whose territory the child or property belonging to the child is present have jurisdiction to take any necessary measures of protection.

If orders are made under Article 11,[39] then, by virtue of Article 23, they shall be recognised by operation of law in all other Contracting States.[40] Alternatively, instead of making a separate order, the court can simply incorporate measures of protection into the return order, with the

[38] See section 2.1.2 above.

[39] Art. 11 provides jurisdiction, as it states that: '(1) In all cases of urgency, the authorities of any Contracting State in whose territory the child or property belonging to the child is present have jurisdiction to take any necessary measures of protection.'

[40] This means that, unlike protective measures taken under Art. 20 of the Brussels IIa Regulation, protective measures taken under Art. 11 of the 1996 Convention are enforceable outside of the territory of the Contracting State where they were issued.

expectation that the requesting State will treat them as urgent measures of protection under the 1996 Convention.[41]

Nevertheless, circulation of the protective measures under Regulation 606/2013 is more advantageous than under the Convention, as the recognition mechanism under the Regulation is simpler than the recognition procedure under the 1996 Convention (no declaration of enforceability is needed under the Regulation). Therefore, circulation of the measures of protection for the child and the mother should be facilitated by Regulation 606/2013, unless the State of habitual residence is a non-EU Member State (e.g. the United Kingdom). In such cases, circulation of the measures would be facilitated by the 1996 Hague Convention.

Pre-Brexit, English judges (both High Court and Court of Appeal) referred to Regulation 606/2013 in return proceedings, recognising its potential to fill the gap in the civil law protection of abducting mothers who return with their children to the requesting State, in child abduction cases involving allegations of domestic violence. In particular, in *Re S (A Child) (Hague Convention 1980: Return to Third State)*,[42] Moylan L.J. noted that measures under Article 11 of the 1996 Convention were also measures under the Protection Measures Regulation.[43] In *In the matter of A (A Child) (Hague Abduction; Art 13(b): Protective Measures)*,[44] Williams J. also acknowledged the potential utility of Regulation 606/2013 in the child abduction context, and commented on the strengths of the Regulation as follows:

> [the Regulation] sets up a mechanism allowing for direct recognition of protection orders issued as a civil law measure between member states, thus

---

41 *In the matter of A (A Child) (Hague Abduction; Art 13(b): Protective Measures)* [2019] EWHC 649 (Fam), para. 25: 'Protective measures may include undertakings, and undertakings accepted by this court or orders made by this court pursuant to Article 11 of the 1996 Hague Child Protection Convention are automatically recognised by operation of Article 23 in another Convention state (see *Re Y (A Child) (Abduction: Undertakings Given for Return of Child)*.' Undertakings can be described as 'promises offered or in certain circumstances imposed upon an applicant to overcome obstacles which may stand in the way of the return of a wrongfully removed or retained child': P. Beaumont and P. McEleavy, *The Hague Convention on International Child Abduction*, Oxford University Press, Oxford 1999, p. 30. See also K. Trimmings, *Child Abduction within the European Union*, Hart Publishing, Oxford 2013, pp. 155–61; and K. Trimmings, O. Momoh and I. Callander, 'POAM UK National Report', p. 98 <https://research.abdn.ac.uk/poam/resources/reports/> accessed 27.12.2021.

42 *Re S (A Child) (Hague Convention 1980: Return to Third State)* [2019] EWCA Civ 352.

43 Ibid., para. 26.

44 *In the matter of A (A Child) (Hague Abduction; Art 13(b): Protective Measures)* [2019] EWHC 649 (Fam).

> a civil law protection order such as a non-molestation order or undertaking issued in one member state, can be invoked directly in another member state without the need for a declaration of enforceability but simply by producing a copy of the protection measure, an Article 5 certificate and where necessary a transliteration or translation.[45]

Williams J. then set out a definition of a protection measure under the Regulation: 'any decision, whatever it is called, ordered by an issuing authority of the member state of origin' that '[i]ncludes an obligation imposed to protect another person from physical or psychological harm'.[46] The learned judge then commented that '[o]ur domestic law provides this court can accept an undertaking where the court has the power to make a non-molestation order', before concluding that 'a non-molestation undertaking given to this court could qualify as a protection measure within the European Regulation on protection measures'.[47] The judge, however, did not develop this reasoning, or take any steps to put it into practice (for example, by issuing the Article 5 certificate, etc.), and, at the end of the judgment, referred only to the 1996 Convention as a means of facilitating the enforceability of undertakings offered by the left-behind parent.[48] Finally, in *RD v. DB*,[49] Mostyn J. issued orders under Article 11 of the 1996 Hague Convention, and noted that these would be 'doubly enforceable'[50] in the State of habitual residence, under the 1996 Convention, and under Regulation 606/2013. The judge then described the Regulation in the following words:

> This Regulation provides for reciprocal enforcement throughout the Union of protection measures ordered for the protection of a person where there exist serious grounds for considering that a person's life, physical or psychological integrity, personal liberty, security or sexual integrity is at risk. For example, it is extended to measures that seek to regulate and control violence, harassment, sexual aggression, stalking, intimidation or any other forms of indirect coercion .... Where such orders are made which might extend inter alia to prohibiting the entering of a place where a protected person resides, works or visits or stays or contact in any form or approaching the protected person, then such measures are, by virtue of the Regulation, to be automatically recognised and

45 Ibid., para. 25.
46 Ibid., para. 26.
47 Ibid.
48 Ibid., paras. 39–41.
49 *RB v. DB* [2015] EWHC 1817 (Fam).
50 Ibid., para. 31.

> enforced without any procedure being required or the need for a declaration of enforceability.[51]

However, like Williams J. (see above), Mostyn J. did not go beyond this outline of the key features of the Regulation. Indeed, no suggestions were made concerning necessary practical arrangements to prepare the protective measures to 'travel' to the requesting State. Interestingly, none of the judges engaged with the text of the Regulation at a deeper level. It would have been interesting to see comments related to issues such as jurisdiction and the relationship between the Brussels IIa Regulation and Regulation 606/2013, in particular.

4. CIRCULATION OF PROTECTIVE MEASURES AND CONTACT

The intersection between parental contact and protection orders is a grey area. If the court issuing the protection measures for the mother is different from the Hague Convention return court, the two courts should cooperate in order to ensure that the resulting protection order takes into account the specific circumstances of the case that stem from the child abduction situation. In particular, the court dealing with the protection order application should determine, taking account of any possibly existing contact rights of the left-behind parent, whether the abducted child should also be included in the protection order (if permitted by national law).[52] If the left-behind parent also poses a risk to the child, and there is a no-contact order in place in the State of habitual residence, the protection order should always include the child (if permitted by national law). If the issuing court considers that the left-behind parent also poses a risk to the child, but there is, nevertheless, a contact order in place in the State of habitual residence, the child should still be included in the protection order (if permitted by national law), but the possibility that the recognition and, where applicable, enforcement of the protection order may be refused upon possible application by the left-behind father, under Article 13(b)

---

51 Ibid., para. 30.

52 Cf. S. Van der Aa, et al., 'Mapping the Legislation and Assessing the Impact of Protection Orders in the European Member States', p. 245 <http://poems-project.com/wp-content/uploads/2015/04/Intervict-Poems-digi-1.pdf> accessed 27.12.2021.

of Regulation 606/2013, must be borne in mind.[53] In such circumstances, the abducting parent should be advised to seek a no-contact order, under Article 11 of the 1996 Hague Convention, as an urgent measure of protection from a competent court in the State of abduction.[54] If the issuing court considers that the left-behind father does not pose a risk to the child, and that the exercise of contact would not hinder the protection of the abducting mother (for example, the handover of the child would be facilitated by a third person), the protection order should allow for continued contact between the child and the left-behind parent.[55] If the issuing court considers that the left-behind parent does not pose a risk to the child, but that the exercise of contact would hinder the protection of the abducting mother, the issuing authority should consider ordering that the exercise of contact be facilitated, for example, through a contact centre. Alternatively, should the prospect of continued contact cause anxiety to the abducting mother, she should be advised to seek a no contact order, under Article 11 of the 1996 Hague Convention, as an urgent measure of protection from a competent court in the State of refuge.[56] This measure would be enforceable in the State of habitual residence, under Article 23 of the 1996 Convention, on a temporary basis, until the substantive matters of custody and contact have been determined by the court of the State of habitual residence.

5. CONCLUSION

Measures for the protection of the abducting mother can be issued in the State of refuge, either in proceedings that are separate from the Hague Convention return proceedings (as self-standing measures), or in Hague return proceedings (as indirect protective measures for the child).

---

53 Art. 13 states: 'The recognition and, where applicable, the enforcement of the protection measure shall be refused, upon application by the person causing the risk, to the extent such recognition is: … (b) irreconcilable with a judgment given or recognised in the Member State addressed.'

54 Depending on the national rules of internal jurisdiction, such competent court may coincide with the court dealing with the return application.

55 Cf S. Van der Aa, et. al, 'Mapping the Legislation and Assessing the Impact of Protection Orders in the European Member States', p. 245 <http://poems-project.com/wp-content/uploads/2015/04/Intervict-Poems-digi-1.pdf> accessed 27.12.2021.

56 Depending on the national rules of internal jurisdiction, such competent court may coincide with be the court dealing with the return application.

Regardless of the jurisdictional basis relied on by the court to issue the protective measures, the most appropriate instrument to facilitate the cross-border circulation of such measures is Regulation 606/2013, unless the State of habitual residence is a non-EU Member State, in which case the 1996 Hague Child Protection Convention should be employed. Regulation 606/2013 provides for the mutual recognition of civil protection measures across the EU by establishing 'rules for a simple and rapid mechanism for the recognition of protection measures ordered in a Member State in civil matters.'[57] Circulation of protective measures under the Regulation is simpler than the recognition procedure under the 1996 Convention, as no declaration of enforceability is needed under the Regulation. Importantly, matters related to contact between the child and the left-behind parent must form an important element of considerations surrounding the cross-border circulation of protective measures, in the context of Hague return proceedings.

57 Reg. 606/2013, Art. 1.

THE POTENTIAL ROLE OF REGULATION 606/2013 IN PROTECTING THE ABDUCTING PARENT IN RETURN PROCEEDINGS

Michael WILDERSPIN*

1. INTRODUCTION: GENERAL FEATURES OF REGULATION 606/2013

Regulation 606/2013 on the recognition of protection measures in civil matters[1] was enacted on 29 June 2013, and has been applicable since 11 January 2015. By virtue of Article 22, it applies to any measures falling within its scope that were taken on or after that date, even where the proceedings had been commenced beforehand.

The purpose of the Regulation is to provide for a simple and rapid mechanism for the recognition of protection measures ordered in Member

* Former Legal Adviser to the European Commission. The views expressed are those of the author alone, and do not necessarily concur with those of the European Commission.

1 Regulation (EU) No 606/2013 of the European Parliament and of the Council of 12 June 2013 on mutual recognition of protection measures in civil matters [2013] OJ L181/4.

States in civil matters (Article 1). This, of course, only tells half the story: the real purpose of the Regulation is to allow the almost automatic circulation in the other Member States of such measures, thereby allowing measures ordered in one Member State to be enforced easily, without the need for a declaration of enforceability, in any other Member State.

Logically enough, the Regulation applies only in cross-border cases (Article 2(2)); in other words, where measures ordered in one Member State are to be enforced in another.

To simplify matters slightly, protection measures are defined as certain prohibitions imposed on a person (such as prohibitions on contact). The addressee of the prohibition is labelled as the 'person causing the risk', and the beneficiary as the 'protected person' (Article 3).

The Regulation contains no rules on jurisdiction, contrary to the Commission's proposal for a Regulation,[2] Article 3 of which would have conferred jurisdiction on the authorities of the Member State in which a person's physical and or psychological integrity was at risk. This proposed rule was removed during the course of negotiations, thereby leaving no uniform rules on jurisdiction.

The legal significance of the absence of any rule on international jurisdiction in the final version of the Regulation implies that such jurisdiction is left up to national law,[3] possibly subject to some unwritten limitation that would restrict jurisdiction to cases in which the protected person has at least some connection with the forum Member State, such as habitual residence, presence, or exposure to the risk of violence there. Since national rules on jurisdiction are, in any event, likely to contain some objective connecting factor, it is probable that the EU legislator simply took the view that there was no real risk of forum shopping, and that the proposed rule would have been unduly restrictive. Had the proposed rule on jurisdiction been adopted, this would, for example, have made it very difficult, under the Regulation, for a court or authority in a Member State in which a person had taken temporary refuge to issue a measure with a view to providing protection (at least temporarily) for the situation in which that person wished to return to the Member State of habitual

2 COM(2011) 276 final.

3 R. Hausmann, *Internationales und Europäisches Familienrecht*, 2nd ed., CH Beck, Munich 2018, p. 1457, para. 59: the author describes this as *'erstaunlich'* (astonishing). However, this view, though correct in the current author's view, is not shared by all commentators; for a summary of the positions to the contrary, see A. Dutta, 'Cross-border protection measures in the European Union' (2016) 12 *Journal of Private International Law* 169, 171.

residence, since such a person might be at risk in the State from which he or she had fled, but be at no immediate risk in the State of refuge.

As it is, the Regulation may be potentially applicable where: (1) the person at risk has obtained a protection measure in Member State *A*, where that person and the person causing the risk are both habitually resident, and the person at risk ('protected person') wishes to go to another Member State, whether temporarily or on a more long-term basis, and benefit from the protection there; or (2) where the person at risk has temporarily fled the Member State of habitual residence, and wishes to obtain a measure of protection in the Member State of temporary presence, even if he or she is not directly at risk there, with a view to enforcing that measure upon return to the Member State of normal residence (whether such a measure can be obtained, in such circumstances, in the Member State of temporary presence is, of course, a matter for that State's law).[4]

As regards the circulation of such protection measures, Chapter II of the Regulation aims to provide for a comparatively light system, which is quite similar to, albeit much less detailed than, that contained in the Brussels Ia Regulation.[5] Article 4 promises much, in that it specifies that a protection measure taken in one Member State is enforceable in the other Member States without the need for a declaration of enforceability, albeit that the effects of the measure will lapse after a maximum of 12 months, even if the validity of the measure in the Member State of origin is longer. However, as always, the devil is in the detail. To be enforceable in another Member State, the protected person must provide the competent authority in the requested Member State with a copy of the decision (if need be, accompanied by a translation), as well as a certificate, which contains information specified in Article 7. The Regulation itself does not contain a standard form for the certificate, but this is rectified by Implementing Regulation 939/2014,[6] Annex I of which contains a standard form, reducing the need for a translation, at least of certain parts of the certificate, in the Member State where the measure is to be enforced.

---

4 This point is made clear in Recital 12, which states explicitly that Member States are not obliged to modify their national systems of protection measures, or to introduce such measures for the application of the Regulation.

5 Regulation (EU) No 1215/2012 of the European Parliament and of the Council of 12 December 2012 on jurisdiction and the recognition and enforcement of judgments in civil and commercial matters [2012] OJ L351/1.

6 Commission Implementing Regulation (EU) No 939/2014 of 2 September 2014 establishing the certificates referred to in Articles 5 and 14 of Regulation (EU) No 606/2013 of the European Parliament and of the Council on mutual recognition of protection measures in civil matters, [2014] OJ L263/10.

In order to ensure the rights of defence of the addressee of the measure (the 'person causing the risk'), the issuing of the certificate is subject to that person being given notice of the measure (Article 6(1)). In addition, Article 6 provides for additional safeguards where the decision has been given *ex parte*, or in default of appearance.

Additionally, once the certificate has been issued, Article 8 requires it to be brought to the attention of the person causing the risk. Unfortunately, this important article is worded very vaguely. In the first place, it does not specify the consequences of failure to comply with that obligation. Logically, for the obligation to have any teeth, non-compliance should mean that the measure is not enforceable in the requested Member State, but this is nowhere made explicit.

Where the addressee (person causing the risk) is resident in the Member State that issued the measure, notification is effected according to the law of that Member State. Where he is resident in another Member State, notification is made by registered letter with acknowledgment of receipt or equivalent. And, lastly, where the addressee's whereabouts are unknown, and in the case of non-acceptance of the letter, 'the situation' is governed by the law of the Member State of origin. Precisely what this means is not spelt out, but presumably it means that the Member State of origin decides what is appropriate notification in such circumstances.

Lastly, the addressee of the measure may challenge its enforcement, but the grounds of challenge are limited, namely public policy and irreconcilability (Article 13(1)). Failure to comply with rights of defence in the Member State of origin of the protection measure is not listed as a discrete ground for refusal of enforcement, but given the importance of this principle, and the need to comply with Article 6 of the European Convention on Human Rights, it is likely that the public policy exception is broad enough to embrace such a failure.[7]

While the underlying objective of the Regulation is laudable, the detailed provisions can be criticised on a number of grounds.[8] Unlike the majority of the private international law instruments adopted by the EU, it does not attempt to establish a complete system. Instead, it is cobbled together on the basis of the simple idea that protection measures taken

---

7 See, e.g. Case C-7/98, *Krombach v. Bamberski*, ECLI:EU:C:2000:164; Case C-394/07, *Gambazzi*, ECLI:EU:C:2009:219; Case C-619/10, *Trade Agency v. Seramico Investments*, ECLI:EU:C:2012:531; and Case C-34/17, *Donnellan*, ECLI:EU:C:2018:282.

8 A. Dutta, 'Cross-border protection measures in the European Union' (2016) 12 *Journal of Private International Law* 169, 171.

in one Member State should be able to circulate in the others. Quite apart from the reservations concerning the rights of the defence, detailed above, the Regulation is unlikely to offer much practical assistance to a person who is protected by a measure issued in one Member State, but who wishes to move to another. In most cases, should protection be needed in the second Member State, it will be simpler and faster for the person to request such measures there; moreover, those measures can be tailored more effectively to local conditions, in particular where the person causing the risk is likely to prove recalcitrant.

The available evidence suggests that the Regulation is hardly used, perhaps for the above reasons. It has been cited only once by a member of the CJEU, namely Advocate General Bobek, in his Opinion in *Pula Parking*,[9] and then only as regards the notion of 'judicial authority'.

However, in England and Wales, the potential usefulness of the Regulation in Hague Abduction Convention return proceedings has been noted, in particular as a means to counter an objection under point b) of the first paragraph of Article 13 of the Abduction Convention that there is a grave risk that the return of the child would expose him/her to physical or psychological harm, or place him/her in an intolerable situation, and it is to this issue that this contribution shall now turn.

2. POTENTIAL APPLICABILITY OF REGULATION 606/2013 IN HAGUE ABDUCTION CONVENTION PROCEEDINGS

As noted in the previous section, the 'grave risk' objection in Article 13 of the 1980 Hague Abduction Convention[10] constitutes one of the exceptions to the obligation, imposed by Article 12 of that Convention, to return the child to the Contracting State in which he or she was habitually resident immediately before the wrongful removal or retention. The statistics show that this provision is the one most frequently relied on by courts in cases of judicial refusal to order the return of the child.[11]

9 Case C-551/15, *Pula Parking*, ECLI:EU:C:2016:825.

10 Convention of 25 October 1980 on the Civil Aspects of Child Abduction.

11 See, in particular, the Statistical Analysis of application under the Convention for 2015 (Global Analysis, Document 11A of September 2017, available at <hcch.net/en/publications-and-studies>).

Article 36 of the 1980 Hague Abduction Convention allows two or more Contracting States to agree among themselves to derogate from provisions of the Convention, in order to limit the restrictions to the return of the child implied by the Convention. It is this provision of the Convention that provides the authorisation for Member States to curtail reliance, inter alia, on the 'grave risk' exception. This has been done in Article 11 of the Brussels IIa Regulation,[12] in particular paragraph 4 thereof. That provision stipulates that 'a court cannot refuse to return a child on the basis of Article 13b of the 1980 Hague Abduction Convention if it is established that adequate arrangements have been made to secure the protection of the child after his or her return'.

Article 11(4) of the Brussels IIa Regulation is couched in general terms: it suffices that 'adequate arrangements have been made to secure the protection of the child' after the return. Such adequate arrangements might take the form of an order protecting the child, taken by the courts of the Member State to which the child is to be returned, which will normally have jurisdiction on the substance of parental responsibility by virtue of either Article 8 or 10 of the Brussels IIa Regulation. However, such 'adequate arrangements' are certainly not limited to such orders, and, in particular, the wording of Article 11(4) does not exclude from its scope measures that are taken by the court in the Member State of 'refuge' that orders the return of the child.[13]

The deficiency in the Brussels IIa Regulation is, of course, that, while Article 11(4) does not exclude such measures from its scope, the Regulation makes no positive provision to allow this to be done. In particular, the court in the Member State of refuge will not normally have jurisdiction on the substance of parental responsibility, and thus cannot take measures that will be recognised and enforced pursuant to the Regulation in the other Member States; at most, it will have the limited local jurisdiction conferred by Article 20, which permits the taking of provisional, including protective, measures in respect of a child present in that State, but does not allow such measures to circulate.[14]

---

12 Council Regulation (EC) No 2201/2003 of 27 November 2003 concerning jurisdiction and the recognition and enforcement of judgments in matrimonial matters and the matters of parental responsibility, repealing Regulation (EC) No 1347/2000 [2003] OJ L338/1.

13 See the contribution by C. Honorati, section 4, in this volume.

14 On this point, see, in particular, Case C-256/09, *Purrucker v. Valles Pérez ('Purrucker I')*, ECLI:EU:C:2010:437.

In England and Wales, courts have grappled with this issue, and have proved quite inventive in finding solutions. Unfortunately, the most popular of those solutions, as we shall see, is (most probably) not permitted by the Brussels IIa Regulation.

In *RB v. DB*,[15] the solution adopted by Mostyn J. was to (purport to) take protective measures under Article 11 of the 1996 Hague Child Protection Convention. That provision bears some similarities to its counterpart in Article 20 of the Brussels IIa Regulation (in particular, jurisdiction is based on the presence of the child and urgency), but also has one crucial difference: there is no impediment to such measures being recognised and enforced in the other Contracting States,[16] albeit that such measures will lapse once they are superseded by any measures that the situation requires.

In that judgment, the judge ordered the return of the child from England and Wales to Austria, pursuant to the Abduction Convention. He also adopted protective measures, purporting to base his jurisdiction on Article 11 of the 1996 Convention, but without giving any consideration as to whether this was legally possible. The difficulty with such an approach, of course, is that it seems to fly in the face of Article 61 of the Brussels IIa Regulation, which governs the relation between that Regulation and the 1996 Convention. It stipulates that, where the child is habitually resident in a Member State, the Regulation applies. This can only mean that, in such a case, in the event of overlap between the two instruments, the provisions of the Regulation prevail.[17]

The enabling provision in the 1996 Convention, namely Article 52, allows groups of Contracting States, including regional organisations, to conclude regional agreements where the child is habitually resident in one of the State Parties to such an agreement. Unlike the equivalent provision in Article 36 of the 1980 Hague Abduction Convention, which, as discussed above, authorises such regional arrangements only where such arrangements make it easier to return the child, Article 52 of the

15 2015 EWHC 1817 (Fam).

16 This conclusion is not stated explicitly in Article 11, but para. 72 of the Explanatory Report to the Convention makes it clear that this is the case.

17 Along the same lines, see R. Hausmann, *Internationales und Europäisches Familienrecht*, 2nd ed., CH Beck, Munich 2018, p. 632: *'Auf dem Gebiet der internationalen Zuständigkeit verdrängt die EuEheVO … das KSÜ immer dann, wenn das Kind seinen gewöhnlichen Aufenthalt in einem Mitgliedstaat hat'* (in the area of international jurisdiction the Brussels IIa Regulation always applies instead of the Convention where the child has his habitual residence in a Member State).

1996 Convention contains a more general authorisation. Article 52 is based solely on the habitual residence of the child, which is not subject to any condition that the regional arrangement must provide for better or more complete remedies than the Convention does. It is, thus, likely that Article 20 of the Regulation prevails over Article 11 of the Convention, despite the fact that the latter provides for a more efficient remedy. The formulation of Article 61 of the Regulation does not allow courts to simply pick and choose whichever of the two instruments provides the more efficient remedies in a given case.

De lege ferenda, there is a strong argument for amending Article 20 of the Brussels IIa Regulation so as to bring it into line with the 1996 Convention. As will be seen below, this has been achieved, at least to a certain extent, with the enactment of the Brussels IIb Regulation.[18]

In *RB v. BD*, Mostyn J. added, almost as something of an afterthought, that he could also base jurisdiction to take such protective measures on Regulation 606/2013. In this he was, it is submitted, correct.[19] Although Article 2(1) of that Regulation specifies that it does not apply to protection measures that fall within the scope of the Brussels IIa Regulation, it would be unnecessarily strict to interpret this as excluding recourse to Regulation 606/2013 where a protection measure technically falls within the scope of the Brussels IIa Regulation, but cannot be enforced in other Member States. If this interpretation were not correct, it could mean that a court could avail itself of Regulation 606/2013 to take measures to protect the abducting parent who accompanied the child back to the Member State from which he or she had been wrongfully removed, but could not do so in the case of the child, which could scarcely have been within the contemplation of the legislature.

It is perhaps surprising that his suggestion has not been more widely taken up in other Member States, since it would provide for an effective solution by plugging the gap left open by Article 20 of the Brussels IIa Regulation.

---

18 Council Regulation (EU) 2019/1111 of 25 June 2019 on jurisdiction, the recognition and enforcement of decisions in matrimonial matters and the matters of parental responsibility, and on international child abduction (recast) [2019] OJ L178/1.

19 Although Recital 11 of Regulation 606/2013 specifies that the functioning of that Regulation should not 'interfere' with the functioning of the Brussels IIa Regulation, there is nothing to suggest that a court seised of a matter may not avail itself of a remedy under the later Regulation, where the Brussels IIa Regulation does not offer one.

3. POTENTIAL APPLICABILITY OF PART III OF THE BRUSSELS IIB REGULATION TO PROTECTION OF THE ABDUCTING PARENT IN RETURN PROCEEDINGS

In the Brussels IIb Regulation, the treatment of international child abduction, which was dealt with quite summarily in Article 11 of the Brussels IIa Regulation, has been greatly expanded, and is now the subject of an entire chapter, Chapter III. Detailed consideration of the new chapter is beyond the scope of this contribution. What is significant for our purposes is that ex-Article 11(4) is replicated (with slight changes) as Article 27(3), and supplemented by a new provision, Article 27(5). This latter provision entitles a court that orders the return of the child to take protective measures to protect the child from the grave risk referred to in Article 13 of the Abduction Convention.

Recital 46 gives as examples of such measures an order that the child continue to reside with the primary carer, or an order on contact. In addition, Recital 45 gives examples of 'adequate arrangements' within the meaning of Article 27(3), citing an order that the applicant (i.e. the applicant in the return proceedings) refrain from approaching the child. Although that Recital seems to envisage that such an order would be made by the courts of the Member State to which the child is being returned, there seems to be no reason why such an order cannot, equally, fall within the scope of Article 27(5).

The legal basis for jurisdiction under the Regulation in these circumstances is Article 15 (the successor of Article 20 of the Brussels IIa Regulation), which confers jurisdiction on the basis of the presence of the child. Normally, as seen above, provisional measures taken on this basis have only a local effect, which would make them of no use where they are intended to protect the child in another Member State.

The legislature did not solve this problem by aligning Article 15 to Article 11 of the 1996 Convention, so as to allow such protective measures to circulate in all cases. However, it provided for a tailor-made solution to accommodate the situation addressed by Article 27(5). By virtue of Article 2(1)(b) of the new Regulation, provisional measures, including protective measures, ordered by a court pursuant to Article 27(5) in conjunction with Article 15, are deemed to be 'decisions' for the purposes of Chapter IV on recognition and enforcement and, thus, can be enforced in the other Member States, in particular the Member State to which the child is to be returned.

This is clearly a sensible solution, which will enable appropriate measures to be taken, and should, thus, allow more abducted children to be returned to the Member State from which they have been wrongfully removed.

One significant question is whether the possibility, conferred by Article 27(5), to protect the child upon his or her return embraces the power to take such measures to protect the abducting parent upon return. The question is clearly of considerable significance in the case where there is a risk of domestic violence. The point will, at some stage, need to be addressed by the CJEU, but, in this writer's view, the expression 'measures to protect the child' is sufficiently broad to cover measures to protect the abducting parent, where it is necessary or desirable for that parent to accompany the child.

If this conclusion is correct, this would effectively make Regulation 606/2013 redundant in this field, since the Brussels IIb Regulation would confer powers on the courts of the Member State of refuge that are at least as effective as those conferred by Regulation 606/2013.

On the other hand, if it is not correct, it would still be possible for a court to take measures to protect the child, pursuant to Article 27(5) of the Brussels IIb Regulation, and to supplement those measures by taking measures on the basis of Regulation 606/2013 to protect the abducting parent who is to accompany the child. In both cases, the protective measures can circulate and, thus, be enforced in the Member State to which the child is to be returned.

4. CONCLUSION

Regulation 606/2013 has had very limited use, but, nevertheless, has a potential role to play where a court seised of a Hague return application wishes to order the child to be returned, despite the taking parent alleging that the child will be exposed to a 'grave risk' within the meaning of Article 13 of the 1980 Abduction Convention, since the court can order measures of protection that can be enforced in the Member State to which the child and parent will be returned.

The existing gap in the Brussels IIa Regulation, which does not allow such protective measures to circulate, is largely (possibly completely) plugged by the new provisions of the Brussels IIb Regulation, which will make Regulation 606/2013 largely redundant in this field.

PROTECTIVE AND RETURN-SEEKING PARENTS

The Power of Language in Child Abduction Law

Johanna NIEMI and Laura-Maria POIKELA

1. INTRODUCTION

The main aim of the international regulation of situations in which a parent has taken their child and moved to another country before a looming divorce proceeding and custody trial has been to secure the child's quick return to the country of shared domicile. The main reasoning behind this approach is that a parent should not be able to manipulate the jurisdiction of the custody dispute to be more favourable to them, and should not be changing the child's environment to gain an advantage in the custody dispute.[1] The primary purposes of the Hague Convention on Child Abduction ('the Convention' or 'HCCA'),[2] as the main instrument governing international child abductions, were, and still are, to preserve the status quo, to ensure the prompt return to the *status quo ante*,[3] and to deter parents from crossing international borders in search of a more sympathetic court. These kinds of motivations led to the adoption of the Convention in 1980, and the European Union (EU) essentially transferred the procedural regulations of the Convention into the Brussels IIa Regulation in 2003.[4] As a result of a complex process of negotiation, the Hague Convention was, ultimately, preserved for intra-member State abductions, but complemented by more stringent EU rules.[5]

Before the Hague Convention on Child Abduction, two other Hague Conventions addressed international family law and child law matters. Neither of these, the Hague Convention on the Guardianship of Infants (1902) or the Hague Convention on the Protection of Minors (1961), mention international child abductions. The need to agree on rules regarding international child abductions was recognised in the late 1970s, when the number of divorces began to increase. Both the Council of Europe and the Hague Conference on International Private Law started to work on a Convention in this area. During the preparations, the US-based lawyer Adair Dyer prepared a research report combining legal and sociological approaches to international child abductions.[6] For decades, researchers,

1 E. Pérez-Vera, *Explanatory Report on the HCCH Child Abduction Convention*, Acts and Documents of the XIVth Session, Hague Conference on Private International Law, The Hague 1981 <https://assets.hcch.net/docs/a5fb103c-2ceb-4d17-87e3-a7528a0d368c.pdf> accessed 26.05.2021, e.g. para. 15.

2 Convention of 25 October 1980 on the Civil Aspects of International Child Abduction, referred to as 'the Convention'.

3 Restoring the circumstances before the abduction, by returning the child to the State of habitual residence.

4 Council Regulation (EC) No 2201/2003 of 27 November 2003 concerning jurisdiction and the recognition and enforcement of judgments in matrimonial matters and the matters of parental responsibility, repealing Regulation (EC) No 1347/2000 [2003] OJ L338/1. From 1 August 2022, Council Regulation (EU) 2019/1111 of 25 June 2019 on jurisdiction, the recognition and enforcement of decisions in matrimonial matters and the matters of parental responsibility, and on international child abduction (recast) [2019] OJ L178/1, shall replace Reg. 2201/2003.

5 P. McEleavy, 'The European Court of Human Rights and the Hague Convention: Prioritising Return or Reflection?' (2015) 62 *Netherlands International Law Review* 365–405, 372.

6 A. Dyer, *Report on International Child Abduction by One Parent ('Legal Kidnapping')*, Preliminary Doc. 1, Actes et Documents of the XIVth Session, Hague Conference on Private International Law (1978).

professionals, officials and courts all over the world have relied on the Dyer Report and the Explanatory Report by Elisa Pérez-Vera in interpreting the Convention. The final draft for the Convention was presented to the Hague Conference in November 1979. The 23 countries participating in the process adopted the Hague Convention on Child Abduction in 1980.[7]

There are several reasons to ask whether the Convention is still adequate today, and its motivations still relevant, especially in Europe. The world is not the same as it was in 1980. First, the regulation of jurisdiction within the EU has evolved in child disputes since the enactment of the Brussels IIa Regulation, which includes rules on jurisdiction within EU countries over such matters. Secondly, and also related to the processing of international disputes, cooperation among the courts across borders has developed to include, for example, possibilities for the electronic presentation of evidence, either in the course of cooperation between the courts, or directly from a witness or a party to a court in another country, as well as efficient service of documents, and enforcement of judgments across borders.

A third development since the 1970s has been an increase in research on violence against women and children (VAW and VAC, respectively).[8] We know much more about these forms of violence today than we did in the 1970s. It has not been good news. There is a greater level of violence within families than was previously known, and such violence is more serious. Domestic violence has an effect on children, even when they are not the direct victims.[9] The European Parliament has commented that:

> violence against women goes hand in hand with violence against children and has an impact on children's psychological wellbeing and lives … violence against women as mothers directly and indirectly affects and has a long lasting

---

7 B. Bodenheimer, 'The Hague Draft Convention on International Child Abduction' (1980) 14 *Family Law Quarterly* 2. The Hague Conference on Private International Law (HCCH) currently has 89 Members (August 2021).

8 European Union Agency for Fundamental Rights, *Violence against Women: An EU-wide Survey*, FRA 2014 <https://fra.europa.eu/sites/default/files/fra_uploads/fra-2014-vaw-survey-main-results-apr14_en.pdf> accessed 29.09.2021; C. Hagemann-White, L. Kelly and R. Romkens, *Feasibility Study to Assess the Possibilities, Opportunities and Needs to Standardise National Legislation on Violence against Women, Violence against Children and Sexual Orientation Violence*, European Union 2011 <https://op.europa.eu/en/publication-detail/-/publication/cc805fb4-c139-4ac0-99b7-b0dad60179f7/language-en#> accessed 29.09.2021.

9 S. Wood and M. Sommers, 'Consequences of Intimate Partner Violence on Child Witnesses: A Systematic Review of the Literature' (2011) 24(4) *Journal of Child and Adolescent Psychiatric Nursing* 223.

> negative impact on their children's emotional and mental health, and can create a cycle of violence and abuse which is perpetuated through generations.[10]

The fourth development, relevant for cross-border relationships, is the change in the nature of violence and harassment. More and more harassment, threats and defamation take place in the electronic world, including through personal communications such as emails and text messages, and social media activities.[11]

The regulation of cross-border child removals (abductions) does not pay much attention to the reasons why the removal has taken place, but prioritises swift return of the child. There are reasons to reconsider how the courts handle cases in which a parent has removed the child from a violent home.

Furthermore, times have also changed regarding international and transnational families and their situations. An increasing number of families, especially within the EU, live either temporarily or permanently in a country in which only one, or neither, of the parents were born. This free movement, where people work and/or study in another Member State, or move within the EU after first settling there from a non-Member State, have contributed to families being more international and multicultural than before. When a parent moves with their child to another country, it is more likely to be to a country where the parent already has social contacts.[12] It is likely that the parents who move with their children to another country are a more diverse group than during the drafting of the Convention in the 1970s.

The purpose of this contribution is to ask how international communities, the EU, and EU States have responded to these changes to the nature of situations in which a child is moved from one country to another EU country. More specifically, we are interested in how the Convention and the Brussels IIa system of a swift return of the child to the country of habitual residence functions in circumstances where there are indications of domestic violence.

---

10 European Parliament resolution 26 November 2009 on the elimination of violence against women (P7-TA (2009) 0098).

11 European Institute for Gender Equality, *Cyber violence against women and girls*, EIGE 2017 <https://eige.europa.eu/publications/cyber-violence-against-women-and-girls> accessed 29.09.2021.

12 Taylor and Freeman have identified the desire to move to a familiar environment with support of the extended family as the main reason for parents to move: N. Taylor and M. Freeman, 'International Research Evidence on Relocation: Past, Present, and Future' (2010) 44(3) *Family Law Quarterly* 3.

The growing body of international law on violence against women seeks to protect both women and children. In the European legal domain, the Istanbul Convention and the European instruments on cross-border enforcement of protection orders[13] strengthen the protection against violence, albeit in different ways. This body of law has evolved separately from the regulations on child abduction. The aim of this contribution is to bring together these two regulatory spheres: child abduction law and the law of protection against violence. Since the aims of these types of law are far apart – rapid return of the child versus protection against violence – it is not surprising that the language of their respective regulations and texts are quite different. Therefore, we start with an analysis of the two discourses: one of swift return, and the other of protection.

The theoretical and methodological basis of this contribution is social constructionism, according to which language not only reflects or corresponds to reality, but also constructs it. Thus, the words and concepts that we use shape social relations, social structures and, finally, concrete reality.[14] This kind of thinking is not unfamiliar to lawyers and legal researchers. Obviously, legislation and legal decisions have effects that change relations, and lead to changes in environments. Social constructionism goes further than this, because the power of language and discourses to construct reality are not limited to such intentional actions as enacting laws and giving legal decisions, but also encompass indirect and unintended effects. Thus, in the legal setting, the attention of the researcher turns to the broader use of language and concepts, and to how the discourses construct identities, actions and relations.[15] As per Carol Bacchi, we are particularly interested in how legal language constructs a certain social problem, such as the removal of a child.[16]

---

13 Council of Europe Convention on the preventing and combating violence against women and domestic violence; referred to as the 'Istanbul Convention' [2011]; Regulation (EU) No 606/2013 of the European Parliament and of the Council of 12 June 2013 on mutual recognition of protection measures in civil matters [2013] OJ L181/4; Directive 2011/99/EU of the European Parliament and of the Council of 13 December 2011 on the European protection order (EPO) OJ L338/2.

14 P. Berger and T. Luckmann, *The Social Construction of Reality*, Penguin Books, London 1991.

15 K. Nieminen, 'The Law, the Subject and Disobedience: Inquiries into Legal Meaning Making', Dissertation, University of Helsinki 2017 <https://helda.helsinki.fi/handle/10138/195911> accessed 29.09.2021.

16 C. Bacchi, *Analysing policy: What's the problem represented to be?*, Pearson Education, London 2009.

Social constructionism is the theory behind several methodological approaches, in particular discourse analysis[17] and narrative analysis.[18] In this contribution, the concept analysis is informed by discourse analysis: in particular, how the key concepts of child abduction and protection against violence depict the *actions* and the *parent*, and what kind of effects these conceptualisations have on the lives of the parents.

Section 2 of this contribution analyses the language of relevant international law. First, in section 2.1, it looks at the language of the central legal instruments – the Convention and the Brussels IIa Regulation – focusing on what is generally referred to as child abduction. The language in these instruments is gender- neutral. Thereafter, section 2.2 comments on the different approach chosen by the recent EU-funded project 'Protection of Abducting Mothers in Return Proceedings' (POAM),[19] which uses gendered language.

Next, section 3 explores the language of international law on violence against women, in which VAW is, today, seen as a violation of human rights. In this context, protection against violence has become a key concept, as is exemplified by the EU documents regulating cross-border enforcement of protection orders. Finally, section 4 brings these two discussions together, and refers to the case law of the European Court of Human Rights (ECtHR), which has in several cases tried to consolidate the requirements of the Convention, on the one hand, and the protection of private and family life according to the European Convention of Human Rights (ECHR), on the other.

2. THE LANGUAGE OF THE REMOVAL OF A CHILD

2.1. THE CONVENTION AND BRUSSELS IIA: WRONGFUL REMOVAL

The private international law term for circumstances in which a parent moves to another country with their child, without permission from

17 J. Niemi-Kiesiläinen, P. Honkatukia and M. Ruuskanen, 'Legal Texts as Discourses' in E.M. Svensson, Å. Gunnarsson and M. Davies (eds), *Exploiting the Limits of Law*, Routledge, Ashgate 2007, 69–88.

18 R. Wharton and D. Miller, 'New Directions in Law and Narrative' (2016) *Law, Culture and the Humanities* 1.

19 Best Practice Guide – Protection of Abducting Mothers in Return Proceedings (hereafter 'POAM Best Practice Guide'), reprinted in this volume.

the other parent who has custody (usually shared) of the child, is child abduction. It is clear even to a non-native speaker of English that the term 'abduction' denotes a serious wrongdoing. The *Cambridge Dictionary* defines abduction as 'the *act* of making a *person* go *somewhere* with you, *especially* using *threats* or *violence*'.[20]

In the Hague Convention on Child Abduction, this terminology is present only in the title. The Convention text itself does not use the word 'abduction'. The State Parties decided to avoid using the word 'abduction' in the Convention text because of the stigmatising connotation of the word. The original Convention countries were of the opinion that the Convention text should not include any criminal connotations.[21] Thus, especially when it seems that domestic violence might be a crucial factor behind the parent's decision to move or even flee with the child, or there is at least evidence or a reasonable suspicion that this is the case, terminology such as 'abduction' and 'abductor' places the situation in a more criminal setting than originally intended by the Convention Member States.

Nevertheless, the catchily worded concept 'child abduction' has conquered the world. Even translations of the word replicate the terms 'abduction' or 'child kidnapping'. The word abduction is part of the legal language in international civil law, as well as national criminal law, and is widely used by authorities, researchers and professionals.

The EU has incorporated the Hague Convention rules on child abduction into EU law with the Brussels IIa Regulation on jurisdiction and recognition of judgments in matrimonial matters and parental responsibility.[22] This Regulation mentions the word 'abduction' in the title of the key article, Article 10: 'Jurisdiction in cases of child abduction'.

---

20 <https://dictionary.cambridge.org/dictionary/english/abduction> accessed 29.09.2021 (emphasis added).

21 A. Passanante, 'International Parental Kidnapping: The Call for an Increased Federal Response' (1996) 34 *Columbia Journal of Transnational Law* 677, 690; D. Leslie, 'A Difficult Situation Made Harder: A Parent's Choice between Civil Remedies and Criminal Charges in International Child Abduction' (2008) 36(2) *Georgia Journal of International and Comparative Law* 381, 383–412 <https://digitalcommons.law.uga.edu/gjicl/vol36/iss2/4> accessed 29.09.2021; B. Bodenheimer, 'The Hague Draft Convention on International Child Abduction' (1980) 14 *Family Law Quarterly* 2: 'The word abduction appears only in the [HCCA] title and is there qualified by the word's civil aspects. It was felt that abduction standing by itself may have a criminal law connotation.'

22 Council Regulation (EC) No 2201/2003 of 27 November 2003 concerning jurisdiction and the recognition and enforcement of judgments in matrimonial matters and the matters of parental responsibility, repealing Regulation (EC) No. 1347/2000 [2003] OJ L338/1.

The Brussels IIb Regulation repeats the same language in its title and chapter title.[23] Otherwise, both the Convention and the Brussels IIa Regulation use the terminology 'wrongful removal or retention' of the child, emphasising that the removal has been in contravention of the right of the child's (other) custodian.[24]

The Hague Convention identifies the child as the main victim of the removal. The purpose of the Convention is 'to protect children internationally from the harmful effects of their wrongful removal or retention'.[25] The Convention does not state who the abductors would be. However, since the Convention is connected to custody disputes, and is intended to deter abductions that are presumed to have occurred for the purposes of forum shopping, and therefore regulates international jurisdiction, it is clear that the main actors will be the parents of the child. The Convention does not even mention the word 'parent', let alone 'mothers' or 'fathers'. Likewise, the Brussels IIa Regulation, notwithstanding its core concept of parental responsibility, defines the party whose rights have been violated, in sterile terminology, as 'a person, an institution or any other body'.[26]

Indeed, even if the aim of these instruments is to protect children, both instruments state that the violation is 'in breach of rights of custody', attributed to a person, an institution or any other body.[27] Neither the Convention nor the Brussels IIa Regulation mentions the possibility that the person moving with the child may have, and often has, custody rights (joint or sole) over the child. Having custody rights includes, in many jurisdictions, the right to decide where the child lives.

Even though the language of the Convention and the Brussels IIa Regulation is gender-neutral, and devoid of the nature of the parental relationship, the *Explanatory Report to the Convention* describes the child's relationship to the person, institution or any other body that has the custody rights in the following terms:

> the true victim of the 'childnapping' is the child himself, who suffers from the sudden upsetting of his stability, the traumatic loss of contact with the parent

---

23 The term 'child abduction' is in the title of the recast Regulation 2019/1111, and Chapter III is titled 'International Child Abductions'.

24 HCCA, Art. 3; Reg. 2201/2003, Art. 2.11; Brussels IIb Regulation 2019/1111 (hereafter 'Brussels IIb Reg.'), Ch. III.

25 HCCA Preamble.

26 Reg. 2201/2003, Art. 10(a); Brussels IIb Reg., Ch. III, Art. 22; also, HCCA, Art. 3.1.

27 Reg. 2201/2003, Art. 3.1; HCCA, Art. 3.1.

> who has been in charge of his upbringing, the uncertainty and frustration which come with the necessity to adapt to a strange language, unfamiliar cultural conditions and unknown teachers and relatives.[28]

The language used by the *Explanatory Report* is such as is typically connected to the mother/child relationship: for example, according to the attachment theory, 'traumatic loss' and 'parent in charge of his upbringing'. In gender-neutral terms, this language assumes that the violated custodian has been in charge of the psychological needs and everyday care of the child.

In addition, the original Convention scenario describes the country to which the child is wrongfully removed as totally strange and unfamiliar to the child. While some child abductions correspond to this description, there are reasons to doubt whether these are typical circumstances in Europe, where people can easily keep contact with their former home countries during holidays, and via various media, such as phones, mail, electronic channels and social media.

During the 1970s, the presumption of the Convention Member States was that the abductor would not hold custody of their abducted child or, at least, was not their primary carer. Thus, the removal or retention would often lead to the breach of the custody rights of the 'left-behind' parent. Only later, through research, and with case law, has it become clearer that the 'abductor' is just as likely to be a parent with sole or joint custody of the child, or the primary carer. In recent times, and with the increasing amount of ECtHR case law on child abduction, the original idea of the abductor not having custody rights over the child, and abducting the child in order to acquire custody rights in a different jurisdiction, has changed significantly.

In addition, a notable share of the parents who move with their children are mothers. Beaumont, Walker and Holliday[29] conclude that, in

---

28 E. Pérez-Vera, *Explanatory Report on the HCCH Child Abduction Convention*, Acts and Documents of the XIVth Session, Hague Conference on Private International Law, The Hague 1981 <https://assets.hcch.net/docs/a5fb103c-2ceb-4d17-87e3-a7528a0d368c.pdf> accessed 26.05.2021, para. 24, quoting A. Dyer, *Report on International Child Abduction by One Parent ('Legal Kidnapping')*, Preliminary Doc. 1, Actes et Documents of the XIVth Session, Hague Conference on Private International Law (1978).

29 P. Beaumont, L. Walker and J. Holliday, 'Conflicts of EU Courts on Child Abduction: the reality of Article 11(6–8) Brussels IIa proceedings across the EU' (2016) 12(2) *Journal of Private International Law* 211–60. The article contains the final findings from a research project that sought to collect data on non-return orders

the majority of cases in which a court has based their refusal of return on Article 13 of the Convention, the majority of the parents moving with the child (84%) have been mothers.[30] Furthermore, the abducting parent was usually returning, with the child, to the State of the parent's nationality. A key finding of the study was that, in just under half of the cases (31 out of 63), the non-return had been ordered on the basis of the Article 13(1)(b) 'grave risk of harm' provision. In 29 of these cases, the parent moving with the child was the mother.[31] The gender-neutral language hides a gendered but varying reality.

2.2. THE POAM PROJECT: ABDUCTIVE MOTHERS AND LEFT-BEHIND FATHERS

The EU-funded POAM project on the protection of mothers who have fled an abusive partner uses different terminology from the Convention and the Brussels IIa Regulation.[32] Unlike these instruments, POAM uses gendered terminology: it speaks about 'abducting mothers' and 'left-behind fathers'.

As already mentioned, research has shown that the majority of 'abducting parents', at least in the EU, are mothers.[33] Studies on abducting mothers indicate that many of them are victims of some degree of abuse, and some even of violence.[34] Against this background, there is reason to ask how appropriate the term 'abduction' actually is, in such cases.

The process of return without delay (without even an investigation into the child's best interest)[35] relies on the original idea that abductions happen

---

made between 1 March 2005 and 28 February 2014, where there were Brussels IIa, Art. 11(6–8) proceedings arising from HCCA, Art. 13. The study identified 63 such cases, but did not look at non-returns based on the HCCA, Art. 13 across the EU. The study covered only non-returns that resulted in Art. 11(6–8) proceedings.

30 The authors of the article use the term 'abducting parent'.

31 There were a further seven cases where the non-return was ordered on the basis of grave risk combined with the child's objections, and two cases where it was combined with one of the provisions in Art. 13(1)(a).

32 POAM, 'Protection of Abducting Mothers in Return Proceedings: Intersection between Domestic Violence and Parental Child Abduction' <https://research.abdn.ac.uk/poam/> accessed 29.09.2021.

33 K. Trimmings, *Child Abduction Within the European Union*, Hart Publishing, Oxford 2013, p. 78.

34 M. Freeman, *Parental Child Abduction: The Long-Term Effects*, International Centre for Family Law, Policy, and Practice, 2014, p. 20 <http://www.famlawandpractice.com/researchers/longtermeffects.pdf> accessed 29.09.2021.

35 The Convention does not mention the best interest of the child. The Explanatory Report includes a discussion of the best interest of the child, concluding: 'Now, the

in connection with, or at the time of, the custody and contact rights being under dispute, or such a dispute being pending, in a national court of the State of habitual residence. In reality, the reasons for such a move could be, for example, the proximity to the parents' own parents, loneliness in the country of the spouse,[36] access to better healthcare and social security, or a new partner or job in the parent's original home country. To lump all of these, and other possible legitimate reasons, under the derogatory term 'abduction' is rather arbitrary, to say the least.

It is suggested that the term 'left-behind fathers', used in recent literature, including that published by the Hague Conference and, indeed, the POAM, is no less problematic in its connotations. It implies pity for the father: a mother who leaves is still a stigmatising label in all cultures. It implies victimhood, and brings to mind popular movies, such as *Three Men and a Baby* or *Kramer vs. Kramer*, which depict the burden of the father left behind with his child, with either humour or compassion. While a parent certainly has a right to seek the return and the custody of their child, generalising assumptions about why parents do so can be dangerous. The reasons may vary from a genuine concern about the well-being of the child, or about being prejudiced in a custody dispute, to a wish to control the protection-seeking parent, or to get an abused spouse to return. The term 'left behind' implies wrongdoing on the part of the other parent, towards the parent without whose consent the removal of the child has happened. Further, 'left behind' is, in our opinion, especially poorly suited to cases where domestic violence has been the reason for fleeing or moving with the child.

Overall, the majority of parents who move to another country, or plead for the return of their child, have a reason to do so. Broad assumptions and moral statements about their reasons are likely to be unjustified in a large number of cases. We suggest that a more neutral terminology would be appropriate, in relation to both the sex of the parent and the reason behind the move. Regarding cases involving abuse and/or domestic violence, a more proper and adequate explanatory term would be 'protecting parent'

right not to be removed or retained in the name of more or less arguable rights concerning its person is one of the most objective examples of what constitutes the interests of the child.': E. Pérez-Vera, *Explanatory Report on the HCCH Child Abduction Convention*, Acts and Documents of the XIVth Session, Hague Conference on Private International Law, The Hague 1981 <https://assets.hcch.net/docs/a5fb103c-2ceb-4d17-87e3-a7528a0d368c.pdf> accessed 26.05.2021, para. 24.

36 In HCCA terminology, the child's habitual residence before the abduction.

or 'protection-seeking parent'. More generally, we could speak about 'parents who move with their children'. To take a step further again, evaluating and recognising all the circumstances of each particular case, and depending on the relevant facts, even 'fleeing parent' might be a more suitable term than 'abducting parent'. As a neutral term for the parent who stays in the country from which the other parent has moved, we suggest 'return-applying parent' or 'parent seeking the return' of the child. In all cases, parents have a right to expect that we use respectful language about their choices.

3. THE LANGUAGE OF PROTECTION AGAINST VIOLENCE

3.1. VIOLENCE AGAINST WOMEN IN INTERNATIONAL LAW

In international law, there has been a thorough paradigmatic change in relation to violence against women and children. Traditionally seen as matters for national law, there are now several international instruments addressing these issues as violations of international law. The CEDAW Committee has even argued that the prohibition of domestic violence is part of customary international law,[37] and thus valid even without an explicit contractual commitment.

Besides the UN instruments, such as the Declaration on the Elimination of Violence against Women[38] and the CEDAW Convention,[39] with the Recommendations and Communications of the CEDAW Committee, the most important European Conventions are the European Human Rights Convention, complemented by the case law of ECtHR, and the Istanbul Convention.[40] According to these instruments, violence against women is a human rights violation, and a form of gender-based discrimination

---

37 Committee on the Elimination of Discrimination against Women (CEDAW), General Recommendation (GR) No. 35 on gender-based violence against women, updating general recommendation No. 19, 14 July 2017.

38 Declaration on the Elimination of Violence against Women, Proclaimed by General Assembly resolution 48/104 of 20 December 1993.

39 UN Convention on the Elimination of All Forms of Discrimination against Women, 18 December 1979.

40 Council of Europe Convention on the preventing and combating violence against women and domestic violence; referred to as the 'Istanbul Convention' [2011].

against women.[41] In the human rights treaties, the States have committed to respecting and ensuring these rights.[42] Regarding violence against women, the ECtHR has specified that States should have adequate legislation and administrative procedures in place, and an obligation for their representatives to act when they are aware of an immediate risk of violence.[43]

While the human rights treaties generally leave the concrete means and ways of fulfilling these commitments to the discretion of the States, a standard of due diligence has evolved for the assessment of such fulfilment.[44] The recommendations on the international law on VAW specify the obligations of the States under such concepts as prevention, protection, prosecution, punishment and redress.[45] The most recent and detailed international instruments – the Istanbul Convention and CEDAW General Recommendation No. 35 – include a long list of measures that a State should implement. Even if the required measures are many, they are not always specific. For example, the Istanbul Convention states that the sanctions for criminal offences of VAW should be punishable by effective, proportionate and dissuasive sanctions (Article 45.1),[46] but does not specify what kind of sanctions qualify as such. Among the measures, the commitment to provide judicial orders for the protection of the victims are most concrete ones. The protection orders may prohibit contact, or order the eviction of the abuser from the shared home.[47] The Istanbul

---

41 E.g. Istanbul Convention, Art. 3. See also Declaration on Violence against Women, 1994, Preamble.

42 E.g. International Covenant on Civil and Political Rights [1966], Art. 1.1; CEDAW GR No. 35 p. 11: respect, protect and fulfil.

43 E.g. *Opuz v. Turkey*, no. 33401/02, ECHR 2009; *Kontrova v. Slovakia*, no. 7510/04, ECHR 2007; *Branko Tomašić v. Croatia*, no. 46598/06, ECHR 2009; *ES. and Others v. Slovakia*, no. 8227/04 ECHR 2009; *Civek v. Turkey*, no. 55354/11, ECHR 2015; *Tërshana v. Albania*, no. 48756/14, ECHR 2020. See also CEDAW, GR No. 35 on gender-based violence against women, updating general recommendation (CEDAW GR No. 35) No. 19, para. 26.

44 E.g. Declaration on the Elimination of Violence against Women, Proclaimed by General Assembly resolution 48/104 of 20 December 1993, Article 4(c); Istanbul Convention, Article 5(2).

45 CEDAW GR No. 35, para. 28; Istanbul Convention, Art. 5(2).

46 In the Istanbul Convention, the monitoring Committee, GREVIO, has a central role in specifying whether the States have concretely fulfilled their duties of due diligence in implementing the Convention.

47 CEDAW, GR No. 35 on gender-based violence against women, updating general recommendation (CEDAW GR No. 35) No. 19, para. 40(b).

Convention is the first binding international instrument that includes a commitment to provide legislation on protection orders: both emergency barring orders and longer protection orders (Articles 52 and 53).

Further, protection is a concept that binds together the general obligation to respect, protect and fulfil human rights, the overall approach of VAW instruments to prevent and protect, and the concrete content of Articles 52 and 53 of the Istanbul Convention. The duty to protect has a specific role and meaning in the European context. Unlike the Anglo-Saxon countries, in which generic temporary protection measures in civil and criminal procedure laws evolved into practical tools for cases of domestic violence during the 1980s and 1990s, the European countries have enacted specific laws for protection against domestic violence. In particular, the Austrian model of a barring order imposed by the police, after which the victim may file for a civil protection order, has been influential in Europe. When the European countries enacted protection order laws in the 1990s and 2000s, they responded to the demands of politicians, and experts on domestic violence. Consequently, the protection order laws do not neatly fall into the division between civil and criminal procedure. Many countries categorise them as administrative, yet the police have a role at the initial stage of the process.[48]

3.2. EUROPEAN UNION AND CROSS-BORDER PROTECTION

The EU is in a unique situation regarding violence against women. Since matters of criminal law generally belong to the competence of the Member States, the role of the EU has been to commission and fund research,[49] as

48 S. Van der Aa et al., *Mapping the Legislation and Assessing the Impact of Protection Orders in the European Member States*, Wolf Legal Publishers, AH Oisterwijk 2015 <http://poems-project.com/> accessed 29.09.2021; T. Freixes and L. Román, *Protection of Gender-based Violence Victims in the European Union: Preliminary Study of the Directive 2011/99/EU on the European Protection Order*, Universitat de Rovia et Virgili/Universitat Autonoma de Barcelona, Tarragona and Barcelona 2014.

49 E.g. European Union Agency for Fundamental Rights, *Violence against Women: An EU-wide Survey*, FRA 2014 <https://fra.europa.eu/sites/default/files/fra_uploads/fra-2014-vaw-survey-main-results-apr14_en.pdf> accessed 29.09.2021; The European Institute for Gender Equality has also carried out studies on the costs of violence, cyber violence and female genital mutilation: <https://eige.europa.eu/gender-based-violence> accessed 29.09.2021.

well as projects and campaigns.[50] In addition, the European Parliament has adopted resolutions on violence against women.[51] The EU recognises VAW within its gender equality framework,[52] which is significant since gender equality has been part of the regulation of the internal market from the beginning of the European Community.[53] Since the Lisbon Treaty of 2009, the EU has committed to combatting discrimination based on sex, among other grounds.[54]

Yet, legal action against VAW at the EU level has been difficult. The EU signed the Istanbul Convention in 2017,[55] but has not ratified it. However, several criminal law and procedural instruments that the EU has adopted, within its wider competences according to Articles 82 and 83 of the Treaty on the Functioning of the European Union (TFEU), are relevant in cases of VAW. In particular, the cross-border recognition of protection orders was a logical step in the EU's work to enhance cross-border cooperation in criminal and civil matters.[56] The adoption of Regulation 606/2013 on Protection Measures and Directive 2011/99/EU on Protection Orders means that the EU has confirmed the protection of victims of violence as a central concept in this judicial cross-border cooperation.

The Regulation and the Directive are generic; that is, they are not gender-specific, nor are they related to violence against women in general, or domestic violence. While the Directive is silent on the specific needs of

---

50 The Daphne Programme has, since 1997, had a significant effect, bringing together research, expert knowledge and stakeholders in VAW and VAC. For a brief history, see <https://ec.europa.eu/justice/grants/results/daphne-toolkit/daphne-toolkit-%E2%80%93-active-resource-daphne-programme_en> accessed 29.09.2021.

51 European Parliament resolution 26 November 2009 on the elimination of violence against women (P7-TA (2009) 0098).

52 <https://ec.europa.eu/info/policies/justice-and-fundamental-rights/gender-equality/gender-based-violence/ending-gender-based-violence_en> accessed 29.09.2021.

53 Consolidated Version of the Treaty on European Union, since Lisbon 2009, Art. 3.3(3).

54 Consolidated Version of the Treaty on the Functioning of the European Union 2009, Art. 19.1, Charter of Fundamental Rights of the European Union (2000/C 364/01) OJ C 364/1.

55 Istanbul Convention, Art. 72.1; The Council Decision (EC) 2017/865, 11 May 2017, on the signing, on behalf of the European Union, of the Council of Europe Convention on preventing and combating violence against women and domestic violence with regard to matters related to judicial cooperation in criminal matters, <https://ec.europa.eu/justice/grants1/programmes-2007-2013/daphne/index_en.htm> accessed 29.09.2021. About the difficulties in the EU decision-making, see: <https://www.europarl.europa.eu/legislative-train/theme-area-of-justice-and-fundamental-rights/file-eu-accession-to-the-istanbul-convention> accessed 04.02.2022.

56 European Parliament resolution of 10 February 2010 on equality between women and men in the European Union (2009/2101(INI)) endorsed the proposal to introduce the European protection order for victims.

protection in relation to domestic or gender-based violence, the preamble to the Regulation states that the protection applies when:

> there exist serious grounds for considering that that person's life, physical or psychological integrity, personal liberty, security or sexual integrity is at risk, for example so as to prevent any form of gender-based violence or violence in close relationships such as physical violence, harassment, sexual aggression, stalking, intimidation or other forms of indirect coercion.[57]

As important as protection is, these instruments are not without complications. They are not frequently applied. A report identified only seven EPOs up until September 2017, compared to the estimated number of 100,000 national protection orders.[58]

Unlike the national European protection measures, the EU Regulation and Directive distinguish between protection in criminal and civil procedures, which is the standard distinction in procedural laws and doctrines. The drafters of the EU instruments have been aware of the varying nature of national protection laws.[59] Thus, the State in which the recognition and execution of the order takes place would recognise the order, notwithstanding its classification in the State that issued the order in the first place:

> Since, in the Member States, different kinds of authorities (civil, criminal or administrative) are competent to adopt and enforce protection measures, it is appropriate to provide a high degree of flexibility in the cooperation mechanism between the Member States under this Directive.[60]

However, the executing State should not execute an order issued by the police as a civil protection measure, according to the preamble of the Regulation.[61] Moreover, the Regulation emphasises the autonomous

---

57 Preamble (6).

58 Committee on Civil Liberties, Justice and Home Affairs; Committee on Women's Rights and Gender Equality, *Report on the implementation of Directive 2011/99 on the European Protection Order* (2016/2329(INI)), 18 March 2018.

59 E.g. Reg. 606/2013, Preamble 15. The 2018 report (ibid.) mentioned that the Directive had not led to notable convergence between the national laws.

60 Dir. 2011/99 Preamble (20).

61 Preamble 13. The articles of the Regulation do not repeat this limitation. On the contrary, Art. 2, defines the 'issuing authority' as any judicial authority, or any other authority designated by a Member State as having competence in the matters falling within the scope of this Regulation.

interpretation of the scope of civil matters in EU law.[62] Consequently, the issuing State and the executing State may classify the order differently. For a recognition process with a purpose of simple and rapid[63] execution of a protection measure, the need for an interpretation of the original order unavoidably causes bureaucratic friction and delay.

As scholars of international private law have pointed out, the Regulation and Directive do not include any rules on international jurisdiction to issue a protection order.[64] The drafters of national and EU protection order laws have not found jurisdiction to be problematic, or in need of regulation, because, in a typical case, a threatened person files for protection in the country where they live or stay, and feel threatened. A standard case includes physical harassment, and the emphasis of the order is on restrictions on physical contact and approach.[65] Even though the orders usually include a prohibition on contacting the threatened party, the focus has been on situations in which both parties reside or stay in the same country. In such situations, both criminal and civil jurisdiction is within that country. The anticipated need for executing the order in another country arises when the protected person moves.[66]

The international jurisdiction becomes more complicated if the parties are in different countries. Such cases are not far-fetched, since electronic threats have become common. For example, in a small sample of interviews with protected persons, all of them had experienced various forms of serious harassment and threats via social media and other electronic media.[67] This should not be an obstacle to cross-border execution of protection, since the EU rules on jurisdiction in civil matters acknowledge jurisdiction in the country where a person has suffered the consequences and harm of an action taken in another EU country.[68] Likewise, national laws regulate international criminal law jurisdiction within the State, and such laws usually acknowledge the damage caused by a crime as a basis for jurisdiction.

---

62 Reg. 606/2013, Preamble 13.

63 Ibid., Art. 1.

64 A. Dutta, 'Cross-Border Protection Measures in the European Union' (2016) 12 *Journal of Private International Law* 169, 171.

65 Reg. 606/2013, Art. 2(1); Dir. 2011/99/EU, Art. 5.

66 Dir. 2011/99/EU, Preamble (24).

67 J. Niemi and S. Majlander, '"Ja ... Minä Jäin Henkiin" Lähestymiskielto ja suojelutarkoitus' [2017] *Lakimies* 747 et seq.

68 Council Regulation (EC) No. 44/2001 of 22 December 2000 on jurisdiction and the recognition and enforcement of judgments in civil and commercial matters OJ L 012, Art. 7.

Thus, the drafters of the EU Regulation and Directive may well have thought that jurisdiction in these matters would not constitute a problem. Private international law scholars, such as Anatol Dutta, are right, however, when they remind us of the EU law principle that recognition of judgments should require clear rules on jurisdiction, particularly if recognition does not require an exequatur.[69] The principles of EU law have evolved, after the Lisbon Treaty. TFEU Articles 81 and 82, which regulate the competence of the EU on recognition of judgments and decisions, do not require EU rules on jurisdiction as a basis of recognition. Furthermore, it is reasonable to think that protection measures against violence and threat, especially against VAW as a human rights violation, are exactly the type of measures that the principle of regulating jurisdiction and recognition in the same EU instrument would not be necessary. Nevertheless, it is understandable that the primacy of protection may turn out to be difficult to reconcile with the regulation of child abduction, which prioritises the swift return of the child.

4. RECONCILIATION OF THE INSTRUMENTS

4.1. THE CONVENTION: GRAVE RISK

The two discourses described above, the 'abduction discourse' and the 'protection against violence discourse', have evolved independently of each other. However, there is a link between the two, in the 'grave risk' exception contained in the Convention and the Brussels IIa Regulation. Article 13(1)(b) of the Convention states that 'the requested state is not bound to order the return of the child if … there is a grave risk that his or her return would expose the child to physical or psychological harm or otherwise place the child in an intolerable situation'.

The grave risk exception seems to be a kind of irritant in the Convention system, which aims at a rapid return of the child. Indeed, as Katarina Trimmings has shown, concern about the overuse of the exception played a major role in the incorporation of the Convention system into the Brussels IIa Regulation in the early 2000s.[70] As a result, the Regulation was

[69] A. Dutta, 'Cross-Border Protection Measures in the European Union' (2016) 12 *Journal of Private International Law* 169.

[70] K. Trimmings, *Child Abduction Within the European Union*, Hart Publishing, Oxford 2013.

complemented by provisions limiting the possibility to refuse the return of a child on the basis of the 'grave risk' exception (Article 11(4)): 'A court cannot refuse to return a child on the basis of Article 13b of the 1980 Hague Convention if it is established that adequate arrangements have been made to secure the protection of the child after his or her return'.[71]

The court should always order the return of the child, if the child can get protection in the Member State of habitual residence. As the Convention and Brussels IIa Regulation do not regulate to where, or to whom, in the country of habitual residence the child should be returned, there is not a straightforward assumption that the child should be returned to the seeking parent, especially in cases where allegations of domestic violence have been made during the process.

Thus, within the EU, the risk of violence, and protection against it – both central concepts in European and national laws and policies against VAW and VAC – are key elements in the evaluation of grave risk, according to the Convention and the Brussels IIa Regulation. Since VAW is increasingly seen as a violation of human rights, there is reason to refer to Article 20 of the Convention: 'The return of the child under the provisions of Article 12 may be refused if this would not be permitted by the fundamental principles of the requested State relating to the protection of human rights and fundamental freedoms'.

According to the Explanatory Report on the Convention, this Article should be used very exceptionally, and its interpretation should not follow the evolving nature of human rights at international level, but refer to the internal interpretations (or lack of them) in the returning State.[72] According to Arenstein, for example, an appeal to Article 20 has never been successful in return proceedings in the United States.[73] However, a distinction

---

71 The Brussels IIb Regulation modifies this point, at Art. 27(3): 'Where a court considers refusing to return a child solely on the basis of point (b) of Article 13(1) of the 1980 Hague Convention, it shall not refuse to return the child if the party seeking the return of the child satisfies the court by providing sufficient evidence, or the court is otherwise satisfied, that adequate arrangements have been made to secure the protection of the child after his or her return.'

72 E. Pérez-Vera, *Explanatory Report on the HCCH Child Abduction Convention*, Acts and Documents of the XIVth Session, Hague Conference on Private International Law, The Hague 1981 <https://assets.hcch.net/docs/a5fb103c-2ceb-4d17-87e3-a7528a0d368c.pdf> accessed 26.05.2021, paras. 11–15. Para. 118 uses the terminology of 'requested state'.

73 R. Arenstein, 'How to Prosecute an International Child Abduction Case under the Hague Convention' (2017) 30 *Journal of the American Academy of Matrimonial Lawyers* 1–26.

between human rights at the international level, and at the national level, is hard to maintain in the EU, where all countries are parties to the ECHR, and adhere to the Fundamental Rights Charter and principles of the EU.[74] In particular, human rights standards regarding gender-based violence, as confirmed by the ECtHR, should be the same for all EU countries. Yet, the ECtHR has found several violations of these.[75]

4.2. ECHR: PROTECTION OF PRIVATE AND FAMILY LIFE IN CHILD ABDUCTION CASES

In the case law of the ECtHR on violence against women, a State violates human rights if either its laws, policies or responses to risk are not at the level of due diligence.[76] Typically, violation of the ECHR occurs when violence is reported to the police, but the police do nothing, or too little in relation to the severity of violence.[77] Thus, the ECtHR makes an assessment, taking into account both the severity of violence and the State's response in protecting or failing to protect against it. The ECtHR has addressed cases of domestic violence as violations of Article 3 (cruel and inhuman treatment), or Article 8 (protection of private life).

Since 2000, the ECtHR has developed valuable case law, under Article 8 of the ECHR, concerning child abduction. First, the Court has concluded that a violation of Article 8 takes place when a country has not taken adequate steps to enforce an applicant's (return-seeking parent's) right to have their child returned,[78] or when the national court has not examined

---

[74] Strictly speaking, the FRC is binding for the Member States only when they implement EU law.

[75] See case law referred to in n. 43.

[76] E.g. Declaration on the Elimination of Violence against Women, Proclaimed by General Assembly resolution 48/104 of 20 December 1993, Art. 4(c); Istanbul Convention, Art. 5(2).

[77] E.g. *Opuz v. Turkey*, no. 33401/02, ECHR 2009. In *Opuz*, the court formulated the duty to take concrete measures if the authorities are aware of an immediate risk. In *Talpis v. Italy* (no. 41237/14, ECHR 2017), the Court concluded that the duty to act cannot be avoided by police passivity. Even though the lethal risk (father killed the son of the applicant) materialised months after the applicant had made a complaint of violence, and after the police inactivity, the Court held that there had been a breach of the Convention.

[78] E.g. *Maire v. Portugal*, no. 48206/99, ECHR 2003: 'the Court considers that each Contracting State must equip itself with an adequate and sufficient legal arsenal to ensure compliance with the positive obligations imposed on it by Article 8 of the Convention and the other international agreements it has chosen to ratify'. Further, 'the Court concludes that the Portuguese authorities failed to make adequate and

the situation adequately.[79] The return-seeking parents in these cases have been both mothers and fathers, but usually fathers.

In cases where the child and/or the protection-seeking parent have been applicants, the Court's focus has been on the procedural requirements of the returning State. The Court has consistently held that the courts in the returning State should give sufficient consideration to the alleged grave risk, in their proceedings.[80]

In the Grand Chamber case *X v. Latvia*, the ECtHR laid down the principles to reconcile the requirements of the Convention and Article 8 of the ECHR. Emphasising the harmonious application of these instruments.[81] The Court stated that, '[t]he decisive issue is whether the fair balance that must exist between the competing interests at stake – those of the child, of the two parents, and of public order – has been struck'.[82] In the following paragraphs, the Court underlined the principle of the best interest of the child, with references to the EU Fundamental Rights Charter and the Brussels IIa Regulation.[83] The conclusion of the Court was that the Convention shares this same philosophy.[84] This is interesting, since the Convention does not include the concept of the 'best interest of the child', besides mentioning the 'interests of children' in its preamble. According to the Explanatory Report, this concept is sociological, cultural, and too vague to be used as a legal standard.[85] According to the Convention, the best interest of wrongfully removed children is their prompt return to the State of habitual residence.

---

effective efforts to enforce the applicant's right to the return of his child and thereby breached his right to respect for his family life as guaranteed by Article 8 of the Convention'. In *Ignaccolo-Zenide v. Romania*, no. 31679/96, ECHR 2000, 'The Court concluded that the Romanian authorities had not taken adequate or appropriate steps to respect the mother's right to have the children returned. By a majority of 6 votes to 1, the Court ruled that Article 8 had in consequence been breached.'

79 E.g. *Ilker Ensar Uyanik v. Turkey*, no. 60328/09, ECHR 2012.

80 E.g., in *B.V. v. Belgium* (no. 61030/08, ECHR 2012) the court had made no risk assessment.

81 *X v. Latvia*, no. 27853/09, 26.11.2013 (Grand Chamber), paras. 93–94.

82 Ibid., para. 95.

83 Ibid., paras. 96–97.

84 Ibid., para. 97, 101.

85 E. Pérez-Vera, *Explanatory Report on the HCCH Child Abduction Convention*, Acts and Documents of the XIVth Session, Hague Conference on Private International Law, The Hague 1981 <https://assets.hcch.net/docs/a5fb103c-2ceb-4d17-87e3-a7528a0d368c.pdf> accessed 26.05.2021, para. 22: 'recourse by internal authorities to such a notion involves the risk of their expressing particular cultural, social etc. attitudes which themselves derive from a given national community and thus basically imposing their own subjective value judgments upon the national community from which the child has recently been snatched'.

The ECtHR, notwithstanding its emphasis on the harmonious interpretation of these instruments, is distant from such an understanding of the best interest of the child. The Court holds that the principle, in the context of Article 8 and the Convention, is mainly procedural: it requires that the States sufficiently evaluate the best interest of the child in the return proceedings, when the grave risk exception has been invoked. Thus, the national court must genuinely take into account the factors allegedly constituting a grave risk, and give a sufficiently reasoned decision on these points.[86]

In *X v. Latvia*, as in other decisions, the ECtHR held that the parent who opposes the return must 'adduce sufficient evidence' of the facts that constitute the exception, such as grave risk.[87] Further, the ECtHR considered that the Latvian courts had not complied with the procedural requirements of Article 8 of the ECHR, in that they had refused to take into consideration an arguable allegation of 'serious risk' to the child in the event of her return to Australia. In *Neulinger and Shuruk v. Switzerland*, the ECtHR considered that the mother would sustain a disproportionate interference with her right to respect for her family life, if she were forced to return to Israel.[88]

It is a common argument that providing evidence of domestic violence and abuse is difficult. However, even in the cases that have come before the ECtHR, there are examples of sufficient evidence. In *OCI v. Romania*, the Court held that a violation of the right to private life had taken place, where there was evidence of ill-treatment of the children in the country of habitual residence.[89] In particular, when the justice system of the habitual State has initiated proceedings concerning such actions, the ECtHR has indicated that the courts in the returning State have a specific duty to examine these.[90] In this regard, protection orders, whether civil or criminal in nature, should give reason for the court in the returning State to examine the situation of the child. Additional evidence, such as

86 *X v. Latvia*, no. 27853/09, 26.11.2013 (Grand Chamber), para. 106.

87 Ibid., para. 116.

88 *Neulinger and Shuruk v. Switzerland*, no. 41615/07, ECHR Grand Chamber 2010.

89 *OCI and others v. Romania*, no. 49450/17, ECHR 2019. The court held that the Romanian authorities had been presented with an arguable allegation of a grave risk of harm, but had failed to examine the allegations of 'grave risk' to the children. The court found that Romania had violated Article 8 of the ECHR: 'The courts should have at least ensured that specific arrangements were made in order to safeguard the children.'

90 *Neulinger and Shuruk v. Switzerland*, no. 41615/07, ECHR Grand Chamber 2010.

the records of child welfare officials, social workers, schools, police and healthcare authorities, should be easy for the actors of the justice system to acquire. Further, cooperation between the officials of the Member States should play a vital role in these cases.[91]

At this point, the criminal justice system provides certain advantages. First, the police have responsibility for collecting the evidence, and the means to do so, including seizure, interrogations and, ultimately, arrest. Criminal protection orders are part of the arsenal of the police, specifically aimed at protection of the victim, and the sanctions for the breach of such orders (usually arrest) are rather straightforward. There is no reason to dismiss civil protection measures, which are equally likely to provoke the duty to examine the grave risk exception. Due to a lower evidentiary threshold, civil protection measures may be easier to obtain.[92] In the light of the case law of the ECtHR, both civil and criminal protection orders should be effective in prompting the returning courts to examine the grave risk exception.

Subsequently, formal questions about jurisdiction and cross-border enforcement of the protection orders and measures should be of lesser importance. The courts in either the State of habitual residence or the returning State may have jurisdiction to impose a protection order, if the threat of violence or harassment is likely to be experienced there. The importance of the orders is primarily evidentiary, and their role is to raise the duty of sufficient examination in the return proceedings.

It is necessary to underline here that a parent can also invoke other types of evidence of grave risk, but since the threshold is 'grave' risk, and there is time pressure, official documents and procedures are most effective.

The Brussels IIa Regulation emphasises the protection of the child in the State of habitual residence (Article 11(4)). It is an open question: what kind of measures would count as adequate protection, according to Article 11(4)? The Brussels IIb Regulation envisions the following:

> Which type of arrangement is adequate in the particular case should depend on the concrete grave risk to which the child is likely to be exposed by the return

---

91 R. Schuz, *The Hague Child Abduction Convention – A Critical Analysis*, Hart Publishing, Oxford and Portland, OR 2013.

92 More about the comparison between civil and criminal protection can be found in L. Sosa, J. Niemi and S. van der Aa, 'Protection Against Violence: The Challenges of Incorporating Human Rights' Standards to Procedural Law' (2019) 41 *Human Rights Quarterly* 939–61.

> without such arrangements. The court seeking to establish whether adequate arrangements have been made should primarily rely on the parties and, where necessary and appropriate, request the assistance of Central Authorities or network judges.[93]

As this quotation indicates, there are no clear guidelines on what qualifies as evidence of adequate protection, nor on how the national courts are to assess and ensure evidence that fulfils the Article 11(4) requirement of 'adequate arrangements to secure the protection of the child'.

The POAM Best Practice Guide endorses the proposition that the allegations of a grave risk of harm should be investigated first and, after this, the court should consider the availability, adequacy and effectiveness of protective measures to dispel the grave risk of harm to the child.[94] We find three problems with this approach. Firstly, in our opinion, domestic violence always constitutes a grave risk to the child. Thus, elaboration of the severity of the 'grave risk' is, in most cases, unnecessary. Secondly, obtaining evidence and elaborating on future protection measures can be difficult and take time, at best, and be speculative, at worst. Thirdly, even though the protection requirement in the Brussels IIa Regulation mentions only the child, in practice the protection is conditional on the returning parent participating in the protection. With a grave risk of harm, the return to the original shared home is not likely to be an option. Many other issues remain, including the question of whether it is enough that the State offers the returning parent a place in a shelter.

A different approach is suggested. The court should, first, examine how the State of habitual residence has responded to the allegations of domestic violence before the abduction. Normally, a victim considers other means of protection before moving to another country. In many cases, the abused parent will already have tried to seek help in the State of habitual residence. Therefore, failures to respond, to offer protection, and to take the necessary and effective steps to protect the child and the parent in the country of habitual residence, will be violations of their fundamental rights. Thus, such failure should encourage the court to refuse the return of the child. In addition, judicial protection orders, either civil or criminal, are often the

---

93 Council Regulation (EU) 2019/1111 of 25 June 2019 on jurisdiction, the recognition and enforcement of decisions in matrimonial matters and the matters of parental responsibility, and on international child abduction (recast), Preamble 45.

94 POAM Best Practice Guide, ss. 5.1.1, 5.1.2, and 5.1.3.1.

first measures to be ordered. However, the perpetrators frequently violate them.[95] Thus, an order, as such, would rarely count as sufficient protection, but can be part of the protective measures. It is important to document any breaches of protection orders, as they are evidence of the insufficiency of protection. Rather than risk lengthening the process, due to investigations into the allegations and available protection measures, the court should focus on evaluating whether, and how, the State of habitual residence has reacted to the family's situation before the abduction.

It is true that some women do not speak about violence to anyone, or make a complaint to the authorities. However, if a victim has evidence of the violence (grave risk), it is possible to produce evidence of other cases in which the State of habitual residence has not protected women who have reported violence. The case law of ECtHR may provide some indicative evidence, and the Committee monitoring the Istanbul Convention provides information about the practices of the State Parties.[96] The investigations into the allegations should be concluded in the same way that the ECtHR investigates and evaluates whether a State has secured that adequate and effective protection measures have been put in place for the child's (and mother's) return.

5. CONCLUSIONS

Since 1980, when the Hague Convention on Child Abduction was adopted, the situations in which a parent may move from one country to another with their child have changed significantly, and, therefore, the original objectives and reasoning behind the Convention might have become, to some extent, outdated. Especially in the EU, with free movement across borders, and common regulations on jurisdiction, the fear of one parent cutting the ties between the child and the other parent by moving the child to an unknown environment and culture may be overstated. Yet, the prejudiced and stigmatising language of 'abductions' persists in the discussion of international moves with children.

Neither the language nor the regulation of cross-border child removals (abductions) pay much attention to the reasons why the removal takes

95 S. Van der Aa et al., *Mapping the Legislation and Assessing the Impact of Protection Orders in European Member States*, Wolf Legal Publishers, AH Oisterwijk 2005. <http://poems-project.com/> accessed 26.05.2021.

96 <https://www.coe.int/en/web/istanbul-convention/grevio> accessed 26.05.2021.

place, but instead prioritise a swift return of the child. The most important exception is a risk of grave harm. Empirical studies have shown that the majority of parents who move with their children are mothers, and that a great majority of parents who invoke the grave risk exception are mothers. This contribution pleads for respectful language towards parents who have experienced the necessity of moving with their children, irrespective of the reasons for the move, which may include fear of violence, ignorance of the international rules on jurisdiction, longing for extended family, or fear of losing the children.

Since 1980, the international law on the protection of children and women, as victims of violence, has evolved remarkably. The Convention on the Rights of the Child, adopted in 1989, gave children protection, and a voice in the international arena. Several international legal instruments seek to protect women against domestic violence and other forms of violence, especially in Europe. These legal instruments, and the growing body of research on the effects of violence, show that living in a violent home is harmful to children. Therefore, there is a strong argument for always holding domestic violence to be a grave risk to a child. The ideology of a rapid return of a child to the country of habitual residence, with limited possibilities to examine the circumstances and the best interest of the child, does not fit in with these developments. The ECtHR has concluded, several times, that returning courts have not made a sufficient examination of the circumstances, and have thus violated the protection of private life, according to Article 8 of the ECHR.

The EU has essentially copied the Hague Convention's rapid return ideology. In addition to this, the Brussels IIa Regulation has underlined the requirement for protective measures after returning the child to the country of habitual residence. However, the Regulation remains silent on what level of protection is sufficient. Moreover, the Regulation only refers to the protection of the child, and not the protection of the parent – usually the mother – who is forced to return, too, if the child is small. According to Bartolini,[97] the ECJ has never reflected on the problems which the return with the child to the place of habitual residence would entail for the parent.[98] Beaumont, Walker and Holliday have suggested that the renewed

---

[97] S. Bartolini, 'In the Name of the Best Interests of the Child: The Principle of Mutual Trust in Child Abduction Cases' (2019) 56 *Common Market Law Review* 1–30.

[98] E.g. P. Beaumont, L. Walker and J. Holliday, 'Parental responsibility and international child abduction in the proposed recast Brussels IIa Regulation and the effect of Brexit on future child abduction proceedings' (2016) 4 *International Family Law Journal* 307–18.

Brussels IIa Regulation could, and should, include a provision that allows urgent protective measures for the returning abducting parent (usually the mother).[99] However, the Brussels IIb Regulation, effective from 1 August 2022, does not include protection measures for the 'abducting parent'. Thus, it remains that the returning parent may file for protection either in the court of the returning State, or in the State of habitual residence. In either case, the EU instruments provide for recognition of both civil and criminal protection measures in other EU countries. While the acknowledgement of the judicial protective measures is welcome, it is necessary to recognise that they are not very effective; breached orders are commonplace. Their most important value is providing proof of grave risk.

This contribution has not examined whether the rather strict time limits in the Convention, and even more so in the Brussels IIa Regulation, are sufficient for the assessment of the grave risk, and the adequacy of protection measures in the country of habitual residence. In the light of the ECtHR case law, an investigation that fulfils the requirements of Article 8 (and possibly Article 6) of the ECHR is hardly possible, in the tight timescales. As long as these two legal instruments – that is, the ECHR and the Brussels IIa Regulation – must be reconciled, the approach of the POAM Best Practice Guide, advocating for the evaluation of the merits of the allegations first, might not be suitable in the majority of cases. Instead of evaluating and considering the level of risk and harm (whether grave or not), we suggest that the court should look at the protection measures first. The rich case law of the ECtHR shows that, in many cases, women seek protection, but the justice system does not respond.[100] Thus, looking at protection measures would provide evidence of both the risk and the protection.

In conclusion, the protection of private life according to the ECHR, and the swift return procedure of the Convention and the Brussels IIa Regulation, seem to be difficult to reconcile. Therefore, there is reason to ask whether the persistent adherence to the Convention abduction system is necessary or sensible in the EU, which has free movement, clear rules on jurisdiction and cross-border enforcement, and, finally, mutual trust in the legal systems of other Member States. Is the situation that different from a situation in which one parent moves out of the house, but settles

---

99 P. Beaumont, L. Walker and J. Holliday, 'Conflicts of EU Courts on Child Abduction: the reality of Article 11(6–8) Brussels IIa proceedings across the EU' (2016) 12(2) *Journal of Private International* 211–60.

100 See n. 43 and section 4.2, for case law.

within the borders of the same State? Why, for example, are there different rules when a parent moves with a child from Maastricht (the Netherlands) to Liege (Belgium), than when they move from Lund to Kiruna (both in Sweden). The distance in the former case is 30 kilometres; in the latter case, 1,800 kilometres. There may be delays in processing child custody cases in national courts, but the automatic return of abducted children does not cure such problems. Rather, the national and EU legislators should work towards better procedures for mediating and adjudicating child custody disputes. Perhaps it is time to rely on the courts to which the Brussels IIa Regulation gives jurisdiction, and the national laws that recognise the best interest of the child.

BEST PRACTICE GUIDE

Protection of Abducting Mothers in Return Proceedings: Intersection between Domestic Violence and Parental Child Abduction

PREPARED UNDER THE AUSPICES OF THE POAM PROJECT

UNIVERSITY OF ABERDEEN PRAVOS Pravni fakultet Osijek Sveučilište J. J. Strossmayera u Osijeku LMU LUDWIG-MAXIMILIANS-UNIVERSITÄT MÜNCHEN BICOCCA

This project has received funding from the European Union's Rights, Equality and Citizenship Programme 2014–2020 under grant agreement No. 810373.

CONTENTS

BEST PRACTICE GUIDE ON THE PROTECTION OF ABDUCTING MOTHERS IN RETURN PROCEEDINGS

Katarina TRIMMINGS, Onyója MOMOH, Costanza HONORATI, Anatol DUTTA and Mirela ŽUPAN

1. INTRODUCTION

1.1. METHODOLOGY

This Guide was prepared under the auspices of the research project 'Protection of Abducting Mothers in Return Proceedings: Intersection between Domestic Violence and Parental Child Abduction' (POAM),[1] funded by the European Commission from the European Union's Rights, Equality and Citizenship Programme. The Guide presents the findings of the POAM project, collated from the project local workshops[2] and project reports[3] prepared by the University of Aberdeen (United Kingdom – Scotland), the Josip Juraj Strossmayer University of Osijek (Croatia), the University of Milano-Bicocca (Italy) and the Ludwig-Maximilian University of Munich (Germany) ('the Project Partners') and the National Points of Contact for Spain, Slovenia and Serbia ('the National Points of Contact'), and refined through a process of consultations with relevant specialists, including experts from the European Commission and the Hague Conference on Private International Law (hereafter 'the Hague Conference').[4]

The Guide was developed taking into consideration the Hague Conference 'Guide to Good Practice under the HCCH Convention

---

1 See https://research.abdn.ac.uk/poam/.

2 See https://research.abdn.ac.uk/poam/events/.

3 See https://research.abdn.ac.uk/poam/resources/reports/.

4 These consultations culminated in the Project Workshop ('POAM Experts' Workshop'), which was originally scheduled to take place at the University of Milano-Bicocca, Italy on 27 March 2020, to be hosted by Professor Costanza Honorati, but had to be rescheduled at a short notice due to the COVID-19 pandemic. The Workshop was then held as a virtual event on 19 June 2020.

of 25 October 1980 on the Civil Aspects of International Child Abduction – Part VI – Article 13(1)(b)' (hereafter 'the HCCH Guide').[5] The HCCH Guide addresses the application of Article 13(1)(b) of the 1980 Hague Abduction Convention[6] and provides guidance to judges and Central Authorities on the approach to, and analysis of, the Article 13(1)(b) 'grave risk of harm' exception. The HCCH Guide's objective is to promote, on an international scale, the correct and consistent application of the Article 13(1)(b) grave risk exception in accordance with the 1980 Hague Convention. There are aspects of the HCCH Guide that are relevant to the issue of protection measures for abducting mothers and, indeed, the protection of children in cases involving domestic violence. The present Guide is intended to complement the HCCH Guide through the provision of in-depth guidance on these specific issues. Among other pertinent matters, the present Guide analyses the utility of Regulation 606/2013[7] and Directive 2011/99[8] in the context of parental child abductions motivated by acts of domestic violence, taking into account the EU child abduction regime of Regulation 2201/2003 ('the Brussels IIa Regulation').[9]

1.2. OBJECTIVES

The Guide is intended to assist child abduction professionals, including judges, legal practitioners, NGO representatives, Central Authorities and other public authorities involved in child abduction cases where allegations of domestic violence by the left-behind father have been made by the abducting mother in return proceedings.

In particular, the Guide seeks to achieve the following objectives:

- To evaluate the difficult issues of protection of abducting mothers in child abduction cases committed against the background of domestic

---

5 Hague Conference on Private International Law, 'Guide to Good Practice under the HCCH Convention of 25 October 1980 on the Civil Aspects of International Child Abduction – Part VI – Article 13(1)(b)', 2020 (hereafter 'HCCH Guide'), available at https://assets.hcch.net/docs/225b44d3-5c6b-4a14-8f5b-57cb370c497f.pdf.

6 Convention of 25 October 1980 on the Civil Aspects of International Child Abduction.

7 Regulation (EU) No 606/2013 of the European Parliament and of the Council of 12 June 2013 on mutual recognition of protection measures in civil matters.

8 Directive 2011/99/EU of the European Parliament and of the Council of 13 December 2011 on the European protection order.

9 Council Regulation (EC) No 2201/2003 of 27 November 2003 concerning jurisdiction and the recognition and enforcement of judgments in matrimonial matters and the matters of parental responsibility, repealing Regulation (EC) No 1347/2000.

violence, and to enhance the protection of such abducting mothers in return proceedings.

- To contribute towards the awareness and implementation of Regulation 606/2013 and Directive 2011/99.
- To contribute towards the objectives of the Hague Conference on Private International Law set out in the Conclusions and Recommendations of the 7th Meeting of the Special Commission to review the practical operation of the 1980 and 1996 Hague Conventions,[10] and its recognition of the value of evidence-based research (paragraph 81).[11]

1.3. SCOPE

The Council of Europe Convention on preventing and combating violence against women and domestic violence ('the Istanbul Convention')[12] contains a wide definition of domestic violence, stating that it includes 'acts of physical, sexual, psychological and economic violence that occur within the family or domestic unit or between former or current spouses or partners, whether or not the perpetrator shares or has shared the same residence with the victim'.[13] Regulation 606/2013 does not introduce an autonomous definition of violence, and refers to behaviour that endangers a victim's life, physical or psychological integrity, personal liberty, security or sexual integrity, and aspires to offer protection from acts such as 'physical violence, harassment, sexual aggression, stalking, intimidation or other forms of indirect coercion'.[14]

---

10 Convention of 19 October 1996 on Jurisdiction, Applicable Law, Recognition, Enforcement and Co-operation in Respect of Parental Responsibility and Measures for the Protection of Children.

11 Paragraph 81 states: 'The Special Commission recognises the value of evidence-based research to strengthen existing knowledge on the effects of wrongful removal or retention of children internationally. In particular, it would be desirable to have further research addressing: (1) the short-term and long-term outcomes for children and relevant family members, including taking and left-behind parents; and (2) the impact and effectiveness of protective measures, other judicial and legal processes, support services and/or arrangements to apply post-return.' Available at https://assets.hcch.net/docs/edce6628-3a76-4be8-a092-437837a49bef.pdf.

12 The Council of Europe Convention on preventing and combating violence against women and domestic violence, Istanbul, 11/05/2011.

13 Istanbul Convention, Art. 3(b).

14 Regulation, Recital 6.

This Guide adopts the Hague Conference terminology,[15] which corresponds with Regulation 606/2013, Recital 6, and uses the term 'domestic violence' to denote a range of abusive behaviours within the family, including physical (including sexual) and psychological abuse.[16] The specific category of domestic violence victims that this project is concerned with is abducting mothers who have been involved in return proceedings under the 1980 Hague Abduction Convention and the Brussels IIa Regulation, in circumstances where the child abduction had been motivated by acts of domestic violence in the form of physical or psychological abuse from the left-behind father who, following the abduction, filed an application for the return of the child to the State of the child's habitual residence.

2. PROTECTION OF ABDUCTING MOTHERS IN RETURN PROCEEDINGS

2.1. IMPORTANCE OF THE TOPIC

2.1.1. High Proportion of Mothers as Abductors

Statistical information on the operation of the 1980 Hague Abduction Convention shows that 73% of parental child abductions are committed by mothers.[17] Alarmingly, many of these mothers are fleeing domestic violence.[18] Although there are no comprehensive statistics on how

---

15 See HCCH Guide, Glossary.

16 Recital 6 of Regulation 606/2013 states that the Regulation is intended to apply to 'protection measures ordered with a view to protecting a person where there exist serious grounds for considering that that person's life, physical or psychological integrity, personal liberty, security or sexual integrity is at risk, for example so as to prevent any form of gender-based violence or violence in close relationships such as physical violence, harassment, sexual aggression, stalking, intimidation or other forms of indirect coercion'.

17 N. Lowe and V. Stephens, 'A statistical analysis of applications made in 2015 under the Hague Convention of 25 October 1980 on the Civil Aspects of International Child Abduction, Part I – Regional (revised) (September 2017); Part II – Global Report (September 2017), Part III – National Reports (July 2018)'.

18 Case study example: when mothers flee from domestic abuse, it is useful to consider two distinctly different circumstances. The first is a foreign mother returning to her home country having fled from the abuse, but also from a country where the language is problematic, family/support network is scant, or even immigration difficulties are present: there is a higher degree of disenfranchisement. The second is a mother

many 1980 Convention cases involve allegations or findings of domestic violence, empirical research has confirmed that this phenomenon frequently plays a role in parental child abduction cases, and it is alleged that it may be present in a large number of child abductions committed by mothers.[19] This suggests that many of the returning abducting mothers may potentially be at risk of revictimisation at the hands of their violent ex-partners.

2.1.2. *Vulnerabilities of Abducting Mothers in Cases Involving Domestic Violence*

Returning mothers in child abductions committed against the background of domestic violence are subject to particular vulnerabilities, including the risk of revictimisation upon their return to the State of habitual residence, the lack of financial and emotional support in the State of habitual residence plus probable financial dependence on the left-behind father on the return, sometimes the lack of credibility as a respondent in return proceedings due to the failure to report the incidents of domestic violence in the State of habitual residence prior to the abduction, and the exposure to 'intimidatory litigation', whereby the left-behind father abusively uses the return proceedings as a means of further harassment, rather than from a genuine desire to secure the return of the child. Such 'intimidatory litigation' adds greatly to the anxiety suffered by the abducting mother, who, as a survivor of an abusive relationship, is likely to be overwhelmed already with the repercussions of that relationship.

---

who, with a good command of English and familial connections in England flees for example from Ireland to England.

19 M. Freeman, 'The Outcomes for Children Returned Following an Abduction' (2003) The Reunite Research Unit. The study conducted by the International Child Abduction Centre, Reunite, revealed that domestic violence and/or child abuse were raised as the main concern relating to return in 67% of the representative sample of mother abductor cases. See also S. De Silva, 'The International Parental Child Abduction Service of the International Social Service Australian Branch' (2006) 11 *The Judges' Newsletter* 61; Permanent Bureau of the Hague Conference, 'Domestic and Family Violence and the Article 13 "Grave Risk" Exception in the Operation of the Hague Convention of 25 October 1980 on the Civil Aspects of International Child Abduction: A Reflection Paper' (May 2011), available at https://assets.hcch.net/upload/wop/abduct2011pd09e.pdf; and M. Župan, M. Drventić and T. Kruger, 'Cross-Border Removal and Retention of a Child – Croatian Practice and European Expectation' (2020) 34 *International Journal of Family Law and Policy* 60.

2.1.3. *Gap: Safety of the Abducting Mothers Upon Return*

Nowadays it is widely understood that 'domestic violence directed towards a parent can be seriously harmful to the children who witness it or who depend upon the psychological health and strength of their primary carer for their well-being.'[20] Yet, neither the 1980 Convention nor the Brussels IIa Regulation have explicit regard to the safety of the abducting mother upon the return. Although the Hague Conference has recognised that, '[i]n some situations, the grave risk to the child may also be based on potential harm to the taking parent by the left-behind parent',[21] and that 'the protection of the child may also sometimes require steps to be taken to protect an accompanying parent',[22] a gap remains as to the enforceability of protective measures intended to safeguard the abducting mother upon the return, with inconsistent practices in place resulting in varying levels of protection across jurisdictions. It is the intention of the Guide to address this gap.

2.2. THE GRAVE RISK OF HARM DEFENCE AND ALLEGATIONS OF DOMESTIC VIOLENCE

The 'grave risk of harm' exception to return, embodied in Article 13(1)(b) of the 1980 Convention,[23] is particularly pertinent to abductions committed against the background of domestic violence.[24] Indeed, it is often raised by abducting mothers opposing the return, based either on the allegations involving the child as the 'direct victim', or as an 'indirect victim', where the child is exposed to the effects of domestic

20 B. Hale, 'Taking Flight – Domestic Violence and Child Abduction' (2017) 70 *Current Legal Problems* 7.

21 HCCH Guide, para. 57.

22 Hague Conference on Private International Law, Conclusions and Recommendations of the Fifth Meeting of the Special Commission (2006), para. 1.1.12, available at https://assets.hcch.net/upload/concl28sc5_e.pdf.

23 Article 13(1)(b) states: 'Notwithstanding the provisions of the preceding Article, the judicial or administrative authority of the requested State is not bound to order the return of the child if the person, institution or other body which opposes its return establishes that … there is a grave risk that his or her return would expose the child to physical or psychological harm or otherwise place the child in an intolerable situation.'

24 See HCCH Guide, paras. 57–59.

violence directed towards the mother.[25] Among such effects are impaired parenting capacities of the mother, resulting from the impact of the violence on her physical and/or psychological health.[26] The 'grave risk of harm' defence may also be raised where the abducting mother is unable to return with the child due to fear of the child's father; the subsequent separation from the primary carer mother may be argued to create a grave risk for the child.[27]

It has, therefore, been recognised that the circumstances of the abducting mother and the child may be intertwined to the extent that domestic violence perpetrated solely against the mother may justify the finding that the return would expose the child to a grave risk of 'psychological harm or other intolerable situation', pursuant to Article 13(1)(b).[28]

In cases involving allegations of domestic violence, the 'grave risk of harm' defence is often invoked, and in some cases successfully made out, in conjunction with the 'child's objections' defence under Article 13(2) of the Convention.[29]

2.3. POLICY CONSIDERATIONS

The underlying philosophy of the 1980 Hague Convention is that international child abduction is harmful to children and should, therefore,

---

25 Permanent Bureau of the Hague Conference, 'Domestic and Family Violence and the Article 13 "Grave Risk" Exception in the Operation of the Hague Convention of 25 October 1980 on the Civil Aspects of International Child Abduction: A Reflection Paper' (May 2011), available at https://assets.hcch.net/upload/wop/abduct2011pd09e.pdf, para. 11.

26 HCCH Guide, para. 57.

27 Ibid, para. 9.

28 E.g. *In the Matter of E (Children)* [2011] UKSC 27 (hereafter '*Re E*'); and *In the Matter of S (a Child)* [2012] UKSC 10 (hereafter '*Re S*'). See also HCCH Guide, para. 58.

29 See POAM Project Report – United Kingdom, p. 85 and POAM Project Report – Italy, p. 3, available at https://research.abdn.ac.uk/poam/resources/reports/. Article 13(2) states: 'The judicial or administrative authority may also refuse to order the return of the child if it finds that the child objects to being returned and has attained an age and degree of maturity at which it is appropriate to take account of its views.' C. Honorati, 'Il ritorno del minore sottratto e il rischio grave di pregiudizio ai sensi dell'art. 13 par. 1 lett. b della convenzione dell'Aja del 1980' (2020) 4 *Rivista di diritto internazionale privato e processuale* 822–24 suggests that courts find it easier and more secure to argue on the opposition of the child or on other available defences, rather than on grave risk of harm caused by domestic violence, especially because of the difficulties related to the burden of proof and the role of protective measures that this ground brings with it.

be discouraged.[30] The Convention also seeks to prevent the abducting parent from establishing 'artificial jurisdictional links' with the requested State with the intention of obtaining an advantage in custody proceedings, and thus benefitting from his/her own wrongdoing.[31] Accordingly, the Convention sets out a legal mechanism designed to ensure the prompt return of a wrongfully removed or retained child to the country of his or her habitual residence. In line with this policy, there are only a limited number of exceptions available to the abducting parent, whilst these exceptions are to be interpreted in a narrow fashion.[32]

As the Convention return policy and the objective of protecting abducting mothers in return proceedings may seem potentially contradictory, it should be emphasised that it is not the intention of this Guide to undermine the return policy of the Convention. Rather, the Guide seeks to ensure that, where appropriate,[33] return can be ordered whilst the abducting mother returning with the child is being protected by means of all available legal avenues, as appropriate in the particular circumstances of the case.

Although the effectiveness of protection measures in the context of domestic violence has been subject to debate, there is strong evidence that protection orders are useful tools in tackling domestic violence.[34] Indeed, even though protection orders are sometimes breached, and satisfactory follow-up measures by relevant authorities may be lacking, in many cases protection orders do halt the undesirable contact, or at least help improve the overall physical, psychological and emotional well-being of the victim as, even if the contact does not stop completely, the overall frequency and intensity of violence tends to decrease.[35] Moreover, protection orders are said to psychologically empower the victim, whilst sending a clear message to the offender that domestic violence is a public concern, and will not be tolerated.[36] However, given the concerns over the effectiveness of protective

---

30 E. Pérez-Vera, 'Explanatory Report on the 1980 Hague Child Abduction Convention', paras. 16–26 (hereafter 'Explanatory Report'), available at https://assets.hcch.net/docs/a5fb103c-2ceb-4d17-87e3-a7528a0d368c.pdf.

31 Ibid.

32 Ibid, para. 34.

33 See section 5, 'In Practice: Step by Step Guide', below.

34 S. van der Aa, et al., 'Mapping the Legislation and Assessing the Impact of Protection Orders in the European Member States' (hereafter 'POEMs Project Final Report'), p. 102, available at http://poems-project.com/wp-content/uploads/2015/04/Intervict-Poems-digi-1.pdf.

35 Ibid, p. 238.

36 Ibid, p. 252.

measures, this Guide recommends that the courts be extremely cautious in accepting protection measures in return proceedings in cases where there is a risk of severe future violence. In essence, the employment of protective measures in such cases should be an exception.[37]

3. PROTECTIVE MEASURES IN THE CONTEXT OF RETURN PROCEEDINGS

3.1. THE NATURE AND TYPE OF PROTECTIVE MEASURES

The Brussels IIa Regulation[38] and its Recast (Brussels IIb)[39] prohibit a non-return order on the basis of Article 13(1)(b) of the 1980 Convention if it is established that adequate arrangements have been made to secure the child's protection upon his/her return. The appropriate protective measures and their effectiveness will differ from case to case, and from jurisdiction to jurisdiction.[40] Therefore, when assessing whether or not protective measures have been taken in the State of habitual residence, and whether they will adequately safeguard the protection of the child upon his or her return, courts may find it helpful to utilise the assistance of the Central Authority of the State of habitual residence[41] and/or the international cooperation arrangements between Hague network judges.[42]

Protective measures in, or related to, return proceedings may be divided into three categories: (1) measures issued by the court seised with the return application ('the Hague Convention return court'); (2) protection orders issued by competent courts in the State of refuge, in proceedings that are separate from the Hague Convention return proceedings (usually on application by the abducting mother); and (3) measures issued by a competent court in the State of habitual residence (See Figure 1 below).

---

37 See section 4.4, 'Recommendations', below.

38 Art. 11(4).

39 Council Regulation (EU) 2019/1111 of 25 June 2019 on jurisdiction, the recognition and enforcement of decisions in matrimonial matters and the matters of parental responsibility, and on international child abduction (recast), Art. 27(3).

40 *Re E*, para. 36.

41 European Commission, 'Practice Guide for the Application of the Brussels IIa Regulation', p. 55 (hereafter 'EC Practice Guide'), available at https://op.europa.eu/en/publication-detail/-/publication/f7d39509-3f10-4ae2-b993-53ac6b9f93ed.

42 *Re E*, para. 36.

This Guide is concerned with the first two types of protective measures (i.e. (1) and (2)).

1) Protective measures issued by the Hague Convention return court in the return proceedings

This category of protective measures involves measures that are ordered by the Hague Convention return court in the State of refuge, and which need to be *recognised* in the State of habitual residence.

In some jurisdictions, courts also endorse and accept undertakings from the left-behind parent as one, or the only, form of protection. Undertakings have, historically, been described as 'promises offered or in certain circumstances imposed upon an applicant to overcome obstacles which may stand in the way of the return of a wrongfully removed or retained child'.[43] In recent precedents, the serious problem of the effectiveness of undertakings was reiterated, echoing the UK Supreme Court case of *Re E*, when Lady Hale referred to concerns about the 'too ready' acceptance by the courts of common law countries of undertakings which are not enforceable in the courts of the requesting State. Schuz highlights that the unenforceability of undertakings is particularly acute in cases involving domestic violence, and spouses who 'will not balk at violating their undertakings'.[44] In essence, the efficacy of undertakings may vary amongst jurisdictions that employ them within their domestic laws. Within cross-border proceedings, voluntary undertakings can be largely ineffective as a means of protection, and therefore the issue of enforceability must be addressed to the court's satisfaction that measures originating from voluntary undertakings have legal effect, i.e. by virtue of the 1996 Hague Convention or mirror orders. Examples of undertakings include: non-molestation/non-harassment undertakings (e.g. 'not to use violence

43 P. Beaumont and P. McEleavy, *The Hague Convention on International Child Abduction* (Oxford University Press, 1999), p. 30. See also K. Trimmings, *Child Abduction within the European Union* (Hart Publishing, 2013) pp. 155–61.

44 R. Schuz, *The Hague Child Abduction Convention: A Critical Analysis* (Hart Publishing, 2013) p. 293. See also the recent decision in *Saada v. Golan*, where the USCA (2nd Circuit), on 19 July 2019, voided the District Court order for the return of the child, stating the assumption that 'in cases in which the district court has determined that repatriating a child will expose him or her to a grave risk of harm, *unenforceable undertakings are generally disfavoured*, particularly where the petitioning parent will comply with the undertakings and *there are no other "sufficient guarantees of performance"*' [at p. 34a, emphasis added]. The Court of Appeal required the District Court to investigate whether alternative, more appropriate and effective protective ('ameliorative') measures were available, and could offer better guarantees for a safe return.

or threats towards the mother, nor to instruct anybody else to do so', or 'not to communicate with the mother directly'); undertakings related to the occupation of the family home (e.g. 'to vacate the family home and make it available for a sole occupancy by the mother and the child'); undertakings related to financial support (e.g. 'to pay for the return tickets for the mother and the child', or 'to provide financial support/maintenance to the mother and the child upon their return'); and undertakings related to residence or access to the child (e.g. 'not to seek to separate the mother from the child', or 'not to seek contact with the child unless awarded by the court or agreed'). As can be seen from the above examples, undertakings do not always contain protective measures as such, but may instead encompass 'more light-touch' practical arrangements to facilitate and implement the child's return and enable a 'soft landing' of the child in the State of habitual residence (e.g. the funding of return flights and financial support upon the return).[45] Given the difficulties with the enforceability of undertakings, this Guide does not endorse the employment of undertakings in return proceedings involving allegations of domestic violence.

Finally, it has been suggested that, when assessing the level of protection available in the State of habitual residence, the Hague Convention return court should also consider the general features of the State of habitual residence (e.g. access to courts and other legal services; State assistance and support, including financial assistance, housing assistance, health services, women's shelters and other means of support to victims of domestic violence; responses by police, and the criminal justice system more generally; and availability of protective measures to victims of domestic violence in the State of habitual residence, such as non-molestation injunctions).[46] This approach is not, however, endorsed by this Guide, as it runs contrary to the Practice Guide for the Application of the Brussels IIa Regulation, which states that '[i]t is not sufficient that procedures exist in the Member State of origin for the protection of the child, but it must be established that the authorities in the Member State of origin have taken concrete measures to protect the child in question'.[47]

---

45 *Re S (A Child) (Hague Convention 1980: Return to Third State)* [2019] EWCA Civ 352, para. 55. See section 3.2, 'Protective measures vs 'soft-landing' measures', below.

46 J. Munby (President of the Family Division), 'Practice Guidance: Case Management and Mediation of International Child Abduction Proceedings', March 2018, England and Wales, para. 2.11 (e), available at https://www.judiciary.uk/publications/practice-guidance-case-management-and-mediation-of-international-child-abduction-proceedings/; and *Re S (A Child) (Hague Convention 1980: Return to Third State)* [2019] EWCA Civ 352, para. 51.

47 EC Practice Guide, p. 55.

2) Protective measures issued in proceedings that are separate from the Hague Convention return proceedings

A protection order may be issued prior to the return (usually on application by the abducting mother) by a competent court in the State of refuge, in proceedings that are separate from the Hague Convention return proceedings. The abducting mother can then travel, with that protective measure, back to the State of habitual residence.

3) Protective measures issued by a court in the State of habitual residence

This category of protective measures covers relevant decisions made in the State of habitual residence either before or after the abduction. In particular, in some cases, there may already be decisions of courts and/or other competent authorities (as appropriate) in the State of habitual residence that can facilitate (or contribute towards facilitating) the protection of the child and/or the mother upon the return. These may include, e.g. civil and/or criminal protection orders in favour of the abducting mother or, where appropriate, (an interim) non-contact order. Alternatively, these measures can be sought from a court in the State of habitual residence, usually after the return of the child has been ordered.

Figure 1. Protective measures issued in or related to return proceedings

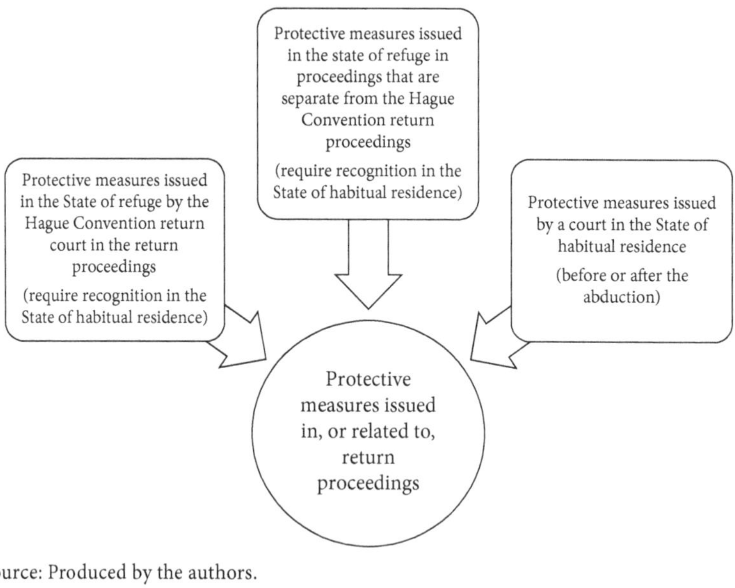

Source: Produced by the authors.

3.2. PROTECTIVE MEASURES vs 'SOFT LANDING' MEASURES

The courts have, in many scenarios, endorsed, or even made, orders giving effect to 'soft-landing' measures within return proceedings. These measures are distinguishable from protective measures against specific and identifiable grave risks of, e.g. domestic violence. Soft landing measures may comprise, e.g. the left-behind parent purchasing return flight tickets for the mother and children to enable them to journey to the country of habitual residence; the provision of a home; financial measures, such as to pay maintenance, or for a down payment for a home, or money to obtain legal advice and to instigate proceedings relevant to the custody of the children. It is of note that soft-landing measures and protective measures may overlap. For example, measures akin to the provision of a home, or money for separate accommodation, for the mother and children share a commonality with non-occupation orders, which constitute an injunctive relief and a means of prohibiting the father from living in the same home, in order that the grave risk of harm is ameliorated. Interestingly, the HCCH Guide makes the point that the court of the State of refuge cannot make orders that are not required to mitigate an established grave risk.[48] However, the HCCH Guide also observes that there are additional measures that, although not directly relevant to the issue of domestic violence, are nevertheless 'practical arrangements' to assist in the implementation of a return order: in order words, 'soft-landing measures'.[49]

Protective measures, on the other hand, are put in place with the explicit intention of addressing the grave risk of harm posed by the domestic violence established in the case. Examples may include non-molestation orders, occupation orders, restraining orders, non-harassment orders, exclusion orders, ouster orders, domestic abuse interdicts, eviction orders, prohibition of access orders, or prohibitive steps orders and other protection orders against (former) spouses, partners and cohabitants, as well as orders to protect children whose well-being is at risk.

4. PROTECTIVE MEASURES WITHIN THE EU

National approaches to protection measures vary across the Member States. Nevertheless, many shared features and common patterns in

48 HCCH Guide, p. 35.
49 Ibid., p. 34.

the regulation of protection measures across the EU can be identified. To facilitate cross-border movement of victims of violence, including domestic violence, the EU legislator has introduced two instruments on mutual recognition of protection orders: Directive 2011/99 on the European Protection Order, and Regulation 606/2013 on mutual recognition of protection measures in civil matters.

This part of the Guide sets out the key features of the Directive and the Regulation. It then outlines the common features and trends in the regulation of protection orders at the national level across the EU, before analysing the potential utility of the Directive and the Regulation in the child abduction context, and making appropriate recommendations.

4.1. MUTUAL RECOGNITION OF PROTECTION MEASURES IN THE EU: OVERVIEW OF REGULATION 606/2013 AND DIRECTIVE 2011/99

The EU legal framework for cross-border recognition of protective measures is represented by Directive 2011/99 on the European Protection Order, and Regulation 606/2013 on mutual recognition of protection measures in civil matters. These instruments provide a legal basis for EU Member States to recognise and, if needed, enforce a protection order that was granted in another Member State.[50] This section provides a brief overview of these two instruments.

4.1.1. Directive 2011/99

The Directive is based on Article 82(1) of the TFEU on judicial cooperation in criminal matters, and aims to facilitate mutual recognition of criminal protection orders that have been issued in one Member State ('the issuing State'), and are sought to be recognised in another Member State ('the executing State').[51]

The Directive aims to protect a person against a criminal act, and therefore applies only if the underlying harmful conduct is criminalised.[52]

---

[50] Ireland does not participate in the Directive (Directive 2011/99, Recital 41), and Denmark does not participate in either the Directive or the Regulation (Directive 2011/99, Recital 42 and Regulation 606/2013, Recital 41).

[51] Directive 2011/99, Art. 2.

[52] Directive 2011/99, Arts. 1 and 2(2).

The relevant crimes are those that may endanger the 'life, physical or psychological integrity, dignity, personal liberty or sexual integrity' of the protected person.[53] Therefore, a European Protection Order ('EPO') can be requested only if the protection order was issued in the context of a criminal matter,[54] and aims to prevent new criminal acts or reduce the consequences of previous criminal acts.[55] Examples include protection orders preventing any form of harassment, abduction, stalking, or other forms of indirect coercion.[56] For a protection measure to fall within the scope of the Directive, it is not necessary for a criminal offence to have been established by a final decision.[57] Interestingly, the issuing authority does not necessarily need to belong to the criminal justice system: it can be of an administrative or civil nature, too.[58]

The restrictions that can be placed on the person causing risk are:

a) a prohibition or regulation on entering the place where the protected person resides, works, or regularly visits or stays;
b) a prohibition or regulation of contact, in any form, with the protected person, including by telephone, electronic or ordinary mail, fax or any other means; and
c) a prohibition or regulation on approaching the protected person closer than a prescribed distance.[59]

The recognition procedure under the Directive departs from the traditional mutual recognition approach based on 'automatic' recognition, as it involves an additional step:[60] the executing Member State has to replace the original protection order with a similar measure available under its national law.[61]

---

53 Ibid.

54 E.g., it is not enough that the violations of the protective measure are subject to criminal act: Directive 2011/99, Art. 1, an EPO can only be requested if the protection order was issued within criminal matters.

55 Directive 2011/99, Recital 9.

56 Ibid.

57 Directive 2011/99, Recital 10.

58 Ibid.

59 Directive 2011/99, Art. 5.

60 See POEMs Project Final Report, p. 205.

61 Directive 2011/99, Art. 9. The procedure will include these steps: 1) an EPO is issued by the competent authority of the issuing State on request of the protected person; 2) the EPO is presented for recognition before the competent authority of the executing State by the protected person; and 3) the competent authority of the executing State considers whether to recognise the EPO, taking account of the possible grounds for non-recognition (Art. 10); and 4) if the EPO has been recognised, the competent

The executing State can choose whether to apply criminal, administrative or civil measures available under its national law;[62] however, it may refuse to recognise the protection order on one of the extensive grounds for non-recognition set out in Article 10.

The enforcement of the protection measure imposed in the issuing State and recognised in the executing State, including the penalties for the breach of the protection order, is left to the national law of the executing State.[63]

4.1.2. Regulation 606/2013

The Regulation is based on Article 81 TFEU, and provides for the mutual recognition of civil protection measures across the EU by establishing 'rules for a simple and rapid mechanism for the recognition of protection measures ordered in a Member State in civil matters'.[64] There are slight differences between the terminology used in the Regulation and the terminology used in the Directive, as the Member State that issued the protection order is referred to in the Regulation as 'the Member State of origin', and the other Member State is termed 'the Member State addressed'.[65] For a protection measure to fall within the scope of the Regulation, the issuing authority does not necessarily need to belong to the civil justice system;[66] however, a protection order issued by the police would not be eligible.[67]

The restrictions that can be placed on the person causing risk, with a view to safeguarding the protected person's physical or psychological integrity, are the same as under the Directive and include:

a) a prohibition or regulation on entering the place where the protected person resides, works, or regularly visits or stays;

---

authority of the executing State adopts a similar measure available under its national law to replace the original protection order (cf. POEMs Project Final Report, p. 207).

62 Directive 2011/99, Art. 9(1).

63 Directive 2011/99, Art. 11(1).

64 Regulation 606/2013, Art. 1.

65 Regulation 606/2013, Art. 3.

66 Regulation 606/2013, Recital 10.

67 Regulation 606/2013, Recital 13.

b) a prohibition or regulation of contact, in any form, with the protected person, including by telephone, electronic or ordinary mail, fax or any other means; and
c) a prohibition or regulation on approaching the protected person closer than a prescribed distance.[68]

The recognition of the protection measure is automatic, meaning that 'a protection measure ordered in a Member State shall be recognised in the other Member States without any special procedure being required and shall be enforceable without a declaration of enforceability being required'.[69]

A protected person who wishes to invoke their protection measure in another Member State is required to produce:[70]

1) A copy of the protection measure;
2) A certificate issued by the Member State of origin;[71] and
3) Where necessary, a translation or transliteration of the certificate.

The protected person can bring enforcement proceedings in the Member State addressed if necessary, and the enforcement, including the sanctions and procedures relating to the breach of the protection order, are left to the law of that Member State.[72]

There are only limited grounds on which a court in the Member State addressed can refuse to recognise and, where applicable, enforce a protection measure issued in another Member State (upon application by the person causing the risk). These grounds include that the protection order is:

- Manifestly contrary to public policy in the Member State addressed; or
- Irreconcilable with a judgment given or recognised in the Member State addressed.[73]

---

68 Regulation 606/2013, Art. 3(1).
69 Protection Measures Regulation, Art. 4(1).
70 Regulation 606/2013, Art. 4.
71 See section 5.2.1.2, 'Practical considerations', below.
72 Regulation 606/2013, Art. 4(5).
73 Regulation 606/2013, Art. 13(1).

4.1.3. *Problems with the Implementation of Regulation 606/2013 in Some Member States*

The Directive belongs to the 'European criminal cooperation' package, and has been transposed into national legislative frameworks through implementation. The Regulation belongs to the 'European civil cooperation' package, and applies directly in all Member States except Denmark.[74] In several Member States, it is still lacking full effect. This non-compliance with the Regulation results either from an omission to notify a body responsible to issue a certificate or enforce a protection order (Ireland), or from a negative declaration to the effect that there are 'no authorities competent for ordering protection measures in civil matters and issuing of certificates' (Croatia, Spain,[75] Sweden, and Portugal).[76]

---

74 Denmark does not participate in either the Directive or the Regulation (Directive 2011/99, Recital 42 and Regulation 606/2013, Recital 41).

75 It is to be pointed out that the information contained in the Judicial Atlas concerning Spain does not align with the findings of the POAM project. The POAM Project Report on Spain explains that, in Spain, criminal courts can issue both criminal and civil protection measures. Whilst the former can circulate under Directive 2011/99, the latter should be able to circulate under Regulation 606/2013: 'Protection measures for victims of domestic violence available under Spanish domestic law can have a criminal, civil and even administrative nature. Whilst civil courts can only adopt civil protection measures, Courts for violence against woman can adopt criminal and civil ones, depending on the case. As such, the so-called protection order in Spanish domestic system can only be issued by courts with criminal jurisdiction. In addition, Law 23/2014 resumes the domestic regulation of the EPO into the Criminal Procedural Law. Therefore, EPO can only be obtained in criminal courts and, obviously, on the basis of the existence of a criminal proceeding. Protection measures with civil nature adopted by criminal courts cannot be covered by the EPO. Nevertheless, those measures, as well as the ones adopted by civil courts, may benefit from the mutual recognition system established under Regulation 606/2013. In this regard, following the respective EU norms, it is important to remain attentive to the nature and purposes of the measure, not of the authority that adopts it': POAM Project Report – Spain, available at https://research.abdn.ac.uk/wp-content/uploads/sites/15/2020/05/National-report_Spain.pdf.

76 The POEMs Project Final Report explains that 'In Portugal POs are mainly, if not exclusively, issued in criminal proceedings. Although it is possible to apply for POs in civil proceedings, this rarely happens in practice': POEMs Project Final Report, p. 54. This is confirmed by the author of the information on Portugal contained in the Judicial Atlas, which adds that civil protection orders can be imposed under Article 70(2) of the Civil Code.

Figure 2. National information concerning Regulation 606/2013[77]

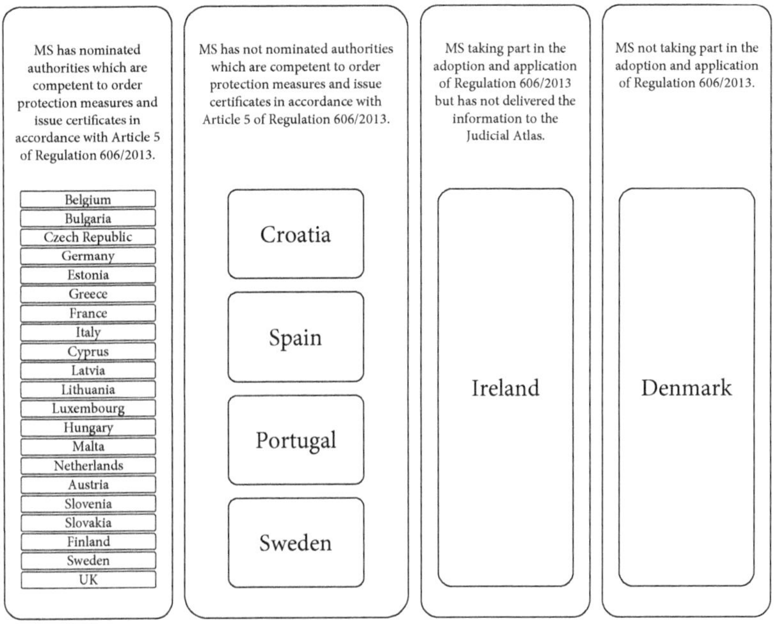

Source: Produced by the authors.

A conclusion on mandatory direct application of the Regulation can be reached in respect of the countries that have not nominated authorities to order protection measures and issue certificates. The Court of Justice of the European Union ('CJEU') has recently rendered a decision in relation to a failure by a Member State to notify the European Commission of notaries as non-judicial authorities exercising judicial functions like courts.[78] The CJEU held that a failure of a Member State to notify the Commission of a body responsible to issue a measure was of a merely indicative value.[79]

77 Source: The European e-Justice Portal, 'European Judicial Atlas in Civil Matters, Mutual Recognition of Protection Measures in Civil Matters', available at https://e-justice.europa.eu/content_mutual_recognition_of_protection_measures_in_civil_matters-352-en.do.

78 Case C-658/17 *WB*, 23 May 2019, ECLI:EU:C:2019:444.

79 Ibid., para. 48: 'Accordingly, the Republic of Poland's failure to notify the Commission of notaries who exercise judicial functions, as provided for in the second subparagraph of Article 3(2) of Regulation No 650/2012, is of merely indicative value.'

It is argued here that such failure cannot deprive a protected person of the right to request a certificate under the Regulation. A logical question arises: Where should the protected person seek the certificate? The Regulation clearly indicates that it does not touch upon a national system of judicial functions, but, on the contrary, relies upon them. A formal failure of notification does not affect the substantive situation that a certain body within the national system is responsible for ordering protection measures. Consequently, it is the court issuing a measure corresponding to measures prescribed by Regulation 606/2013 (and Directive 2011/99) that should issue the certificate.

4.2. NATIONAL APPROACHES TO PROTECTION MEASURES[80]

4.2.1. Civil vs Criminal Protection Orders

The Regulation and the Directive were drafted on the assumption that protection orders can be procured mainly through civil and criminal law. Even though most Member States provide for both civil protection orders and criminal protection orders, not all systems fit neatly into the 'civil vs criminal protection orders' dichotomy envisaged by the EU legislator.[81] In particular, civil protection orders are not available in EU countries such as Croatia: instead, protection orders can be obtained in either criminal or misdemeanour proceedings;[82] and criminal protection orders, as such, are not available in Finland, Denmark and Sweden; instead, a distinct 'quasi-criminal' route is used whereby no link with substantive criminal proceedings is required,[83] although the protection order is imposed by the public prosecutor, the Chief of Police, or a district court.[84]

---

80 This overview is based on the POAM Project Reports, available at https://research.abdn.ac.uk/poam/resources/reports/, and the POEMs Project Final Report.

81 POEMs Project Final Report, pp. 231 and 240.

82 POAM Project Report – Croatia, available at https://research.abdn.ac.uk/wp-content/uploads/sites/15/2020/05/National-report_Croatia.pdf.

83 POEMs Project Final Report, pp. 231 and 240.

84 Ibid., p 59.

4.2.2. *Substantive Similarities*

Protection orders available to victims of domestic violence may be regulated in generic law,[85] or in specific laws on domestic violence.[86] Although the terminology denoting individual types of protection orders may differ across the Member States, all Member States make it possible to impose (in the sphere of civil and/or criminal law) the three prohibitions set out in Regulation 606/2013 and Directive 2011/99: (1) the ban on contacting the protected person; (2) the ban on entering certain areas; and (3) the ban on approaching the protected person.[87]

4.2.3. *Protection Order Procedures*

A civil protection order can normally be applied for by a claimant in civil summary proceedings, and can often be imposed *ex parte*.[88] It can generally be issued as a (preliminary) injunction via interlocutory proceedings (although sometimes it is dependent on other (substantive)

---

85 E.g. Criminal Code (Kazneni zakon), Official Gazette No. 125/11, as amended by the Act on Amendments to Criminal Code (Zakon o izmjenama i dopunama Kaznenog zakona), Official Gazette No. 56/15 (Croatia), see POAM Project Report – Croatia available at https://research.abdn.ac.uk/wp-content/uploads/sites/15/2020/05/National-report_Croatia.pdf; Civil Code (Italy), Arts. 342-*bis* and 342-*ter*, Code of Civil Procedure (Italy), Art. 737-*bis*, and Code of Criminal Procedure (Italy), Arts. 282-*bis* and 282-*ter*, see POAM Project Report – Italy, available at https://research.abdn.ac.uk/wp-content/uploads/sites/15/2020/02/National-report_Italy.pdf; and § 1666 Bürgerliches Gesetzbuch – BGB (Civil Code) (Germany), para. 1666, see POAM Project Report – Germany, available at https://research.abdn.ac.uk/wp-content/uploads/sites/15/2020/02/National-report_Germany.pdf.

86 E.g. Domestic Violence Prevention Act (Zakon o preprečevanju nasilja v družini), Official Gazette, No. 16/08, 68/16 (Slovenia), see POAM Project Report – Slovenia, available at https://research.abdn.ac.uk/wp-content/uploads/sites/15/2020/02/National-report_Slovenia.pdf; Domestic Abuse (Scotland) Act 2018, see POAM Project Report – United Kingdom, available at https://research.abdn.ac.uk/wp-content/uploads/sites/15/2020/02/National-report_UK.pdf; Act on Protection against Domestic Violence (Zakon o zaštiti od nasilja u obitelji), Official Gazette No. 137/2009, 14/2010, 60/2010 (Croatia) POAM Project Report – Croatia.

87 POEMs Project Final Report, p. 234.

88 I.e. without hearing the left-behind father (as long as he has been summoned, and is allowed to appeal the decision, in order to guarantee procedural fairness): POEMs Project Final Report, p. 234. See also POAM Project Reports, available at https://research.abdn.ac.uk/poam/resources/reports/. E.g. In Italy, when the measure is granted *ex parte*, the defendant is heard within a few days for the purposes of a confirmation of the measure. POAM Project Report – Italy, available at https://research.abdn.ac.uk/wp-content/uploads/sites/15/2020/02/National-report_Italy.pdf.

proceedings, e.g. divorce or proceedings on the merits of the case).[89] Although evidentiary requirements for civil protection orders, to some extent, differ among the Member States, the evidentiary threshold is usually not very high.[90] The victim merely has to demonstrate that she is in need of protection.[91]

In contrast, a criminal protection order is normally imposed by a criminal (investigative) court (usually on request by the police or the public prosecutor) as a pre-trial coercive measure or bail (as a means of preventing the suspect from interfering with the criminal procedure); a restraining order (as a means of preventing the suspect from harassing a specific person(s)); a condition to probation; a condition to a suspended prison sentence, or a condition to a conditional release from prison.[92] Some Member States allow criminal protection orders in pre- or post-trial stages only, although in most Member States they are available in both stages.[93] A criminal protection order is always inseparably linked to criminal proceedings (i.e. there must be a suspicion of a crime),[94] and may be imposed for different types of crimes, some of which are more general (e.g. assault, stalking and rape), and some more specific (e.g. intimate partner violence or domestic abuse).[95] It is usually required that the offender be heard first. *Ex parte* criminal protection orders are possible only in a few Member States, and only in exceptional circumstances (e.g. the suspect cannot be located in spite of serious attempts, or the case requires urgent intervention), and only to the extent that the defendant can challenge the decision in subsequent hearings.[96]

Unlike civil protection orders, most criminal protection orders were developed as substitutes for detention or prison and, as such, require a level of violence that will justify an arrest.[97] Moreover, because criminal

---

89 POEMs Project Final Report, p. 59.
90 Ibid., p. 242.
91 Ibid., p. 242.
92 Ibid., p. 59.
93 Ibid., p. 231. Only in England and Wales, and the Republic of Ireland, criminal protection orders can be imposed upon the acquittal of the defendant: Ibid., p. 237. See also POAM Project Report – United Kingdom, available at https://research.abdn.ac.uk/wp-content/uploads/sites/15/2020/02/National-report_UK.pdf.
94 POEMs Project Final Report, p. 70.
95 For more details, see POAM Project Reports.
96 POEMs Project Final Report, p. 71. This may be different in Cyprus, where it possibly suffices that a prosecutor swears under oath that the offence is serious, and that the victim is in need of protection (ibid., fn. 49).
97 Ibid., p. 242.

protection orders are connected to criminal proceedings, the behaviour that will justify an arrest has to be criminalised.

4.2.4. Procedural Variances in National Legal Systems

Despite many commonalities in the regulation of protection order procedures across the Member States, there are also important procedural variances.[98] These concern, inter alia: (1) the range of persons who can apply for a protection order; (2) the interdependence with other proceedings; (3) the application requirements for criminal protection orders, in particular the requisite level of evidence;[99] (4) the possibility of *ex parte* protection orders; (5) the immediate effect of protection orders; (6) the inclusion of mutual children in protection orders; (7) the length of protection order proceedings; (8) the costs of protection of proceedings (i.e. the administrative and court fees involved); (9) the requirement of a legal representation for the victim; (10) the access of the victim to free legal representation;[100] (11) the statutory maximum (if any) and average duration of protection orders; (12) the range of persons who qualify for a protection order; (13) the formal requirements for the formulation of protection orders; and (14) the type of sanctions for breaches of civil protection orders.[101]

4.3. REGULATION 606/2013 AND DIRECTIVE 2011/99 IN THE SPECIFIC CONTEXT OF INTERNATIONAL PARENTAL CHILD ABDUCTION

When it comes to potential utility of the Regulation and the Directive in the specific context of child abduction, the Regulation clearly outclasses the Directive. This is for two sets of reasons: first, reasons pertaining to the key characteristics of criminal protection orders, and second, reasons related specifically to the mutual recognition procedure under the Directive (see below, sections 4.3.1 and 4.3.2 respectively). Nevertheless, the Regulation itself is not flawless, and section 4.3.3 addresses the relative weaknesses of this instrument. This analysis is followed by a set of recommendations, in section 4.4, that have been formulated on the basis of the information set out in the preceding sections.

---

98 As identified by the POEMs project research team in the Project Final Report.

99 Ideally, a civil protection order should be available merely based on a written (statutory) declaration of the victim (ibid., p. 237).

100 Ibid., p. 233.

101 Ibid., pp. 233 and 234.

4.3.1. *Reasons Related to the Key Characteristics of Criminal Protection Orders*

a. The requirement of a link with criminal proceedings
Criminal protection orders are not 'autonomous' measures that could be imposed outside the context of criminal proceedings; rather, they are inseparably linked to criminal proceedings. Such proceedings would have to be initiated in the Member State of refuge as a consequence of a criminal act committed by the left-behind father. As the left-behind father usually remains in the State of habitual residence, this scenario is not very likely. Nevertheless, a situation can be envisaged whereby the left-behind father travels to the State of refuge and assaults/stalks/threatens the abducting mother there. Criminal proceedings can then be initiated in the Member State of refuge. Another exception can be envisaged where relevant national legislation of the State of habitual residence has extraterritorial application. For example, in Scotland, an offence of abusive behaviour towards a partner or ex-partner under the Domestic Abuse (Scotland) Act 2018 can be prosecuted in the Scottish courts, even if the course of behaviour by the perpetrator takes place outside the UK (either wholly or partly). This is as long as, at the time the course of conduct occurs, the perpetrator is a UK national or a habitual resident of Scotland.[102] For example, in a case involving a Scottish couple living in Spain, the mother wrongfully removes the child from Spain to Scotland following an extended period of physical and emotional abuse by the father in Spain. If the mother reported the abuse in Scotland, and criminal proceedings were initiated by the State, a protection measure could be issued by the court to protect the mother, if the father was found guilty of the offence.
↕ *Civil protection orders: can be obtained in simple fast-track proceedings,*[103] *usually independent from proceedings on the merits of the case (although a few Member States have linked them to divorce or other substantive proceedings).*[104]

102 Domestic Abuse (Scotland) Act 2018, s. 3.
103 POEMs Project Final Report, p. 242.
104 See section 4.3.3, '(Relative) weaknesses of the civil protection orders and the Regulation', below.

b. The complexity and length of criminal protection order proceedings
As criminal protection orders are issued in the course of criminal proceedings, the entire procedure is usually complex and, potentially, lengthy. It is normally required that the offender be heard first. The underlying behaviour must be criminalised, and of sufficient severity to justify an arrest, meaning that the evidential threshold is high. Consequently, if the behaviour (e.g. threatening behaviour, stalking, domestic abuse) is not criminalised, or the crime/requisite level of violence cannot be proven, or the victim does not wish to press criminal charges,[105] no protection will be available to the victim.[106]
↕ *Civil protection orders: can normally be obtained as a (preliminary) injunction via interlocutory proceedings, usually on application by the victim.*[107] *Even though there is no uniform evidentiary standard across the Member States, the evidentiary threshold is usually not very high, with the victim having to merely demonstrate that she needs protection.*[108] *A civil protection order can often be imposed* ex parte.

4.3.2. *Reasons Related to Aspects of the Mutual Recognition Procedure under Directive 2011/99*

a. The recognition of the protection measure is not automatic
Continuation of the protection measure is not automatic, but presupposes a decision by the executing Member State.[109] As even a mere recognition requires a decision by the executing Member State, the abducting mother will not be protected immediately upon her return to the State of habitual residence, exposing her to a risk of continued violence by the left-behind father.

105 This is not unusual, as the victim may fear retaliation from the abuser, or not want him to have a criminal record.

106 POEMs Project Final Report, p. 242.

107 Ibid. See section 4.3.3, '(Relative) weaknesses of the civil protection orders and the Regulation', below.

108 POEMs Project Final Report, p. 242.

109 Directive 2011/99, Art. 9. In particular, the competent authority of the executing State shall (without undue delay) recognise the protection order, and take a decision adopting any measure that would be available under its national law in a similar case.

Moreover, as the recognition procedure requires the executing State to replace the original protection order with a measure that would be available under its national law in a similar case,[110] it may well be that no such measure will be available under the national law of the executing State. In such circumstances, the executing State merely has to report to the issuing State 'any breach of the protection measure described in the European protection order of which it is aware'.[111]

↕

Regulation 606/2013: Automatic recognition procedure. A 'protected person' does not need to undertake any court proceedings in the Member State addressed to secure recognition of the measure, because recognition is automatic. The only formal requirement is the presentation of a certificate issued by the Member State of origin. The protection measure is treated as if it had been ordered in the Member State addressed. The Member State addressed does not need to replace the original protection measure with a protection measure under its national law, and it is irrelevant whether the Member State addressed has a protection measure available for similar cases under its own law.[112]

b. The length of the recognition proceedings

In the light of the summary nature of the return proceedings under the 1980 Hague Convention, the fact that the procedure under Directive 2011/99 requires an 'extra step' before the protection order can be recognised raises serious concerns. The length of the recognition proceedings will also be affected by factors such as the overall effectiveness of the criminal justice system in the executing State, and the particulars of the case in question. For example, if the left-behind father was not heard in the protection order proceedings in the issuing State, he will have to be heard in the recognition proceedings.[113]

↕

Regulation 606/2013: No need to hear the defendant. Once a certificate under Article 5 has been issued, the issuing authority of the State of origin must notify the defendant of the certificate,[114] *but, unlike under the Directive, there is no requirement of a prior hearing of the defendant.*

---

110 Directive 2011/99, Art. 9(1).
111 Directive 2011/99, Art. 11(3).
112 POEMs Project Final Report, p. 210; Directive 2011/99, Art. 13(3).
113 Directive 2011/99, Art. 6(4).
114 Directive 2011/99, Art. 8.

c. The behaviour underlying the protection measure must be recognised as criminal in both Member States

Mutual recognition under Directive 2011/99 can only ensue if both the issuing and the executing Member State criminalise the behaviour underlying the protection order. Some behaviours, e.g. stalking, may be recognised as a crime in the issuing Member State, but not be criminalised in the executing Member State. Therefore, abducting mothers who are returned to a State of habitual residence that does not recognise stalking as a criminal offence may experience difficulties with having their protection orders recognised.[115] Another example is the criminal offence of 'abusive behaviour towards partner or ex-partner', created in Scotland by the Domestic Abuse (Scotland) Act 2018. The Act explicitly recognises the range of behaviours that can constitute domestic abuse, including behaviours amounting to coercive and controlling behaviour and psychological abuse, such as controlling activities, behaviour or finances, or isolating the victim from friends or family.[116] This very novel approach to tackling domestic violence is not yet a common occurrence in other Member States. Consequently, as such behaviours are not likely to be recognised as criminal in other Member States, a non-harassment order issued following conviction under the 2018 Act is likely to be refused recognition under the Directive.

↕

Regulation: N/A.

d. Extensive grounds for non-recognition

The grounds for non-recognition of a protection order under Directive 2011/99 are much more extensive than those under the Regulation. In particular, it is open to the executing State to refuse recognition of the protection order on one (or more) grounds set out in Article 10, of

115 Cf. POEMs Project Final Report, p. 213.

116 POAM Project Report – United Kingdom, available at https://research.abdn.ac.uk/wp-content/uploads/sites/15/2020/02/National-report_UK.pdf. Note that the offence needs to be constituted by a course of conduct, so must be, at a minimum, two incidents: Ibid., p. 111.

which the following two are particularly relevant in the child abduction context:

- the protection measure relates to an act that does not constitute a criminal offence under the law of the executing State;[117] and
- the protection measure relates to a criminal offence which, under the law of the executing State, is regarded as having been committed, wholly or for a major or essential part, within its territory.[118]

↕

Regulation 606/2013: much more limited grounds for refusal. The grounds for refusal under the Regulation are much more limited than those available under the Directive. Importantly, unlike under the Directive, it is not possible to refuse recognition of the protection measure on the ground that the law of the Member State addressed does not allow for such a measure, based on the same facts.[119] *Also, importantly, the Member State addressed may 'under no circumstances' review the substance of the protection measure.*[120]

e. Limited scope of Directive 2011/99

In order for a protection order to fall within the scope of the Directive, it must be aimed at preventing new criminal acts or reducing the consequences of previous criminal acts.[121] This means that Member States are not under obligation to issue an EPO based on an order that primarily serves aims other than the protection of the victim (e.g. the social rehabilitation of the offender[122] or witness protection).[123] This means that many orders will not be eligible for recognition under the

117 Directive 2011/99, Art. 10(1)(c). Given the differences among the Member States in tackling domestic violence through criminal law legislation, this ground for non-recognition is likely to limit the level of protection of abducting mothers through criminal protection orders. See sub-section 4.3.2 (c), 'The behaviour underlying the protection measure must be recognised as a criminal offence in both Member States', above.

118 Directive 2011/99, Art. 10(1)(i). See sub-section 4.3.1 (a) 'The requirement of a link with criminal proceedings' above, concerning extraterritorial application of the Domestic Abuse (Scotland) Act 2018.

119 Regulation 606/2013, Art. 13(3).

120 Regulation 606/2013, Art. 12.

121 Regulation 606/2013, Recital 9.

122 Directive 2011/99, Recital 9.

123 Directive 2011/99, Recital 11.

Directive as, in many Member States, criminal protection orders are typically imposed with different motives in mind.[124]

↕

Regulation 606/2013: In the case of civil protection orders, it is not possible to exclude from the scope of the Regulation protection orders that would not primarily serve the objective of protecting the victim, as civil protection orders always promote the interests of the victim first.[125]

f. Assessment of the duration of the victim's stay and the need for protection

The issuing Member State has considerable discretion when deciding whether to issue an EPO. In particular, Directive 2011/99 directs the issuing Member State to take account of the duration of the victim's stay in the executing Member State, when deciding whether to issue an EPO.[126] It is uncertain how this provision would be applied in the child abduction context, as it is unclear how long the abducting mother would need to stay in the State of habitual residence upon the return. This will depend on the outcome of the substantive proceedings on custody and contact, in the State of habitual residence.

Similarly, the issuing Member State must consider the seriousness of the victim's need for protection when deciding whether to issue an EPO.[127] This requirement 'brings with it a "double risk" assessment for the victim who already had the seriousness of the need for protection recognised in the issuing State'.[128]

↕

Regulation 606/2013: The duration of the victim's stay in the executing Member State is irrelevant under the Regulation, and there is no such 'double-check', as is permitted under the Regulation.

124 POEMs Project Final Report, p. 240. See e.g. POAM Project Report – Croatia, available at https://research.abdn.ac.uk/wp-content/uploads/sites/15/2020/05/National-report_Croatia.pdf, p. 24.

125 Ibid., p. 213.

126 Directive 2011/99, Art. 6(1).

127 Ibid.

128 POEMs Project Final Report, p. 214.

4.3.3. *(Relative) Weaknesses of Civil Protection Orders and the Regulation*

a. Victim as the applicant

Civil protection orders are normally issued on application by the victim (or the victim's representative).[129] The abducting mother should, therefore, be informed of the possibility to apply for a protection order that would then be circulated under Regulation 606/2013. Nevertheless, the decision as to whether to apply for a protection order rests with the abducting mother, and should not prejudice her position in the return proceedings.

b. Effectiveness of civil protection orders

The utility of protection measures is determined by their effectiveness. In theory, criminal protection orders are more effective, as breaches of such orders carry criminal penalties. Nevertheless, although the suspect can be detained for breaching the order, this is not always the case in practice.[130] In contrast, breaches of civil protection orders are often not criminalised,[131] and civil protection orders are often criticised for lacking rigorous enforcement mechanisms. Therefore, caution is needed when determining whether a civil protection order would be appropriate in an individual child abduction case, in particular where credible allegations of severe violence have been made, and there is a future risk of violence of such severity.[132]

c. Sanctions for violations of civil protection orders

Some Member States have criminalised civil protection orders violations, whereas others impose only civil sanctions in response to such breaches. This will lead to a problem where a civil protection order has been issued in a Member State that has criminalised breaches, and

---

129 Ibid., p. 68.

130 Ibid., p. 242.

131 Nevertheless, generally, there appears to be a trend towards criminalising civil protection orders (e.g. in the UK, breaches of a non-molestation order, a non-harassment order or a domestic abuse interdict have been criminalised: see POAM UK National Report). See also POEMs Project Final Report, p. 149.

132 POEMs Project Final Report, p. 242.

the protection order has been violated upon the abducting mother's return to a State of habitual residence that has not criminalised such breaches and has only civil sanctions available. In such situation, it is expected that an extra court procedure will be required to determine the appropriate civil sanction for the violation.[133]

d. Time limit on the effects of recognition

The Regulation provides that '[i]rrespective of whether the protection measure has a longer duration, the effects of recognition ... shall be limited to a period of 12 months, starting from the date of the issuing of the certificate'.[134] This restriction, however, is not considered significant in the context of child abduction, as the protection of the abducting mother by the protection order is intended to be only temporary – until the substantive issues of custody and contact have been addressed by the courts of the State of habitual residence. In many cases, leave to remove the child from the State of habitual residence will be granted to the abducting mother by the court of the habitual residence, in the substantive proceedings following the return.

e. Characterisation

The problem of characterisation, in this context, refers to determining whether the measure falls within the civil or criminal law domain. As mentioned above, Regulation 606/2013 facilitates the recognition of protection measures issued in civil law matters, whereas Directive 2011/99 applies to protection measures issued in criminal law matters. Neither the Regulation nor the Directive define what gives a protection measure a criminal or a civil character; nevertheless, it is clear that the instruments are not intended to overlap. The Directive is intended to apply only if the harmful conduct is criminalised,[135] i.e. only if the measure is taken to protect against acts that are criminal per se, and it is not sufficient that violations of the protection order are subject to criminal sanctions. Therefore, protection measures against harmful but not criminal conduct do not fall within the scope of the Directive.

133 See ibid., pp. 241 and 224.
134 Regulation 606/2013, Art. 4(4).
135 Directive 2011/99, Art. 1.

The civil, administrative or criminal nature of the authority ordering a protection measure is not determinative for assessing the civil character of the measure,[136] although a protection order issued by the police would not qualify.[137] The Regulation does not leave the interpretation of the term 'civil matters' to national law, but instead provides that the notion should be interpreted autonomously, in accordance with the principles of Union law.[138] This means that the term is to be defined by the CJEU; however, there is no CJEU case-law on this point in the specific context of Regulation 606/2013 yet.

Against this background, one may ask whether it is left to the issuing Member State to decide which of the two instruments applies to its protection measures. In other words, does the issuing of a certificate under the Regulation, rather than of an EPO under the Directive, bind the other Member States? The answer seems to be 'yes', as, based on the principle of mutual recognition, protection measures ordered in civil matters 'should' be recognised in the Member State addressed as protection measures in civil matters, in accordance with the Regulation,[139] and the necessary adjustments the Member State addressed is allowed to make in the protection measure (e.g. change of address of the protected person) may not affect the 'civil nature' of the measure.[140]

f. Jurisdiction

Unlike other private international law instruments, Regulation 606/2013 does not contain rules on international jurisdiction.[141] Interestingly, the European Commission's proposal for the Regulation[142] contained a jurisdictional rule; however, this rule was not included in the final

[136] Regulation 606/2013, Recital 10; Directive 2011/99, Recital 10.
[137] Regulation 606/2013, Recital 6.
[138] Regulation 606/2013, Recital 10.
[139] Regulation 606/2013, Recital 14.
[140] Regulation 606/2013, Recital 20.
[141] The same is true of the Directive.
[142] Proposal of the Commission for a Regulation of the European Parliament and of the Council on mutual recognition of protection measures in civil matters, COM (2011) 276 final.

version of the instrument. The proposed rule was as follows: 'The authorities of the Member State where the person's physical and/or psychological integrity or liberty is at risk shall have jurisdiction.'[143] Had this rule been adopted, how would have it applied in a child abduction scenario? Would the State of abduction have had jurisdiction to issue a protection measure if the left-behind abuser father was still in the State of habitual residence, as would normally be the case? In some cases, the left-behind father may travel to the State of refuge, posing a danger to the abducting mother, or may threaten her with abusive phone calls or correspondence whilst he remains in the State of habitual residence. In both situations, the abducting mother's 'physical and/or psychological integrity or liberty' would be at risk, and the authorities of the State of refuge would have jurisdiction to issue a protection measure.

Does the failure to include a jurisdictional rule for issuing protection measures in the final version of the Regulation mean that jurisdiction is to be governed by other EU instruments or national law? There is no clear answer to this question, as the intention of the legislator on this point is uncertain. Nevertheless, although the jurisdictional basis is unclear, the Regulation seems to accept the possibility that the person causing the risk may reside in a Member State other than the Member State where the protection order was issued. In particular, Articles 8 and 11, which deal with the obligation to notify the person causing the risk of the issuing of the certificate, and of the adjustment of the protection measure, both refer to a situation 'where the person causing the risk resides in a Member State other than the Member State of origin or in a third country'.

Alternative pathways to determine jurisdiction for issuing a protection order, for circulation under the Regulation in a child abduction case, are set out in section 5.2.1.1 ('In Practice: Step by Step Guide') below.

[143] Ibid., Art. 3.

g. Applicable law

The Regulation contains no rules on applicable law either.[144] This raises the question whether the law governing protection measures should be determined by the *lex fori* (because of the procedural nature of these measures), by the 1996 Hague Convention (as a matter connected to parental responsibility), by Regulation (EC) No 864/2007 of the European Parliament and of the Council of 11 July 2007 on the law applicable to non-contractual obligations ('Rome II') (in the case of general protection measures), or by national conflict rules.[145]

Nevertheless, Article 3(1) of the Regulation[146] seems to suggest that the *lex fori* is applicable. This provision defines protection measures as decisions ordered by the issuing Member State 'in accordance with its national law.' Although, technically, the reference to 'national law' may be interpreted as including relevant provisions of private international law, it is more convincing to assume that the EU legislator adopted this wording precisely with the opposite intention, i.e. in order to make it clear that courts should apply their national law for protection measures without having regard to private international law rules. Otherwise, Article 3(1) would be without any content, as it is clear that the courts should not order a protection measure where it would be against their national law. Therefore, the most convincing interpretation is that the *lex fori* should be applied.

4.4. RECOMMENDATIONS

Based on the above analysis, this Guide makes the following recommendations:

1) In the light of concerns over the effectiveness of protective measures, the employment of civil protection orders with a view to making a return order should not be considered in cases where it has been established that there is a future risk of severe violence.

144 The same is true of the Directive.
145 See A. Dutta, 'Cross-Border Protection Measures in the European Union' (2016) 12 *Journal of Private International Law* 169, 171–172.
146 The same is true of the Directive: see Art. 2(2).

2) Given the advantages of civil protection orders over criminal protection orders, and the strengths of the Regulation over the Directive, civil protection orders should be employed in return proceedings. Accordingly, where a type of a protection does not fit neatly into the civil–criminal dichotomy, such protection orders should preferably be circulated under the Regulation rather than under the Directive. This recommendation is supported by the fact that protection measures against harmful, but not criminal, conduct do not fall within the scope of the Directive; accordingly, the Directive should be applied only in circumstances where the harmful conduct is criminalised.[147]
3) In the protection order proceedings, the issuing Member State should apply the *lex fori*.
4) In the absence of a jurisdictional rule in the Regulation, in the protection order proceedings, the issuing Member State should determine its jurisdiction to issue the protection order in accordance with one of the 'pathways' set out in section 5.2.1.1 ('In Practice: Step by Step Guide') below.
5) The abducting mother should be informed of the possibility to apply for a protection order that would then be circulated under Regulation 606/2013. Nevertheless, the decision as to whether to apply for a protection order rests with the abducting mother, and should not prejudice her position in the return proceedings.

5. IN PRACTICE: STEP BY STEP GUIDE

5.1. APPLICATION OF ARTICLE 13(1)(B) IN CASES INVOLVING ALLEGATIONS OF DOMESTIC VIOLENCE

5.1.1. General Points

Although domestic violence against the abducting mother may present an Article 13(1)(b) defence, '[e]vidence of the existence of a situation of domestic violence, in and of itself, is … not sufficient to establish the existence of a grave risk to the child'.[148] The key question is whether the effect of domestic violence on the child upon his/her return to the State of habitual residence will meet the high threshold of the Article 13(1)(b) exception.[149] This assessment can only reliably be carried out if a prior

147 Directive 2011/99, Art. 1.
148 HCCH Guide, para. 58.
149 Ibid.

evaluation of the merits of the allegations of domestic violence has been undertaken by the court in the return proceedings (see section 5.1.2, 'The court's approach to grave risk of harm', below). As Article 13(1)(b) is forward-looking, the court must focus on evaluating the future (as opposed to the past) risks.[150]

The appraisal of the Article 13(1)(b) defence is a general process,[151] meaning, inter alia, that the court *must* take into account all relevant matters, including all available protective measures.[152] Therefore, also where the evaluation of the merits of the allegations of domestic violence has led the court to the conclusion that the effects of domestic violence on the child upon his/her return to the State of habitual residence meet the high standard of the 'grave risk of harm' exception (see section 5.1.2, 'The court's approach to grave risk of harm', below), the court must consider 'the availability, adequacy and effectiveness' of protective measures.[153]

Figure 3. Application of Article 13(1)(b) in cases involving allegations of domestic violence – General points

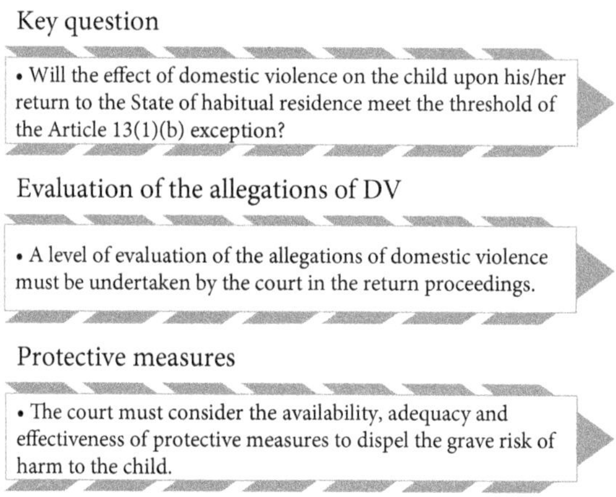

Source: Produced by the authors.

---

150 *Re E*, para. 35. See also *Re C (Children) (Abduction Article 13(B))* [2018] EWCA Civ 2834, para. 48, and HCCH Guide, p. 27. See also POAM Project Report – United Kingdom, available at https://research.abdn.ac.uk/wp-content/uploads/sites/15/2020/02/National-report_UK.pdf, p. 95.

151 *Re S*, para. 22; and *Re C (Children) (Abduction Article 13(B))* [2018] EWCA Civ 2834, para. 40.

152 *Re C (Children) (Abduction Article 13(B))* [2018] EWCA Civ 2834, paras. 40–41.

153 HCCH Guide, para. 59; C. Honorati, 'Il ritorno del minore sottratto e il rischio grave di pregiudizio ai sensi dell'art. 13 par. 1 lett. b della convenzione dell'Aja del 1980' (2020) 4 *Rivista di diritto internazionale privato e processuale* 816, 820.

In the sections below, this Guide advocates for a 'thorough, limited and expeditious'[154] investigation of the merits of the allegations of domestic violence (see section 5.1.2, 'The court's approach to grave risk of harm'), and provides guidance on how such investigation should be approached, including matters such as evidence, burden of proof and the factors to consider (see section 5.1.3, 'Assessing the grave risk of harm where allegations of domestic violence have been made').

5.1.2. The Court's Approach to Protective Measures in Grave Risk of Harm Cases

Two distinct approaches to cases where factual allegations of domestic violence have been made under the 'grave risk of harm' defence have been identified:[155] (1) 'the assessment of allegations approach', where the asserted facts relevant to the disputed allegations of domestic violence are tested by the court, considering all available documentary evidence and, at times, oral accounts (Figure 4); and (2) 'the protective measures approach',[156] where the court assumes the allegations of domestic violence

154 *X v. Latvia* (Application no. 27853/09) Grand Chamber [2013] (hereafter '*X v. Latvia*').

155 See also HCCH Guide. Previous drafts of the HCCH Guide approached the matter as follows: the initial draft Guide set out and endorsed two alternative approaches – Approach 1 (assumption that the asserted grave risk of harm exists and going straight to considering protective measures) and Approach 2 (investigating whether the facts asserted are of sufficient detail and substance, before proceeding to considering protective measures) – see Hague Conference on Private International Law, 'Draft Guide to Good Practice on Article 13(1)(b) of the Hague Convention of 25 October 1980 on the Civil Aspects of International Child Abduction', Preliminary Document No. 3 (June 2017), paras. 114–121. The revised draft Guide proposed only Approach 2: see Hague Conference on Private International Law, 'Draft Guide to Good Practice on Article 13(1)(b) of the 1980 Convention', Preliminary Document No. 4 (February 2019). For further discussion, see O. Momoh, 'The Interpretation and Application of Article 13(1) b) of the Hague Child Abduction Convention in Cases Involving Domestic Violence: Revisiting *X v. Latvia* and the Principle of "Effective Examination"' (2019) 15 *Journal of Private International Law* 626, 651. See also POAM Project Report – United Kingdom, available at https://research.abdn.ac.uk/wp-content/uploads/sites/15/2020/02/National-report_UK.pdf, pp. 87–95. The report further notes that, '[a]dditionally, isolated incidences of alternative approaches have been recorded, although these remain largely non-theorized and conceptually underdeveloped' (Ibid., p. 87).

156 See, e.g. *Re E.*

to be true and, without any assessment of the veracity of the claims, decides whether there are adequate protective measures to ameliorate the grave risk (Figure 5). The latter approach focuses on assessing the adequacy of protective measures as a substitute for investigating the disputed facts.

Figure 4. Assessment of allegations approach (i.e. investigating, first, the merits of the allegations)

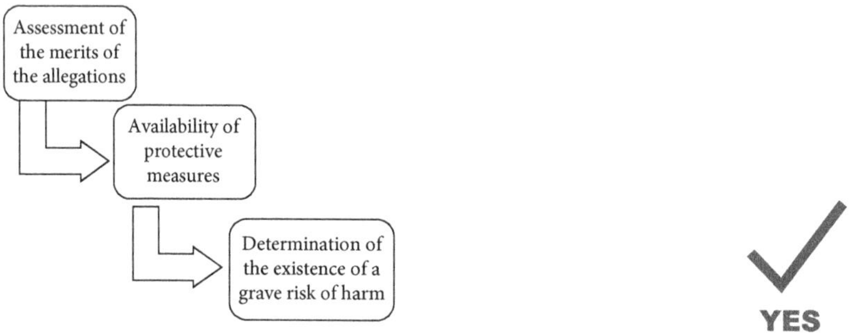

Source: Produced by the authors.

Figure 5. Protective measures approach (i.e. assuming the allegations are true, and considering protective measures first)

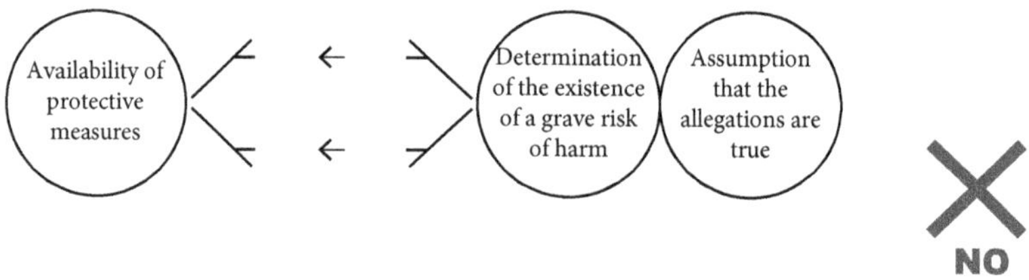

Source: Produced by the authors.

This Guide endorses the assessment of allegations approach over the protective measures approach. Importantly, the assessment of allegations approach seems also to correspond with the relevant proposal in the HCCH Guide.[157] The assessment of allegations approach

[157] HCCH Guide, p. 31.

is considered more appropriate as, without determining whether domestic violence is present, it is difficult to see how 'grave risk' could reliably be assessed, and effective protective measures determined. The protective measures approach seems to be illogical – as if 'putting the cart before the horse' – as it 'involves the consideration of protective measures to mitigate risk before that risk has been established and assessed'.[158]

Admittedly, the assessment of allegations approach may raise concerns over the length of the return proceedings. Speed, however, should not take priority over the proper assessment of risk, and consideration of the safety of the child and the abducting mother, especially when there is an alleged case of domestic violence which is at least prima facie credible. Indeed, the emphasis on speed may encourage courts to minimise or ignore allegations of domestic violence rather than determining them, thus leaving an unassessed risk of harm.

This is, however, not to suggest that the summary nature of return proceedings should be undermined in cases involving allegations of domestic violence. Rather, the assessment of the allegations should be carried out within the boundaries of the return proceedings, through a process of 'thorough, limited and expeditious' examination ('effective examination').[159] Accordingly, a 'thorough, limited and expeditious' examination of disputed allegations of domestic violence should be carried out by the court in return proceedings *before* it proceeds to determining the availability of protective measures. This is important not only for the sake of the child and the abducting mother, but also of the left-behind

---

158 A. Barnett, 'Draft Guide to Good Practice on Article 13(1)(b) of the Hague Convention on International Child Abduction – a perspective from England and Wales', p. 18, in *Eight Letters Submitted to the United States Department of State and the Permanent Bureau of the Hague Conference on Private International Law about a Draft Guide for Article 13(1)b) and Related Draft Documents that were circulated for comment prior to the October 2017 meeting of the Seventh Special Commission on the 1980 Hague Child Abduction Convention at The Hague*, available at https://law.ucdavis.edu/faculty/bruch/files/Letters-re-Hague-Convention.pdf.

159 *X v. Latvia*. For further analysis as to how to strike this difficult balance, see section 5.1.3, 'Assessing the grave risk of harm where allegations of domestic violence have been made', below.

father who, in the interests of fairness and justice, deserves a degree of adjudication on allegations that may well be exaggerated or, even worse, false.[160] Indeed, the left-behind father may be seriously prejudiced by the stigma attached to measures made against him, either by way of undertakings or injunctions or such as non-molestation orders, occupation orders, or orders that there be no interim contact between him and the child.

5.1.3. Assessing the Grave Risk of Harm where Allegations of Domestic Violence have been Made

5.1.3.1. Evidence

As domestic violence, by its very nature, usually occurs behind closed doors, supporting or corroborative documentary evidence can be scarce. Indeed, the absence of police or other authority intervention is not untypical of a disempowered victim of domestic violence, demonstrated by psychological conditions such as battered women syndrome. Notwithstanding this, there are cases where the alleged victim is equipped with documentary evidence, usually relating to previous proceedings in the State of habitual residence, seeking protection from domestic violence. Such evidence may take the form of police and/or medical reports, previous non-molestation orders, ouster orders, non-harassment orders, child arrangements orders, or even criminal proceedings relating to specific acts of violence.

Nevertheless, in the context of return proceedings, obtaining such documentary evidence in a cross-border setting, even with the support of Central Authorities, may prove challenging, and at times unsuccessful, within the strict timescales afforded to Hague Convention cases. These dilemmas may tempt the court to avoid undertaking an evaluation of the merits of the allegations of domestic violence, and to

160 O. Momoh, 'The Interpretation and Application of Article 13(1) b) of the Hague Child Abduction Convention in Cases Involving Domestic Violence: Revisiting *X v. Latvia* and the Principle of "Effective Examination"' (2019) 15 *Journal of Private International Law* 626, 651.

simply proceed to considering protective measures (see section 5.1.2, 'The court's approach to grave risk of harm', above, on the 'Protective measures approach'). This resultant circumstance must be discouraged. Relying on the European Court of Human Rights (Grand Chamber) guidance in the case of *X v. Latvia*, the court should consider the disputed allegations of domestic violence, with the examination leading to a ruling on 'specific reasons [for the decision] in light of the circumstances of the case'.[161] This presupposes that, where available, the court will seek to obtain relevant documentary evidence from the State of habitual residence.

However, where documentary evidence is unavailable (either because it does not exist, or cannot be obtained from the State of habitual residence in a timely manner) the court should hear limited oral evidence to determine the merits of the disputed allegations of domestic violence. Such hearings are sometimes referred to as finding-of-fact or fact-finding hearings. The terminology does appear to carry with it the suggestion of a detailed, highly litigious and contested hearing of great length. This, however, is not what is envisaged here. Indeed, as e.g. English case law demonstrates,[162] it is possible to undertake a limited finding-of-fact hearing to determine disputed allegations of domestic violence, well within the confines of the summary nature of return proceedings.

Further, there are cases where expert psychological or psychiatric evidence is required to address the question of psychological abuse of

---

161 *X v. Latvia*, para. 107. However, bearing in mind the scope and object of return proceedings, the court should take care to avoid pursuing full proceedings on domestic violence. The likelihood of future coercive and violent behaviour should suffice to meet the requirement under Article 13(1)(b), and to examine the availability of protection measures. See C. Honorati, 'Il ritorno del minore sottratto e il rischio grave di pregiudizio ai sensi dell'art. 13 par. 1 lett. b della convenzione dell'Aja del 1980' (2020) 4 *Rivista di diritto internazionale privato e processuale* 815.

162 E.g. *Klentzeris v. Klentzeris* [2007] EWCA Civ 533, where the court explicitly highlighted the requirement in Art. 11(3) of the Brussels IIa Regulation for child abduction cases to be dealt with within six weeks. Thorpe L.J. held that this extended to appeal hearings and, as such, recommended that applications for permission to appeal should be made directly to the trial judge, and that the normal 21-day period for lodging a notice of appeal should be restricted.

the mother, and the impact thereof on the child. The diagrams below set out 'the evidence roadmap', separately for documentary evidence (Figure 6), oral evidence (Figure 7) and on navigating the evidence types (Figure 8).

Figure 6. Evidence roadmap

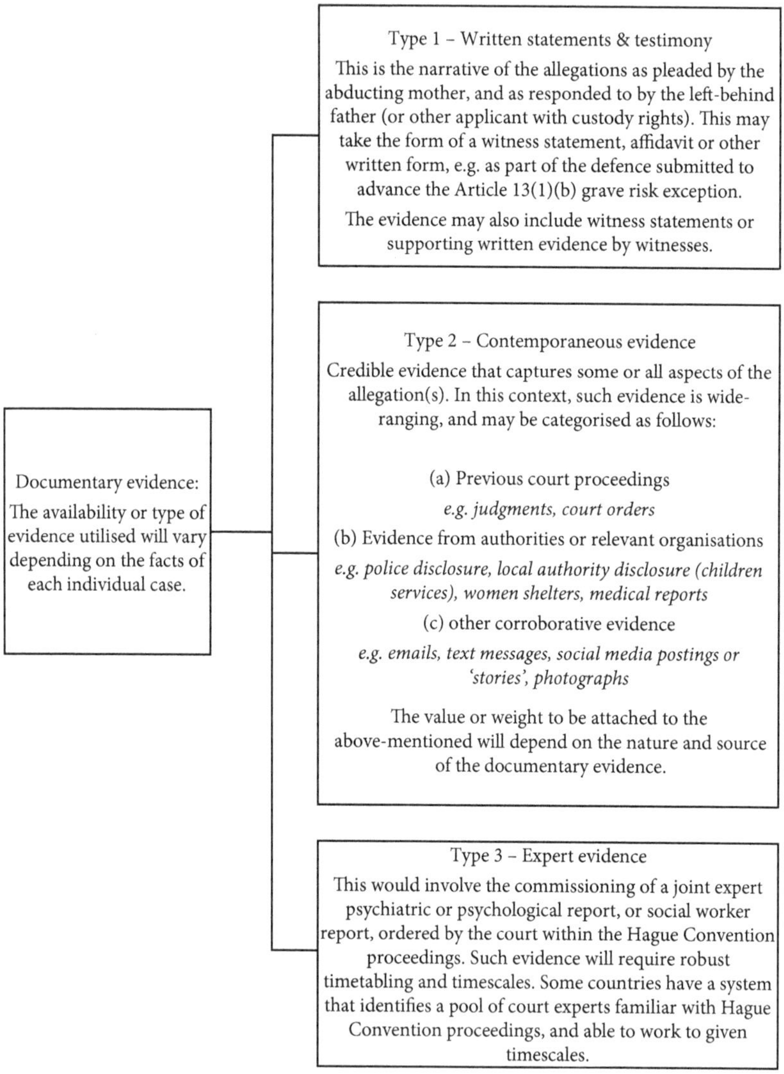

Source: Produced by the authors.

Figure 7. Oral evidence

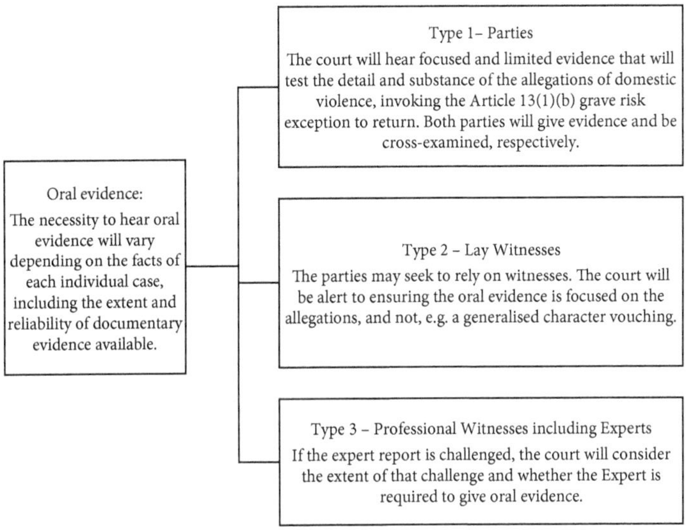

Source: Produced by the authors.

Figure 8. Navigating the evidence types

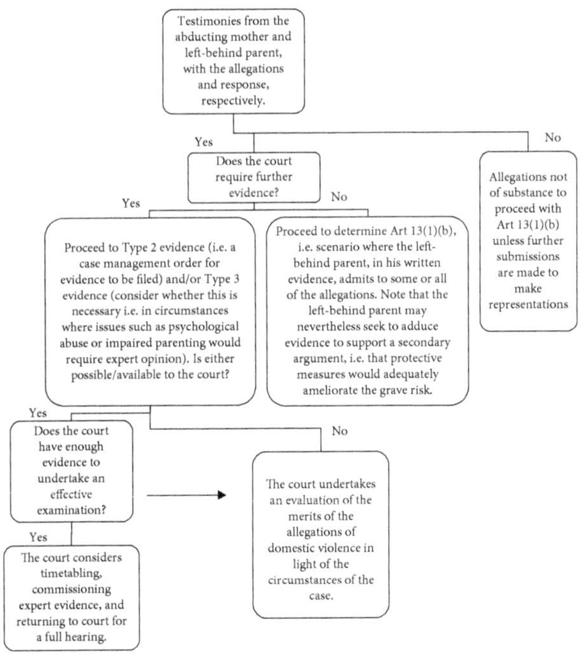

Source: Produced by the authors.

5.1.3.2. Burden and Standard of Proof

The burden of proof that Article 13(1)(b) (or any other exception to return) applies, rests with the person opposing the child's return.[163] It is, therefore, for the abducting mother to produce evidence to corroborate the defence raised.

The court should be required to evaluate the evidence against the civil standard of proof, i.e. the ordinary balance of probabilities.[164]

5.1.3.3. Factors to Consider

a) The level of harm

Firstly, Article 13(1)(b) requires that the risk to the child must have reached such a level of gravity that it can be classified as 'grave'. It is not enough for the risk to be 'real'. Although 'grave' denotes the risk rather than the harm, there is a connection between the two.[165] This means that 'a relatively low risk of death or really serious injury might properly be qualified as "grave" while a higher level of risk might be required for other less serious forms of harm'.[166] The Guide adopts case law interpretation that: (1) the risk must be real and of a level of seriousness to constitute 'grave';[167] and (2) the level of harm must be one which a child should not be expected to tolerate.[168]

As set out above, situations which a child should not be expected to tolerate include not only physical or psychological abuse or neglect of the child himself, but also exposure to the harmful effects of witnessing physical or psychological abuse of his own parent, and/or the consequences of such abuse, such as reduced parenting capacities of that parent, or ensuing separation from the abducting parent, should she not be able to return with the child[169] (see Figure 9 below). It follows that, in child abductions motivated by domestic violence, the risk of harm to the mother and the risk of harm to the child may be intertwined to

[163] See e.g., *Re E*, para. 32.
[164] Ibid.
[165] *Re E*, para. 33.
[166] Ibid.
[167] HCCH Guide, p. 26.
[168] Ibid.
[169] See section 2.2, 'The grave risk of harm defence and allegations of domestic violence', above.

the extent that, even if the domestic violence had been directed solely towards the mother, possible return may constitute a grave risk of harm to the child under Article 13(1)(b) of the Convention. Accordingly, protective measures for the abducting mother should also be considered as protective measures for the child.

Figure 9. The effect on the child of domestic violence directed soley towards the mother

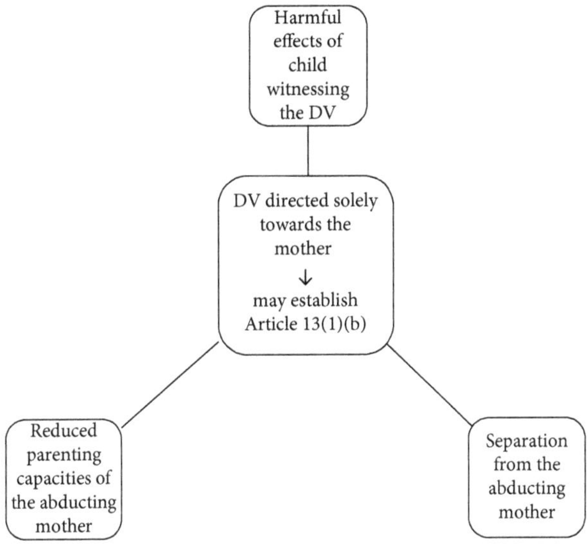

Source: Produced by the authors.

Secondly, case law shows that the level of harm, where it relates to domestic violence, may be categorised into three groups: (i) cases where the abuse is relatively minor; (ii) cases that 'fall somewhere in the middle'; and (iii) cases where 'the risk of harm is clearly grave'.[170] The third category refers to cases where protective measures would not ameliorate the risk, i.e. grave physical, sexual or psychological abuse, significant, severe and repeated violence, with a disregard for the law, to include breaches of previous protection orders. The second category is perhaps the most common, i.e. cases that fall somewhere in the middle, where the abuse is substantially more than minor, but is less obviously intolerable.[171]

---

170 *Simcox v. Simcox*, 511 F.3d 594 (6th Cir. 2007).
171 Ibid.

The nature, frequency, intensity and circumstances in which the violence was committed will all be relevant considerations.[172]

b) The type of harm

In line with the wording of Article 13(1)(b), the harm to the child may take the form of 'physical harm, 'psychological harm', or 'other intolerable situation'. The words 'physical or psychological harm' are not qualified; however, they 'gain colour' from the third limb of the defence (i.e. 'or otherwise … placed in an intolerable situation').[173] 'Intolerable' is a strong word, but when applied in the context of Article 13(1)(b) refers to 'a situation which this particular child in these particular circumstances should not be expected to tolerate'.[174]

The Guide recognises the significance of, and impact on, the victim of domestic violence at all levels, and acknowledges that different jurisdictions use different definitions of domestic violence/domestic abuse, with 'domestic violence' often denoting physical violence, whilst 'domestic abuse' usually refers to acts of psychological and emotional abuse.

c) Impact of domestic violence on the abducting mother's mental health

Anxieties of an abducting mother about a return with the child which are not based on objective risk to her but are, nevertheless, of such intensity as to be likely, if she is returned, to affect her mental health so as to destabilise her parenting of the child to a point where the child's situation would become intolerable, can constitute a 'grave risk of harm' defence under Article 13(1)(b).[175] Therefore, the court may determine whether the risk is the result of objective reality, or of the abducting mother's subjective perception of reality,[176] or whether the mother's anxieties are reasonable or unreasonable.[177] This means that if the court concludes that there is a grave risk of harm to the child, the source of the risk is not

172 HCCH Guide, p. 38.
173 *Re E*, para. 34.
174 *Re D (A Child) (Abduction: Rights of Custody)* [2006] UKHL 51, para. 52; and *Re S*, para. 27.
175 *Re E*, para. 34; *Re S*, para. 34.
176 *Re E*, para. 34; *Re S*, para. 31.
177 *Re S*, para. 34.

the determining factor. It follows that the 'grave risk of harm' defence may successfully be established, for example, 'where a mother's subjective perception of events leads to a mental illness which could have intolerable consequences for the child'.[178]

The court shall, however, examine an assertion of intense anxieties not based upon objective risk very critically, and shall consider whether it can be dispelled through protective measures.[179] However, if there is enough evidence for the court to make a conclusion as to what the objective reality is for the child, the court does not need to proceed to examining the mother's subjective perceptions.[180]

The above reasoning can, analogically, be applied to a situation where it is the child (rather than the abducting mother) who holds intense anxieties about a return, not based on the objective reality, which would amount to the child's situation on return being intolerable.[181]

5.2. PROTECTIVE MEASURES AS CIVIL LAW MEASURES: REGULATION 606/2013

5.2.1. *Outgoing Protection Measures*

5.2.1.1. Jurisdiction, Cross-Border Circulation and Applicable Law

For protection measures ordered in the State of refuge to be circulated (i.e. recognised and enforced) in other Member States, including the State of habitual residence, the court issuing the protection measures must first establish its international jurisdiction. As explained above,[182] the Regulation, strangely, contains no rules on jurisdiction. Therefore, other international instruments must be resorted to for this purpose. The 'pathways' below, to establish jurisdiction to issue protection measures and secure their enforceability, under the Regulation, offer five different approaches for application in different jurisdictions and/or factual case scenarios.

---

178 *Re E*, para. 34.
179 *Re S*, para. 27.
180 Ibid., para. 29. See also *B v. P* [2017] EWHC 3577 (Fam), para. 67.
181 *B v. P* [2017] EWHC 3577 (Fam), para. 66.
182 See section 4.3.3, '(Relative) weaknesses of civil protection orders and the Regulation', above.

As explained above,[183] Regulation 606/2013 does not contain any rules on applicable law. In the absence of such rules, the court or other authority of the Member State of origin that has been seised with an application for a protection measure under the Regulation shall apply the *lex fori* in the protection order proceedings.

a) Protective measures for the abducting mother as indirect protective measures for the child – issued by the Hague Convention return court in the return proceedings

The underlying rationale for the three pathways below is that protective measures to protect the mother also serve as measures for the protection of the child, i.e. to ameliorate the grave risk of psychological harm or other intolerable situation to the child. As such, each of these pathways presumes that the measures for the protection of the abducting mother will be taken by the Hague Convention return court in the course of the return proceedings. These measures will then be circulated under Regulation 606/2013, which establishes 'rules for a simple and rapid mechanism for the recognition of protection measures ordered in a Member State in civil matters'.[184] Although Article 2(3) of Regulation 606/2013 states that the Regulation shall not apply to protection measures falling within the scope of the Brussels IIa Regulation, it is suggested here that a 'functional' interpretation of Article 2(3) be adopted.[185] Accordingly, as Regulation 606/2013 contains no rules on international jurisdiction, Brussels IIa jurisdictional rules, namely Article 20 or Article 11(4), have to be relied on (see below, Figures 10 and 11, respectively). However, measures for protection against domestic violence taken under either

183 Ibid.

184 Regulation 606/2013, Art. 1.

185 In other words, it is proposed here that the purposive approach to statutory interpretation should be adopted when interpreting Article 2(3). According to this approach, the courts should construe statutory language in accordance with the object and intent of the legislation. A principal corollary to the teleological method is the doctrine of 'effectiveness', invariably called by its French name, '*effet utile*'. The doctrine provides that, once the purpose of a provision is clearly identified, its detailed terms will be interpreted so 'as to ensure that the provision retains its effectiveness': K. Gombos, 'EU Law Viewed Through the Eyes of a National Judge', p. 4, available at https://ec.europa.eu/dgs/legal_service/seminars/20140703_gombos_speech_en.pdf, citing K. Lenaerts, 'L'égalité de traitement en droit communautaire. Un principe unique aux apparences multiples en Cahiers de droit européen' 1991, pp. 3–41, particularly p. 38.

of these jurisdictional bases cannot be recognised and enforced under Brussels IIa (see below). Therefore, such measures for protection against domestic violence as 'special' measures of protection should be able to circulate under Regulation 606/2013.[186]

Pathway 1: Jurisdiction based on Article 20 of the Brussels IIa Regulation (matters related to parental responsibility)

Article 20 of the Brussels IIa Regulation gives jurisdiction to the courts of the State of refuge, based on the presence of the child on the territory of that Member State. Article 20(1) states:

> In urgent cases, the provisions of this Regulation shall not prevent the courts of a Member State from taking such provisional, including protective, measures in respect of persons or assets in that State as may be available under the law of that Member State, even if, under this Regulation, the court of another Member State has jurisdiction as to the substance of the matter.

The problem with Article 20, however, is that protective measures taken under this provision are not enforceable outside of the territory of the Member State where they were taken, according to the CJEU decision in *Purrucker*[187] (although this will change after 1 August 2022, when Brussels IIb becomes applicable).[188] Nevertheless, on a functional construction of Regulation 606/2013, this Guide envisages the possibility that protective measures are circulated under Regulation 606/2013 (see above, and Figure 10 below).

186 It is believed that such interpretation does not contradict Recital 11, which explains that Regulation 606/2013 'should not interfere with the functioning of the Brussels IIa Regulation' and, where possible, '[d]ecisions taken under the Brussels IIa Regulation should continue to be recognised and enforced under that Regulation'.

187 *Purrucker v. Vallés Pérez*, Case C-256/09, 15 July 2010.

188 Brussels IIb (Council Regulation (EU) 2019/1111 of 25 June 2019 on jurisdiction, the recognition and enforcement of decisions in matrimonial matters and the matters of parental responsibility, and on international child abduction (recast)), Art. 100. After 1 August 2022, cross-border circulation of protection measures issued under Article 20 of the Brussels IIa Regulation will not need to be secured through Regulation 606/2013, as it will be facilitated by the Brussels IIb Regulation. Nevertheless, the underlying considerations concerning the approach to the grave risk of harm set out in section 5.1, 'Application of Article 13(1)(b) in cases involving allegations of domestic violence', above will remain relevant.

Figure 10. Pathway 1

Source: Produced by the authors.

Pathway 2: Jurisdiction based on Article 11(4) of the Brussels IIa Regulation ('adequate arrangements' to secure a safe return of the child)

Arguably, Article 11(4) of the Brussels IIa Regulation can be seen as a ground of jurisdiction for 'adequate arrangements' which would guarantee a safe return of the child in cases involving the 'grave risk of harm' defence. Article 11(4) of Brussels IIa states:

> A court cannot refuse to return a child on the basis of Article 13b of the 1980 Hague Convention if it is established that adequate arrangements have been made to secure the protection of the child after his or her return.

Article 11(4) can be used also as a jurisdictional ground for measures to protect the mother in return proceedings involving allegations of domestic violence. On a functional construction of Regulation 606/2013, this Guide envisages the possibility that such protective measures are then circulated under Regulation 606/2013 (see above, and Figure 11 below).

Figure 11. Pathway 2

Source: Produced by the authors.

Pathway 3: Jurisdiction based on Article 11 of the 1996 Hague Protection Convention

Article 11 of the 1996 Hague Convention provides for the jurisdiction to issue measures based on the presence of the child on the territory of the State of refuge. Article 11(1) provides:

> In all cases of urgency, the authorities of any Contracting State in whose territory the child or property belonging to the child is present have jurisdiction to take any necessary measures of protection.

Unlike protective measures taken under Article 20 of the Brussels IIa Regulation, protective measures taken under Article 11 of the 1996 Hague Protection Convention are enforceable outside of the territory of the Contracting State where they were issued. Nevertheless, circulation of the protective measures under Regulation 606/2013 is more advantageous than under the Convention, as the recognition mechanism under the Regulation is simpler than the recognition procedure under the 1996 Convention (no declaration of enforceability is needed under the Regulation). Therefore, circulation of the measures of protection for the child and the mother should be facilitated by Regulation 606/2013, unless the State of habitual residence is a non-EU Member State (e.g. the United Kingdom). In such cases, circulation of the measures would be facilitated by the 1996 Hague Convention (Figure 12 below).

Figure 12. Pathway 3

Source: Produced by the authors.

b) Protective measures for the abducting mother as self-standing measures – issued in proceedings that are separate from the Hague Convention return proceedings

The below 'pathway' to establish jurisdiction to issue protection measures, and secure their circulation under Regulation 606/2013, offers an approach that is distinct from those explored in the section 'Protective measures for the abducting mother as indirect protective measures for the child – issued by the Hague Convention return court in the return proceedings' above. The underlying rationale for the pathway below is that protective measures are taken in the State of refuge in proceedings that are separate from the Hague Convention return proceedings. The protective measures will then be circulated under Regulation 606/2013.

Pathway 4: Jurisdiction based on Article 7(2) of the Brussels Ia Regulation[189]

Article 7(2) of the Brussels Ia Regulation makes provision for the jurisdiction to make protective measures on the basis of a tort 'where the harmful event may occur' (i.e. the State of refuge).

Article 7(2) states:

> A person domiciled in a Member State may be sued in another Member State:
>
> ...
>
> (2) in matters relating to tort, delict or quasi-delict, in the courts for the place where the harmful event occurred or may occur.

In order for Article 7(2) to be applicable, the left-behind father would either need to be physically present in the State of refuge, or have threatened the abducting mother via electronic means (telephone, email) of his intention to cause harm to/assault the mother in the State of refuge. It is envisaged here that the protection order would be circulated under Regulation 606/2013 rather than under Brussels Ia. The rationale is that the judgment is concerned with a specific type of protection measure that is governed by a dedicated instrument – Regulation 606/2013. However, the question is open whether Regulation 606/2013 ousts Brussels Ia. This was suggested by the European Commission in their Proposal, but Regulation 606/2013 – despite setting out its delineation with Brussels IIa – remains silent on that question. Therefore, one could apply both instruments as alternatives to one another. At least once the expiry date of the Article 5 certificate under Regulation 606/2013 has been reached, a cross-border enforcement under Brussels Ia could be possible.

---

189 Regulation (EU) No 1215/2012 of the European Parliament and of the Council of 12 December 2012 on jurisdiction and the recognition and enforcement of judgments in civil and commercial matters.

Recital 16 to Regulation 606/2013 points in this direction, as it says that the provisions of the Regulation 'should be without prejudice to the right of the protected person to invoke that protection measure under any other available legal act of the Union providing for recognition'. It has, however, to be noted that, according to the CJEU,[190] provisional measures are only enforceable under the Brussels I regime if the respondent was heard (cf., now, Article 2(a)(2) Brussels Ia). However, even in terms of such *ex parte* measures, these preconditions will be met after the expiry period of the certificate under Regulation 606/2013 has elapsed. An *ex parte* protection measure can only be enforced under Article 8 of Regulation 606/2013 if the certificate has been brought to the notice of the person causing the risk.

Figure 13. Pathway 4

Source: Produced by the authors.

5.2.1.2. Practical Considerations

Formulation of the prohibitions in the protection order

Within the limits of the national law, the scope and duration of the protection order should be formulated carefully, taking account of the facts of the case.[191] The protection order should afford protection to the abducting mother at her place of residence, place of work, or any other place which she visits regularly, e.g. the residence of close relatives, or the child's school.[192]

- Regardless of whether the place in question is described in the protection order by a specific address, or by reference to a designated area which the left-behind father may not approach or enter, the

190 *Denilauler*, Case 125/79, 21 May 1980.
191 Cf. POEMs Project Final Report, p. 244.
192 Regulation 606/2013, Recital 20.

recognition of the obligation imposed by the protection order relates to the purpose which the place serves for the abducting mother, rather than to the specific address.[193]

- Nevertheless, ideally, the prohibited areas should be designated in radiuses (i.e. metres/kilometres/miles) rather than by naming streets. This will make it easier to transpose the protection order in the State of habitual residence upon the abducting mother's return.[194]

Inclusion of mutual children in the protection order

If the issuing authority is different from the Hague Convention return court, the two authorities should cooperate in order to ensure that the resulting protection order takes into account the specific circumstances of the case that stem from the child abduction situation. In particular, the authority dealing with the protection order application should determine, taking account of possible existing contact rights of the left-behind father, whether the abducted child should also be included in the protection order (if permitted by national law).[195] If the left-behind father also poses a risk to the child, and there is a no contact order in place in the State of habitual residence, the protection order should also always include the child (if permitted by national law). If the issuing authority considers that the left-behind father also poses a risk to the child, but there is nevertheless a contact order in place in the State of habitual residence, the child should still be included in the protection order (if permitted by national law), however, the possibility that the recognition and, where applicable, enforcement of the protection order may be refused upon possible application by the left-behind father, under Article 13(b) of Regulation 606/2013, should be borne in mind.[196] In such circumstances, the abducting mother should be advised to seek a no-contact order, under Article 11 of the 1996 Hague Convention, as an urgent measure of protection from a competent court in the State of refuge.[197] If the issuing

193 Ibid.

194 Cf. POEMs Project Final Report, p. 222.

195 Cf. POEMs Project Final Report, p. 245.

196 Article 13 of Regulation 606/2013 states: 'The recognition and, where applicable, the enforcement of the protection measure shall be refused, upon application by the person causing the risk, to the extent such recognition is: … (b) irreconcilable with a judgment given or recognised in the Member State addressed.'

197 Depending on the national rules of internal jurisdiction, such competent court may coincide with the court dealing with the return application.

authority considers that the left-behind father does not pose a risk to the child, and the exercise of contact would not hinder the protection of the abducting mother (e.g. the handover of the child would be facilitated by a third person), the protection order should allow for continued contact between the child and the left-behind father.[198] If the issuing authority considers that the left-behind father does not pose a risk to the child, but the exercise of contact would hinder the protection of the abducting mother, the issuing authority should consider ordering that the exercise of contact be facilitated, for example, through a contact centre. Alternatively, should the prospect of continued contact cause anxiety to the abducting mother, she should be advised to seek a no-contact order, under Article 11 of the 1996 Hague Convention, as an urgent measure of protection from a competent court in the State of refuge.[199] This measure would be enforceable in the State of habitual residence under Article 23 of the 1996 Hague Convention on a temporary basis, until the substantive matters of custody and contact have been determined by the court of the State of habitual residence.

The certificate under Article 5 of Regulation 606/2013

- *Application for Article 5 certificate by the abducting mother*

An abducting mother, as a protected person under the Regulation who has been granted a protection order, will apply to the court or other authority that issued the order ('the issuing authority') for a certificate, so that the measure is recognised across the EU.[200] Ideally, the abducting mother should apply for the certificate at the same time as applying for the protection order; however, it shall be open to the abducting mother to apply for the certificate at any time after such application, provided that the protective measure is still in force.[201] Alternatively, it is suggested here that the court issuing the protection order should consider issuing the certificate *ex officio*, given the presence of the cross-border element from the outset of the proceedings.[202]

198 Cf. POEMs Project Final Report, p. 245.
199 Depending on the national rules of internal jurisdiction, such competent court may coincide with the court dealing with the return application.
200 Regulation 606/2013, Art. 5.
201 Cf. Family Procedure Rules 2010, SI 2010/2955, r. 38.2 (England and Wales).
202 As opposed to the cross-border element arising subsequently.

► *Standard form*

Upon a receipt of such application, the issuing authority shall issue the certificate, following a multilingual standard form established by the European Commission in accordance with Article 19 of the Regulation, and available at https://eur-lex.europa.eu/legal-content/EN/TXT/?qid=1600253873672&uri=CELEX:32014R0939. There is no right of appeal against the issuing of the certificate.[203]

► *Requirements for the issuing of the certificate*

The Regulation sets out three requirements that need to be met before the certificate may be issued:

1) The certificate may only be granted where the protection measure has been brought to the notice of the left-behind father (i.e. the person causing the risk).[204] This obligation must be carried out in accordance with the law of the Member State of origin.
2) Where the protection measure was ordered in default of appearance, the left-behind father must have been informed of the initiation of the proceeding in sufficient time, and in such a way, as to enable him to arrange for his defence.[205] This obligation will normally be met by serving the left-behind father with the document which instituted the protection order proceeding (or an equivalent document).[206] The service shall be carried out in accordance with the law of the Member State of origin.
3) Where the protection measure was ordered in *ex parte* proceedings (i.e. under a procedure that does not provide for prior notice to be given to the person causing the risk), the certificate may only be issued if the left-behind father had the right to challenge the protection measure.[207] The right to challenge the protection measure must have existed under the law of the Member State of origin.

---

203 Regulation 606/2013, Art. 5(2).
204 Regulation 606/2013, Art. 6(1).
205 Regulation 606/2013, Art. 6(2).
206 Ibid.
207 Regulation 606/2013, Art. 6(3).

► *Content of the certificate*

The certificate must contain the following information:

(a) the name and address/contact details of the issuing authority;
(b) the reference number of the file;
(c) the date of issue of the certificate;
(d) details concerning the abducting mother: name, date and place of birth, where available, and an address to be used for notification purposes, preceded by a conspicuous warning that that address may be disclosed to the left-behind father;
(e) details concerning the left-behind father: name, date and place of birth, where available, and address to be used for notification purposes;
(f) all information necessary for enforcement of the protection measure, including, where applicable, the type of the measure and the obligation imposed by it on the left-behind father and specifying the function of the place and/or the circumscribed area which the left-behind father is prohibited from approaching or entering, respectively;[208]
(g) the duration of the protection measure;
(h) the duration of the effects of recognition pursuant to Article 4(4);
(i) a declaration that the above requirements for the issuing of the certificate have been met (Article 6);
(j) information on the rights granted under Articles 9 and 13;
(k) for ease of reference, the full title of the Regulation.[209]

► *Notification of the certificate*

The certificate, and the fact that it results in the recognition and, where applicable, in the enforceability of the protection measure in all Member States, must be brought to the notice of the person causing the risk.[210]

- The notification obligation rests on the issuing authority of the Member State of origin.[211]

---

208 See also Regulation 606/2013, Recital 21.
209 Regulation 606/2013, Art. 7.
210 Regulation 606/2013, Art. 8(1).
211 Ibid.

- The notification of the left-behind father shall be effected by registered letter with acknowledgment of receipt or equivalent.[212]

► *Transliteration or translation*

The abducting mother may request the issuing authority to provide her with a transliteration and/or a translation of the certificate.[213] Ideally, the abducting mother should make such request at the time of the application for the certificate; however, it shall be open to her to make the request at any time after the application for the certificate, as long as the certificate is still in force.[214]

- For this purpose, the issuing authority will use the previously mentioned multilingual form.
- The transliteration or translation shall be into the official language, or one of the official languages, of the Member State addressed, or into any other official language of the EU institutions which that Member State has indicated it can accept.[215]

► *No legalisation of documents*

Importantly, no legalisation of documents or other similar formality is required under the Regulation.[216]

► *Rectification or withdrawal*

The certificate may only be rectified or withdrawn if there is a clerical error, or if it was clearly granted wrongly.[217]

- An application for rectification of an Article 5 certificate shall be made to the court or other authority that issued the order. It should be

---

212 Regulation 606/2013, Art. 8(2). This rule applies as the left-behind father is resident in a Member State other than the Member State of origin. In England and Wales, for example, the notification is carried out 'by sending it by registered letter with acknowledgement of receipt or confirmation of delivery or equivalent to the last known place of residence of that person'.: Family Procedure Rules 2010, SI 2010/2955, r. 38.7.

213 Regulation 606/2013, Art. 5(3).

214 Cf. Family Procedure Rules 2010, SI 2010/2955, r. 38.4 (England and Wales).

215 Regulation 606/2013, Art. 16(2).

216 Regulation 606/2013, Art. 15.

217 Regulation 606/2013, Art. 9(1).

possible for the certificate to be rectified either on application by the abducting mother or the left-behind father, or by the issuing authority on its own initiative.[218]

- An application for withdrawal of an Article 5 certificate shall be made by the abducting mother or the left-behind father to the issuing authority. It should also be possible for the issuing authority to withdraw the certificate on its own initiative.[219]

► *Further certificate following suspension, limitation or withdrawal of the original certificate*

A further certificate may be granted, reflecting any suspension, limitation or withdrawal of the original protection measure.[220] Like for Article 5, the European Commission has established a standard multilingual form for the purpose of Article 14.[221] The form is available at https://eur-lex.europa.eu/legal-content/EN/TXT/?qid=1600253873672&uri=CELEX:32014R0939.

5.2.2. *Incoming Protection Measures*

5.2.2.1. Adjustment of Factual Elements (Article 11(1))

Upon the abducting mother's return to the State of habitual residence, the protection order may need to be adapted to suit the new circumstances. This shall be carried out through adjusting the factual elements of the protection measure in the Member State addressed, with a view to giving the protective measure effect in that Member State,[222] for example by replacing the address of the abducting mother in the State of refuge with her address in the State of habitual residence.

► *Factual elements*

Factual elements include the address; the general location; or the minimum distance the person causing the risk must keep from the protected person, the address or the general location.[223]

---

218 Cf. Family Procedure Rules 2010, SI 2010/2955, r. 38.8. (UK – England and Wales).
219 Ibid, r. 38.9.
220 Regulation 606/2013, Art. 14.
221 Regulation 606/2013, Art. 19.
222 Regulation 606/2013, Art. 11(1).
223 Regulation 606/2013, Recital 20.

- *The procedure for the adjustment*

The adjustment shall be carried out on application to the court made by the protected person.[224] The procedure for the adjustment of the protection measure is governed by the law of the Member State addressed.[225] Similarly, in the event that an appeal is lodged by either the abducting mother or the left-behind father against the adjustment of the protection measure, the appeal procedure will be governed by the law of the Member State addressed.[226] Importantly, the lodging of an appeal does not have suspensive effect.[227]

- *The notification of the left-behind father of the adjustment of the protection measure*

The left-behind father must be notified of the adjustment of the protective measure.[228] The notification shall be effected in accordance with the law of the Member State addressed.[229] The law of the Member State addressed will also govern situations such as when the whereabouts of the person causing risk are unknown, or that person refuses to accept receipt of the notification.[230]

- *The type and civil nature of the protection measure must not be affected*

The adjustment of factual elements may not affect the type and the civil nature of the protection measure.[231]

6. CONCLUSION

The POAM project has affirmed that the protection of abducting mothers in return proceedings is not 'one size fits all', and the mechanisms

224 Cf. Family Procedure Rules 2010, SI 2010/2955, r. 38.12 (England and Wales).
225 Regulation 606/2013, Art. 11(2).
226 Regulation 606/2013, Art. 11(5).
227 Ibid.
228 Protection Measures Regulation, Art. 11(3).
229 Protection Measures Regulation, Art. 11(4).
230 Regulation 606/2013, Art. 11(4).
231 Protection Measures Regulation, Recital 20.

for jurisdiction and enforcement also require careful thought and consideration, taking account of the pertinent national law. As highlighted in the Guide, the approach to the assessment of the grave risk of harm plays a vital part in this process, as to understand properly the grave risk of harm posed is to be better placed to effectively assess and protect children through protecting their mothers. The POAM research project critically analysed and identified four pathways to jurisdiction and cross-border circulation of measures for the protection of abducting mothers. These pathways fall into two separate categories: (1) protective measures for the abducting mother as indirect protective measures for the child, i.e. issued by the Hague Convention return court in the return proceedings; and (2) protective measures for the abducting mother as self-standing measures, i.e. issued in proceedings that are separate from the Hague Convention return proceedings. In the first category, to achieve jurisdiction and cross-border circulation of protective measures, there are three pathways, all using *lex fori* as the applicable law. These pathways are:

a) Jurisdiction based on Article 20 Brussels IIa Regulation, with circulation under Regulation 606/2013;
b) Jurisdiction based on Article 11(4) Brussels IIa Regulation with circulation under Regulation 606/2013;
c) Jurisdiction based on Article 11 of the 1996 Hague Convention, with circulation under Regulation 606/2013 or the 1996 Hague Convention (non-EU state).

In the second category, the following pathway is recommended, again using *lex fori* as the applicable law:

a) Jurisdiction based on Article 7(2) Brussels Ia Regulation with circulation under Regulation 606/2013.

There are individual factors to be considered in deciding which pathway to adopt. These factors comprise circumstances of the individual case, and requirements of the national law of the State of refuge. Accordingly, whilst there is no singular 'best practice' to fit all child abduction cases committed against the background of domestic violence, there will inevitably be a Best Practice for each individual case. Thus, the Best Practice Guide aims to achieve a uniform appreciation and understanding of each pathway, to enable the best protective outcome for each individual child, through their mother, in the Hague Convention return proceedings.

INDEX OF CASES CITED IN THE BEST PRACTICE GUIDE

Court of Justice of the European Union, 21 May 1980, Case 125/79, *Denilauler v. Couchet Fréres*

United Kingdom House of Lords, [2006] UKHL 51, *Re D (A Child) (Abduction: Rights of Custody)*

England and Wales Court of Appeal, [2007] EWCA Civ 533, *Klentzeris v. Klentzeris*

United States Court of Appeals for the Sixth Circuit, [2007] 511 F.3d 594, *Simcox v. Simcox*

Court of Justice of the European Union, 15 July 2010, Case C-256/09, *Purrucker v. Vallés Pérez*

United Kingdom Supreme Court, [2011] UKSC 27, *In the Matter of E (Children)*

United Kingdom Supreme Court, [2012] UKSC 10, *In the Matter of S (A Child)*

European Court of Human Rights (Grand Chamber), 21 November 2013, no. 27853/09, *X v. Latvia*

England and Wales High Court, [2017] EWHC 3577 (Fam), *B v. P*

England and Wales Court of Appeal, [2018] EWCA Civ 2834, *Re C (Children) (Abduction Article 13(B))*

Court of Justice of the European Union, 23 May 2019, Case C-658/17, *WB v. Notariusz Przemysława Bac*

England and Wales Court of Appeal, [2019] EWCA Civ 352, *Re S (A Child) (Hague Convention 1980: Return to Third State)*

GLOSSARY

Abducting mother – a mother who has wrongfully removed or retained her child(ren) across international borders, and is involved in return proceedings under the 1980 Hague Child Abduction Convention and the Brussels IIa Regulation.

Brussels IIa Regulation – Council Regulation (EC) No 2201/2003 of 27 November 2003 concerning jurisdiction and the recognition and enforcement of judgments in matrimonial matters and the matters of parental responsibility, repealing Regulation (EC) No 1347/2000.

1980 Hague Abduction Convention – the 1980 Hague Convention of 25 October 1980 on the Civil Aspects of International Child Abduction.

Left-behind father – a father who has filed an application under the 1980 Hague Abduction Convention and the Brussels IIa Regulation for the return of his child(ren).

Regulation 606/2013 – Regulation (EU) No 606/2013 of 12 June 2013 on mutual recognition of protection measures in civil matters.

Directive 2011/99 – Directive 2011/99/EU of 13 December 2011 on the European Protection Order.

1996 Hague (Protection) Convention – Convention of 19 October 1996 on Jurisdiction, Applicable Law, Recognition, Enforcement and Co-operation in Respect of Parental Responsibility and Measures for the Protection of Children.

State of habitual residence – the State where the child was habitually resident prior to the wrongful removal or retention, i.e. the child's 'home' country (sometimes referred to as 'the requesting State').

State of refuge – the State to which the child has been wrongfully removed, or retained in (sometimes referred to as 'the requested State').

Hague Convention return court – the court of the State of refuge competent for the return proceedings under the 1980 Hague Convention and the Brussels IIa Regulation.

ABOUT THE EDITORS

Katarina Trimmings is a Senior Lecturer in Law at the University of Aberdeen, and the Director of the Aberdeen Centre for Private International Law. She has written extensively on cross-border parental child abduction, and published a monograph titled *Child Abduction within the European Union* (Hart Publishing, 2013), and is one of the authors of the 15th edition of *Cheshire's Private International Law* (Oxford University Press, 2017). She led the EU-funded project 'Protection of Abducting Mothers in Return Proceedings: Intersection between Domestic Violence and Parental Child Abduction' (https://research.abdn.ac.uk/poam/ POAM, 2019–2021).

Anatol Dutta holds a Chair of Private Law, Private International Law and Comparative Law at the Ludwig Maximilian University of Munich. Previously, he was Fellow at the Max Planck Institute for Comparative and International Private Law in Hamburg (2003–2014) and was Professor at the University of Regensburg (2014–2017). Anatol Dutta is a member of the editorial board of *Zeitschrift für das gesamte Familienrecht* (FamRZ), a leading family law journal for practitioners and academics in Germany, and is a member of the German Council of Private International Law. He has a special interest in family and succession law, from a private international law as well as a comparative and interdisciplinary perspective.

Costanza Honorati is a Full Professor of European Union Law at the University of Milano-Bicocca, School of Law where she also holds the Chair of EU Private International Law. She has been Co-ordinator of the PhD Program in European Union Law since 2017 and was the Head of the PhD School between 2009 and 2013. She is currently Chair of the EU Commission's Working Group on a Guide to the Maintenance Regulation and was previously a member of the Expert Group assisting the Commission on the Recast of the Brussels IIa Regulation (2015). She has been a Visiting Scholar and Visiting Professor at several institutions. She is a member of the Editorial Board of *Rivista di diritto internazionale privato e processuale* and the Special Editor for private international law of *European Papers*.

Mirela Župan is a Full Professor at the Josip Juraj Strossmayer University of Osijek, Faculty of Law, and Head of the PhD Programme in Law. Her main professional interests include private international law of family and contractual matters, as well as the impacts of ICT on law and the protection of the vulnerable (children, adults, companion animals). She was awarded the Max-Planck Society Doctoral and Postdoctoral Grant from the Max Planck Institute for Comparative and International Private Law in Hamburg. As a member of several research groups, she has organised and participated in conferences, seminars and workshops, and has published a number of books, chapters and papers. She has acted as a member of the Expert Group assisting the Commission on the Recast of the Brussels IIa Regulation and was nominated as a national reporter for European Commission studies.

www.ingramcontent.com/pod-product-compliance
Ingram Content Group UK Ltd.
Pitfield, Milton Keynes, MK11 3LW, UK
UKHW021845100926
8556IPUK00019B/1061